Volume 6

THE AMERICANIZATION OF A
RURAL IMMIGRANT CHURCH

ACKNOWLEDGMENTS

Writing a dissertation makes one debtor to a host of people. One of the most satisfying obligations in the completion of a manuscript is to express appreciation for help received.

Financial assistance from the Addison E. Sheldon Fellowship Foundation, the Henry J. Amen Fund, and Vennard College made convenient the efficient research and writing of this dissertation. A number of my colleagues at Vennard College carried a significant portion of my responsibilities during frequent absences from campus. I am also indebted to the Faith Missionary Church in Weeping Water, Nebraska, for relieving me of several normal pastoral responsibilities during the early stages of research.

No one can write on General Conference Mennonite history without a stay at the Mennonite Library and Archives on the campus of Bethel College in North Newton, Kansas. Archivists Robert Kreider and David Haury, along with their staff, went out of their way to make my work there profitable and enjoyable. A special word of gratitude is due Professor James C. Juhnke of Bethel College for his insightful reflection on an early draft. At times I was overwhelmed by the warm hospitality of the fine people at the Mennonite Library and Archives.

John Horning and Ronald Wilson allowed me to take advantage of friendships by consenting to read early drafts and discuss important concepts, thus rescuing me from many stylistic blunders.

i

I have benefitted from the close readings and criticisms of
Professors Ann Kleimola and James Rawley of the University of Nebraska.
Professor Frederick C. Luebke directed the project from start to finish
with the proverbial fatherly hand and penetrating eye. He has been
both my greatest critic and most coveted source of encouragement.
I have profitted from his teaching, good counsel, and thoughtful reading
of more drafts than we care to count. Naturally, no one but myself
is to blame for errors and infelicities which remain.

I reserve the most notable appreciation for my family. Countless
letters and encouraging calls from my parents have served to spur
me on at crucial junctures. My two sons, Nathan and Aaron, have made
the ultimate sacrifice of allowing me hours of solitude for research
and writing. Finally, a special acknowledgment goes to my wife, Karla,
who not only typed the early drafts of this study, but whose love
and understanding inspired me in the initial stages, and whose refusal
to take this project more seriously than it deserved in the final
stages aided me more than she realized.

TABLE OF CONTENTS

TABLE OF CONTENTS (continued)

LIST OF ILLUSTRATIONS

LIST OF TABLES

CHAPTER I

INTRODUCTION

In the summer of 1882 a newspaper editor from Atchison visited
several settlements of Mennonites from Russia in central Kansas. Nobel
Prentis was no stranger to Mennonite settlers in Harvey, McPherson, and
Marion counties. He had visited them in 1875 following their first year
in America. His observations, recorded in the Topeka Commonwealth,
revealed a fascination for quaint Mennonite villages and a Russian
oven that heated with straw.[1] As a champion of settlement in Kansas,
Prentis was a regular visitor to numerous immigrant settlements throughout the state and frequently printed interviews with successful prairie
pioneers. He made no secret of the fact that the Mennonites of central
Kansas were model settlers. In a mere seven years they had transformed
the bare prairie into a "garden of the plains" with miniature forests,
fenced fields of wheat and corn, and farms surrounded by orchards that
nearly hid their houses. Prentis traveled from home to home recording
the stories of poor immigrants who in less than a decade had developed
into self-sufficient settlers. Success came with a price, however, and
Prentis, in spite of his zeal to promote settlement in young Kansas,
suspected that the cost would be even higher for the peaceloving,
separatist Mennonites. He predicted that they would continue to prosper
in their new homeland but in the process they would lose the very dignity
they sought to preserve by leaving Russia:

The orchards will bud and bloom, and amid them will stand the
solid brick houses, like those of Russia, and the richest farmers
of Kansas will dwell therein. But there is a danger that this
will not come to pass. Jacob and David will go to work on the
railroad, and let the plow take care of itself; and Susanna and
Agantha will go out to service in the towns, and fall to wearing
fine clothes and marrying American Gentiles; and the evil day
may come when the descendant of the Mennonites of the old stock
will be cushioning store-boxes, saving the Nation with his mouth,
of even going about like a roaring lion, seeking a nomination
for Congress. I wish I could belief it otherwise. I wish our
atmosphere did not make us all so smart that we cannot enjoy
good health. Were it not for that accursed vanity and restlessness which is our heritage, I could indulge in a vision of
future--of a peaceful, quiety, wealthy people, undistrubed by
the throes of speculation or politics, dwelling in great content
under the vines and mulberry trees which their fathers planted
in the grassy wind-swept wilderness.[2]

Mennonites who settled on the American frontier departed Russia
in hopes of securing an autonomous peoplehood that had been threatened
under the Czar. Instead of community autonomy they were offered individual self-sufficiency on the Great Plans. This individual American
freedom, as Prentis predicted, eroded Mennonite community autonomy and
replaced it with prosperity making the greater loss quite bearable.[3]

The Russian Mennonites who settled central Kansas in the late
nineteenth century were the dominant group in a Mennonite polychotomy.
Numerous European countries and eastern states were represented amongst
the first settlers and after 75 years in Kansas eight Mennonite denomi-
nations existed within a five county region. The largest group of
Russian Mennonites affiliated with the General Conference Mennonite Church.
They formed the Kansas Conference in 1877 which in turn became the
Western District Conference in 1892. The Russian Mennonites of Dutch-
Prussian ancestry were joined in the Western District of the General
Conference by Dutch Mennonites from West Prussia, Polish Russia, and
Volhynia; and Swiss Mennonites from Volhynia, Galicia, South Germany and

Switzerland. By 1921 these groups formed some thirty-four General Conference churches in central Kansas and several more daughter congregations
in Oklahoma and western Kansas. It is these thirty-four congregations
that serve as the focus for this study. Smaller related groups such as the
Mennonite Brethren, Church of God in Christ, Mennonite, Krimmer Mennonite
Brethren, and American Mennonite and Amish groups in central Kansas are
not included. The implications of an Americanization study inclusive of
all Mennonites in Kansas are simply too great for the restrictions of
this project.

One of the immigrant institutions that played a significant role
in the acculturation of immigrants in America during the nineteenth and
twentieth centuries was the church. The church served to meet several
immigrant needs, both in urban centers and rural areas. In the country,
as in the city, culturally distinct behavior required community reinforce-
ment in order to retain ethnic distinctiveness.[4] The rural church often
functioned as the institutional rallying point for this cultural distinctiveness, while at the same time easing the process by which the newcomer
was assimilated.[5] In the Old World the church served as the hub of
village life, what Will Herberg refers to as "the repository of sacred
symbols of community existence."[6] Upon arrival in the New World, the
immigrants' first concern was its re-establishment. This was not accom-
plished without difficulties; in the process the immigrants inevitably
transformed the very institution they attempted to duplicate in America.[7]
Thus the story of the immigrant church is two-fold: first, its role in
the Americanization of the immigrants; second, the Americanization of the
church itself.

Although much has been written in the past three decades concerning the Americanization of immigrants, little has been directed at the rural setting. Kathleen Conzen noted in 1980 that in recent surveys of immigrant history there is nothing in the treatment of rural America that approaches the depth of attention given the urban experience. She decries the fact that "there has been little focus on either the emergence of ethnic identity or the process of immigration adaptation per se."[8] Yet in the late nineteenth century, a fifth to a quarter of all foreign born males reported agricultural occupations. As late as 1910, ten per cent of all farm operators were foreign born.[9] However, the explanatory models of the immigrant church have largely been urban. The roots of ethnic identity, community formation, acculturation, various levels of assimilation, ethnic continuity, and the struggle between Americanizing and non-Americanizing clergy battling for the survival of the immigrant church and its transplantation have all been examined in the hostile world of the industrial metropolis. The Mennonite experience in nineteenth century Kansas gives opportunity for an examination of the rural immigrant church, its role in the Americanization of immigrants, and the subsequent Americanization of the church.

Milton Gordon has developed an assimilation model which lists seven stages in the assimilation process: behavioral assimilation (acculturation), structural assimilation, marital assimilation, identificational assimilation, absence of discrimination, absence of prejudice, and absence of value and power conflict.[10] According to Gordon, behavioral assimilation or acculturation is likely to be the first stage for Americanizing immigrants. This entails a language transition and the acceptance of American behavior patterns. There is a significant distinction between

behavioral assimilation (acculturation) and the next step, structural
assimilation. Behavioral assimilation is involved in the development of
secondary relationships (Gesellschaft) while structural assimilation is
involved in the development of primary relationships (Gemeinschaft).
Behavioral assimilation usually occurs with first generation immigrants
but is not necessarily completed with their passing. The second generation continues this process usually at an accelerated rate. Once structural assimilation occurs all other types of assimilation will naturally
follow. This usually takes place with second generation immigrants.
Structural assimilation is defined by Gordon as that stage which includes
large-scale entrance into cliques, clubs, and institutions of the host
society on a primary group level. The rapidity and success of acculturation varies for each group but generally the first generation initiates
behavioral assimilation while the second moves on to the structural
assimilation stage. Gordon makes two exceptions for his generalizations:
1) minority groups who are spatially isolated and segregated in a rural
area; and 2) racially distinct minorities such as American Blacks who
are easily marked for discrimination. Both of these groups are slowed
in their behavioral assimilation while structural assimilation is postponed for a generation or more. In both instances, the Americanization
process is delayed but not halted.[11]

The Mennonites from Russia and eastern Europe who settled central
Kansas in 1874–1880 initially were spatially isolated and segregated in
a rural society. True to Gordon's theory, their acculturation was slowed
but not eliminated. There were rapid assimilators among the Kansas
Mennonites such as Bernhard Warkentin, a well-to-do immigrant who married

a non-Mennonite, attended a Presbyterian Church, and established the Newton
Milling and Elevator Company and the Kansas State Bank. However, the story
of Mennonite Americanization is not simply that of Bernhard Warkentin and
those who eventually left the Mennonite fold. The story of Mennonite
Americanization is etched in the record books of the immigrant church
established on the Kansas prairies in the late nineteenth century and
serving as a hub of village life well into the twentieth century. Central
Kansas was not the final resting ground for all Russian and eastern
European Mennonites after 1874. Many left central Kansas for Oklahoma,
western Kansas, California, Colorado, and Texas. Others left the Mennonite
church. Once severed from the mother church, acculturation accelerated.
For those who remained in central Kansas the story of Americanization was
linked to the institution of the church, its role and its transition from
1874 until 1939. During that time American revivalism, modernism, the
Spanish-American War, World War I, the Great Depression, public schools,
and American politics all had a significant impact upon the Mennonite
Church.

In 1904, three decades after their departure from Russia and
eastern Europe, Mennonite historian and Bethel College president,
C.H. Wedel, marveled at the progress of Mennonites in central Kansas.
The immigration experience had produced a cosmopolitan view, something
rare in 1874. Public schools in a number of districts were controlled
by Mennonites. Several Mennonites held public offices. During the
Spanish-American War General Conference Mennonites in Kansas voluntarily
participated in Red Cross work. Mennonites were being recognized across
the nation for their unique contributions to society. Wedel was obviously
proud of the adjustments made by his brethren during their first thirty

years in central Kansas. However, he quickly pointed out the precarious

predicament of Mennonites: they were in danger of losing their heritage.

Recognizing this he challenged the church to engage in a "systematic

fostering of Mennonite faith" to preserve their unique values and ethno-

religious cohesiveness without rejecting Americanization and at the same

time maintaining a progressive posture in modern society.[12]

Wedel's warnings went unheeded by most Mennonites in 1904.

America was unlike Russia with its systematic Russification policy aimed

at assimilating ethnic minorities. The Spanish-American War posed little

threat of a universal military conscription. German-language parochial

schools in central Kansas were given a free hand in perpetuating Mennonite

ethnoreligious identity. Kansas Mennonites appeared comfortable with an

atmosphere of American Protestant revivalism in the late nineteenth century.

Transplanted immigrant churches thrived in America's denominational society.

In fact, the behavioral assimilation of Mennonites during their first four

decades in America was relatively smooth and without significant conflict.

However, when war broke out in Europe in 1914 and three years later the

United States declared war on Germany, Mennonites in central Kansas

suddenly realized the truth of Wedel's warning. The structural assimila-

tion demanded of Mennonites by a growing mood of American superpatriotism

was more than a Mennonite heritage permitted. World War I ended the gradual

assimilation of Mennonites in central Kansas and awakened them to group

consciousness.

Gordon's model of assimilation makes a crucial distinction between

behavioral assimilation and structural assimilation. The former refers to

the absorption of the cultural behavior patterns of the host society; the

latter refers to the actual entrance of immigrants and their descendants

into the various institutions of the host society on a primary group level.
Gordon contends that while behavioral assimilation has taken place among
ethnic groups in America to a considerable degree, structural assimilation
has not been nearly as extensive.[13] This observation tends to apply to
General Conference Mennonites in central Kansas from 1874 to 1939. As
long as Mennonites pursued behavioral assimilation, conflicts were minimal.
However, World War I and subsequent political and religious movements in
the 1920s and '30s called for the structural assimilation of Kansas Mennonites to complete the Americanization process. These events produced the
sharpest conflicts encountered by Mennonites in their Americanization.

The approach of this research to Mennonite acculturation in
central Kansas is that of the assimilation hypothesis, rather than a
pluralistic emphasis. The assimilationist motif is less concerned with
unique features that distinguish an ethnic group from the host society.
Instead it emphasizes emerging similarities and a gradual accommodation
of Americanization. That is not to imply that a cultural pluralistic
view is any less legitimate. The assimilationist perspective tends to
place less emphasis on ethnic exclusiveness and puts more stock in
behavioral and structural assimilation.[14]

In the traditional view of immigrant history, the theme of this
project would center on the Mennonite "contribution" to American Protestantism. However, the recent challenge of immigrant history has been to
focus on the process of Americanization and the development of an ethnic
awareness over long periods of time. In the case of the Kansas Mennonites, the character of this process was embellished in an encounter of
Mennonite nonconformity with American religiosity, secularism, and
nationalism. The result is the story of the Americanization of the

Mennonite church from 1874 to 1939.

CHAPTER I - ENDNOTES

1. Nobel L. Prentis, Kansas Miscellanies (Topeka: Kansas Publishing House, 1899), pp. 147-54.

2. Ibid., pp. 166-67.

3. James C. Juhnke, "Freedom for Reluctant Citizens," Mennonite Life 29 (January 1974): 30.

4. Kathleen Neils Conzen, "Historical Approaches to the Study of Rural Ethnic Communities," in Ethnicity on the Great Plains, ed. Frederick C. Luebke (Lincoln: University of Nebraska Press, 1980), p. 5.

5. Frederick C. Luebke, Immigrants and Politics: the Germans of Nebraska, 1880-1900 (Lincoln: University of Nebraska Press, 1969), p. 35.

6. Will Herberg, Protestant, Catholic, Jew; an Essay in American Religious Sociology (Garden City, New York: Doubleday, 1955), p. 11.

7. Ibid.

8. Conzen, p. 2.

9. Ibid.

10. Milton M. Gordon, Assimilation in American Life (New York: Oxford University Press, 1964), pp. 70-71.

11. Milton M. Gordon, Human Nature, Class, and Ethnicity (New York: Oxford University Press, 1978), pp. 166-80, 184-95.

12. C. H. Wedel, Abriss der Geschichte der Mennoniten, vol. 4 (North Newton, Kansas: Bethel College, 1904), pp. 199-205.

13. Gordon, Human Nature, Class, and Ethnicity, pp. 202-08.

14. John Higham, "Current Trends in the Study of Ethnicity in the United States," Journal of American Ethnic History 2 (Fall 1982): 5-15; Timothy L. Smith, "New Approaches to the History of Immigration in Twentieth-Century America," American Historical Review 71 (July 1966): 1265-79.

CHAPTER II

EUROPEAN BACKGROUND, 1525-1874

Anabaptism and Early Migration

The story of the Americanization of Mennonites in Kansas
began in Europe three and one-half centuries before their arrival
on the Great Plains. Shortly after the outset of the Protestant
Reformation, a group of religious leaders calling themselves
"Brethren" began pulling away from the main bodies of the Reformation.
Led by Conrad Grabel, Felix Manz, and George Blaurock, they set out
to complete (as they saw it) what Luther, Zwingli, and Calvin had
initiated. Amongst their opponents they were referred to as "Anabaptists" because they rejected infant baptism and insisted upon a believer's
baptism.[1] The Anabaptist movement began in Zurich, Switzerland in the
year 1525 and spread to Holland in 1530. In 1536 the Anabaptist cause
won to its ranks a Catholic priest named Menno Simons. Because of Menno's
numerous and powerful writings, he became the most widely known figure
of the new movement and by the middle of the sixteenth century people
gradually referred to the Anabaptists as "Mennonites."[2]

Although Menno Simons was not the founder of the nonresistance
faction of the Anabaptist movement, he was its most influential leader.
Under his leadership the Mennonite faith grew and spread throughout
Europe in spite of intense persecution and martyrdom. From the very
beginning Mennonite beliefs came into conflict with the state church.

The Mennonite faith was founded on the apostolic model of New
Testament Christianity. This included:

1. A church for only true believers based on voluntary membership and a believer's baptism

2. Nonconformity of the church to the world

3. Practice of true brotherhood and material aid to the needy

4. Nonresistance

5. Separation of church and state [3]

These five principles represented the core of Mennonite dogma. Their
concrete application could be traced to various aspects of Mennonite life
and often evoked persecution. In the first ten years over five thousand
Swiss Brethren were executed in Switzerland.[4] For many emigration was the
only alternative to martyrdom. By the middle of the sixteenth century the
Swiss Mennonite movement had shifted to southern Germany. Late in the
seventeenth century a growing stream of emigration from South Germany
and Switzerland carried thousands of Swiss Mennonites to the New World,
especially Pennsylvania, to escape persecution. This migration lasted
two hundred years and was a part of the great Atlantic migration from western
Europe to America. Swiss Mennonites and Amish in this migration settled east
of the Mississippi from eastern Pennsylvania to Illinois and represent the
largest segment of North American Mennonites. Not all Swiss and South
German Mennonites left Europe for the new world at this time. Smaller
groups accepted the invitation of Austrian Emperor Joseph II in the 1780s
to settle his newly acquired Polish territory of Galicia. A portion of
these Galician Mennonites later responded to an invitation of Catherine
the Great and left for Russia before the close of the eighteenth century
finally settling in the province of Volhynia.[5] Although persecution was

the initial cause of migration, economic conditions soon played an important role (fig. 2-1).

While the major Swiss Mennonite migration pattern moved initially south and eventually west to the new world, the harried Dutch Anabaptists resettled east along the North Sea coast and southern Baltic area from Antwerp to the Vistula delta, where by the middle of the sixteenth century, Mennonites concentrated in the triangle of Danzig-Elbing-Marienburg. West Prussian landowners in this area enlisted experienced Dutch Mennonites in a program to convert swamps into productive farm lands. Their success enabled them to acquire lands and numerous Mennonite villages developed in the Vistula delta. When the Danzig-Elbing-Marienburg area had been occupied, the surplus population established settlement along the Vistula delta as far as Poland. Although Mennonites of this region shared a common origin, they found themselves living under four separate political divisions.[6] However, by 1772 all four divisions were united under the king of Prussia, Frederick the Great.

Although Frederick was a comparatively tolerant ruler, Mennonite privileges lasted only a brief period as a growing spirit of militarism in Europe spread into Prussia. After the death of Frederick, an edict was issued in 1789 by his successor, King Frederick William II, revoking earlier Mennonite privileges. The purchase of new lands by Mennonites in Prussia was forbidden, heavy taxes were levied, and the threat of universal military conscription was real.[7] At this point the Dutch-Prussian Mennonites considered several possibilities, including a notion to join their Swiss Brethren in America. Some established the congregations of

Fig. 2-1. Mennonite migration patterns in Europe, 1525-1884.

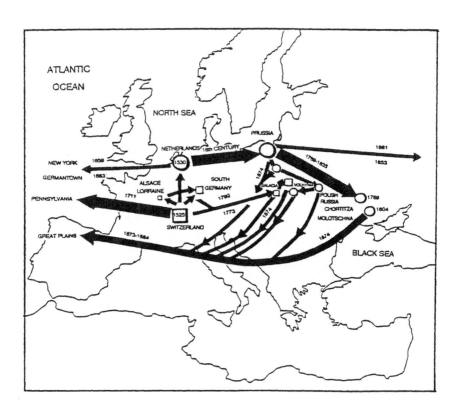

☐Swiss Mennonites
○Dutch Mennonites
◄Migration flow

Deutsch-Wymysle and Deutsch-Kazun northwest of Warsaw. Others were

enticed deeper into Poland with generous offers of land, tax exemption,

and religious freedom by the Polish Count Potocki. Here Dutch-Prussian

Mennonites established the village of Michalin in 1791 and joined their

Swiss Brethren from Galicia and the Palatinate. Still later at the

beginning of the nineteenth century the Dutch-Prussian Mennonites accepted

Prince Lubanersky's offer to settle on his estates near Ostrog in Volhyni

This same offer had attracted Swiss Mennonites and again the paths of the

Dutch and the Swiss Anabaptists converged but did not meet. Contact was

established between the two factions but little, if any, intermingling

occurred.[8]

The largest group of Dutch Mennonites in Prussia responded to an

offer made in 1784 by Catherine the Great to settle the frontier steppes

of Russia. About one-half of the Prussian Mennonite churches accepted

Catherine's offer and nearly 8,000 left the fertile delta of the Vistula

between 1786 and 1870 to start life over on the fertile, though desolate,

steppes along the lower Dnieper and Molotschna.[9] Up to this point Dutch

Mennonite migration had been on a scale involving small groups. Hence-

forth organized large-scale migration of Mennonites of Dutch background

was common.

The Prussian Mennonite Church

During the two centuries of their sojourn in Prussia the

Dutch Mennonites underwent Germanization. This process commenced slowly

in the late seventeenth and early eighteenth centuries in West Prussia

and shortly thereafter in the free city of Danzig. Gradually the

Mennonites substituted a dialect of Low German, Plautdietsch, for Dutch

and Dutch dialects as the conversational language.[10] By the time they
had migrated to the Black Sea area High German had also replaced Dutch
as the literary and church language. However, most Mennonites learned
High German only in Russia due in part to Czar Paul's instruction that
all government agencies carry on all official correspondence with German
settlers in High German in an attempt to remedy colonists' ignorance of
the law.[11] If two centuries of Germanization had instilled a sense of
"Deutschtum" in Prussian Mennonites, this loyalty quickly dissolved as
a growing Prussian militarism restricted Mennonite land purchases.
Mennonite identity lay not in a grand Germanhood nor in their previous
Dutch background. By the late eighteenth century there could be found
a distinctive Gemeindechristentum.[12] Mennonite loyalties were to the
church, not to the Prussian state. The church, whether in the city or
in the country, functioned as the rallying point for cultural cohesiveness. In Prussia, as later in Russia and for a time in America, the
Mennonite congregation served as the center of village life, "the repository of the sacred symbols of community existence."[13] The local church
was the dominant influence in the lives of Prussian Mennonites in the
eighteenth century. Church buildings were simple, usually constructed
from wood without paint inside or out, reflecting the influence of the
"hidden church of Holland."[14] By the end of the century pulpits were
common in most churches and sermons were read from manuscripts.

Men and women sat segregated from each other. Worship was
plain and simple in form. Musical instruments were not generally
accepted until the late nineteenth century. The ministry was divided
into three ranks: Aeltester (elder), Vermaaner (minister), and
Armendiener (Deacon). The Vorsaenger (song leader) was selected for

life just below the deacon in dignity.[15] All ranks were elected from among the laity and served without either pay or special preparation. When there were several candidates, selection was by lot. The elders exercised strong leadership and greatly influenced their flocks. Their term was for life and they were seldom removed from office except for gross sin.

Church government was strictly congregational. Membership was restricted to baptized adults. Communion was limited to members who were at peace with God and usually concluded with the footwashing ordinance. Discipline was strictly enforced with the ban of excommunication enacted in case of flagrant sin.[16] Marriage was a sacred rite and therefore performed on Sunday in the church. Marriage with non-Mennonites was not performed by Mennonite elders and resulted in excommunication in most churches. By the end of the eighteenth century High German had replaced Dutch as the worship language in most Prussian congregations.

Three factions of the Dutch Mennonites resulted from serious divisions in sixteenth century Holland: the Flemish, the Frisians, and the Waterlanders. The Frisians originated in 1566 in the Dutch province of Friesland. Newly arrived Belgian (Flemish) Mennonites offended the Frisian notion of dress and manner. In turn the Flemish thought the Frisians were too worldly in the adornment of their homes. In 1567 the parties separated and banned each other, maintaining their dispute for three centuries throughout Europe. Both the Frisian and Flemish divisions spawned further schisms with conservative and progressive wings in both groups. In Prussia the split lasted longer than in the Netherlands where the Dutch initiated mergers early in the seventeenth century. A third faction, the Waterlanders, was the most liberal branch of the three divisions. Originally they had rejected

the stricter interpretations of church discipline by Menno Simons and his
co-elders at the Strasbourg Conference of 1557. Unlike the Frisians and
the Flemish, the Waterlanders did not consider their own church as the
only true Mennonite church and by 1800 had merged with various progressive
factions of the Frisian and Flemish Mennonites.

The Frisian and Flemish schism revealed variant church practices
in Prussia. In Flemish congregations the preachers read their sermons while
seated whereas in the Frisian congregations the sermons were extemporaneous.
The Flemish mode of baptism involved pouring while the Frisians sprinkled.
In the Flemish communion the preacher distributed bread to the members, who
remained seated, while Frisian congregations filed past the elder who
placed bread in their handkerchiefs. Only late in eighteenth century
Prussia was intermarriage between the two groups quietly accepted. At the
time of their original settlement in Russia, the opposition was still
strong enough that settlements were organized maintaining a separation.
Only gradually did the distinction between the groups disappear in Russia.[17]
As a result of these numerous schisms, the Mennonites who settled in central
Kansas in the 1870s brought with them various practices which differed
significantly with each congregation.

Settlement in Russia

To Prussian Mennonites Catherine's invitation was a timely
act of providence. A law in 1774 compelling Mennonites to pay annually
exorbitant fees for military exemption was followed by an edict in 1789
forcing landed Mennonites to support Lutheran churches, schools, and
parish homes. The further purchase of land by Mennonites was not
permitted except with special permission from the king. It was obvious

that Prussian Mennonites could not remain without making major concessions. Under these circumstances a special invitation was sent to Mennonites along the lower Vistula in 1784. Actually Catherine had initiated a colonization program with an imperial manifesto in 1763. She was in need of farmers to cultivate the virgin soil of the Russian Steppe and develop a buffer between Russia and her enemies to the south. Prospective colonists were extended the following rights and privileges as a result of the July 22, 1763 manifesto:

1. Free board and transportation from the Russian boundary to the place of settlement.

2. The right to settle in any part of the country and to pursue any occupation.

3. A loan for the building of houses, the acquisition of farm implements, the establishment of factories, etc.

4. Perpetual exemption from military and civil service, though this was not to preclude anyone from joining such services at his own volition.

5. Exemption from the payment of taxes for a varying period of time, depending upon the place of settlement and type of occupation.

6. Free religious practice and, to those who founded agricultural colonies, the right to build and control their own churches and schools, but not to establish monasteries.

7. The right to proselytize among the country's Moslem population, even "to enserf them", but under no condition whatsoever to proselytize among other Christian subjects, especially members of the Russian Orthodox Church.

8. The right of local self-government for all those who established agricultural communities.

9. The right to import free of duty family belongings as well as goods for sale up to a specified amount.

10. The right of those who established factories at their own expense to buy serfs and peasants.

11. Finally, if these terms were not satisfactory, prospective colonists were invited to send delegates to Russia to negotiate specific terms with the government.[18]

There is no record that any Mennonites were recruited to go to Russia during the two decades following the 1763 imperial manifesto. None of the 104 German colonies established on the banks of the Volga River from 1764-67 were Mennonite.[19] It was not until twenty-five years after the 1763 manifesto that Mennonites began migrating to recently obtained Turkish lands called "New Russia". Although numerically one of the smallest contingents of foreign colonists brought to South Russia under Catherine and her successors, the Mennonites were successful farmers who reportedly received a great deal of praise during their sojourn on the steppes. The regional viceroy, Potemkin, recognized the quality of Mennonite immigrants and personally conducted negotiations with two Mennonite deputies in 1787, approving a twenty-point petition. The petition was not that of desperate migrants in search of an immediate haven; it was a carefully weighed and prepared statement of a people who knew their worth and were fully conscious of the needed concessions compatible to their religious convictions.[20] Taking advantage of the final point in the 1763 manifesto, the Mennonite deputies negotiated beyond those outlined in the original document. The response of the Prussian Mennonites to the special concessions was enthusiastic. In spite of Prussian government interference, two groups of emigrants from the Danzig area numbering 228 families departed for the Black Sea area in the fall of 1788. Viceroy Potemkin ordered them in June 1789 to establish their first colonies in the province of Ekaterinoslav on one of his numerous personal estates instead of the location in Taurida as specified in the official agreement concluded in 1787. This colony became known as the Chortitza settlement, so named after a tributary of the Dnieper River. In 1797 an additional 118 families joined the original settlers forming a settlement of 400 families by 1800.[21] Later the Chortitza settlement would be referred to as the "Old Colony" since it was the first Mennonite settlement in southern Russia.

The first Russian Mennonite settlers were not by trade the farmers Catherine tried to induce. For the most part they were Flemish tradesmen and craftsmen who were hard-pressed by economic difficulties. The Frisian wing was more agrarian than the Flemish and usually possessed a larger supply of livestock.[22] The conflict between the Frisian and Flemish factions of Prussian Mennonites continued in Russia. In fact, the settlement was initially bankrupt of spiritual leadership due to the inability of both sides to agree on an acceptable elder. This lack of unity contributed significantly to the early difficulties of the Chortitza group. The first pioneers soon settled in separate villages according to their Frisian/Flemish background and organized separate churches. The largest number of settlers belonged to the Flemish group and organized the Chortitza Mennonite Church while Frisian Mennonites organized the Kronsweid Mennonite Church. Both churches served as the hub of village life and as daughter colonies were established branch congregations were likewise founded. As long as branch congregations had no officially appointed and installed elder, the elders of the two mother churches performed baptisms, conducted the Lord's supper, and served as leaders. In this fashion the Chortitza Mennonites of both the Frisian and Flemish wings separately maintained a common ethno-religious identity with little deviation from the mother church.

The church schism was further complicated by agricultural
inexperience, unkept promises by a bureaucratic Russian government,
the theft of household goods enroute, and poor soil in the Chortitza
region. In the midst of these difficulties the early settlers turned
their wrath on the two Mennonite deputies who had negotiated the
original conditions of settlement with the Russian government, Hoeppner
and Bartsch. Lacking both experience in self-government and the
necessary spiritual leadership, the early Chortitza Mennonites were
devoid of conflict management skills.

Meanwhile conditions for Dutch Mennonites still in Prussia
continued to deteriorate. Supplements of previous decrees served
to increase the anxieties among an even larger number of Mennonites
with regard to their future in Prussia. Recognizing the opportunity
of the moment, Czar Alexander I issued in Imperial Manifesto stressing
quality rather than quantity of immigrants, specifically favoring
Mennonites. From 1803 to 1840 approximately 1,200 Mennonite families
responded to Alexander's wooing and founded the second and largest
settlement on the Molotschna River some one hundred miles from the
Chortitza settlement.[23] The Molotschna settlers were generally more
prosperous and more experienced at farming than their Chortitza brethren.
They came with strong ecclesiastical leadership and in 1805 organized
the first eighteen villages into one congregation under elder Jakob Enns.
Most of the Molotschna Mennonites were of the Flemish branch with only
one Frisian village. If the Chortitza settlers were the trailblazers
for Mennonite settlement in Russia, the Molotschna settlers were the
model for subsequent Mennonite migrations. Even though confronted with
many of the same difficulties and adjustments of the Old Colony, they

learned from the mistakes of the Chortitza group and benefited from their experience.

The Dutch Mennonites from Prussia found what they were looking for on the Russian steppes--religious toleration, military exemption, self-rule, and land. Like many of the other 500,000 German colonists who settled in Russia during the century following the 1763 manifesto, the Mennonites had been victims of religious intolerance common to eighteenth century German duchies. Overpopulation (Europe doubled in population from 1750 to 1850), the effects of war and revolution, and the fear of a reduction in status from landowner to paid laborer blended with religious discontent to cause immigration to the Russian steppes.[24] Initially the push factors were predominant but once settlements were established pull factors took over. Although early Mennonite historians emphasized the religious factors in immigration, seldom was religion the sole cause of migration. Economic pressure and religious discontent usually accompanied the immigrant to a new land. Maldwyn Jones may well be correct in his assumption that "one can safely say that the prospect of earthly lure was a stronger stimulus to emigration than that of heavenly bliss."[25]

There were numerous sources of the Mennonite migration to Russia. For whatever reasons, around 8,000 Prussian Mennonites settled in the Black Sea region of Russia from 1789 to 1874.[26]

Life in Russia

Throughout the nineteenth century foreign visitors touring the Russian countryside were inevitably directed to the Black Sea region to observe the colonial development of the Czar's stepchildren.

Alexander I made no secret of his fondness for Mennonite settlers.
He had made a gift of 6,000 rubles for a church building in the
Molotschna colony and on two occasions had personally visited the
settlement.[27] He was proud of their development of the steppes. Two
English observers in the first half of the nineteenth century were also
impressed with the Black Sea Mennonites. Mary Holderness reported
as a result of her 1816-20 tour of Russia that the Mennonites were a
"most industrious and religious class of people, deservedly held
in high esteem."[28] She was particularly impressed with their immense
farms and extensive orchards. Three decades later another English
observer, H. D. Seymour, went to the extent of comparing the Molotschna
colony to an oasis in the desert:

> Their neat cottages, well-built barns and out-houses, surrounded
> by trees and gardens, and by highly cultivated fields, bear
> the signs of wealth and comfort, and of care bestowed upon them
> by an industrious and intelligent population. The German col-
> onies form a striking contrast to the dreary country in which
> they are situated, and to the miserable Russian villages . . . .[29]

Of utmost interest to the Mennonites upon their arrival in New
Russia was the land. One of the original promises of the 1763 manifesto
was the allotment of sixty-five dessiatines (175 acres), consisting of
arable land, meadow, pasture, and woodland where available. Unlike
the Volga Germans who used the repartitional tenure form of land
ownership commonly known as the mir system, the Black Sea Mennonites
used the hereditary household tenure in which the oldest son took over
the farm and financially compensated the other members of the family
for their shares of land inheritance. Furthermore, Mennonite land
holdings were kept in separate districts from Lutheran, Catholic,
Reformed, and Pietists to avoid religious conflicts. A portion of

a colony's land holdings were set aside so that future generations
could settle them. Although the land holdings of a colony were collectively held, every family had its allotted portion that they treated
as their own. Thus, theoretically the landless people of the future
had an equal right to village land since its ownership was invested
in the village commune.[30] In practice, however, the landless had
no claim to the land because the original family allotment could
not legally be divided among the heirs of a household nor sold or
given away. This proved to be a grave defect in the land ownership
regulations.

The administration of the colonies was also of great concern
to the Mennonites. In Prussia they had been under the rule of either
a Catholic or Lutheran royalty and were often victimized by the whims
of economic and political fortunes. Their status was always changing
and never guaranteed. For the most part they were granted autonomy
in purely local issues concerning education, health, and welfare in
Russia. Alexander I (1801-1825) and Nicholas I (1825-1885) left them
to their own devices of self-rule because they were model colonists.
No other religious group of colonists had developed and maintained their
own hospitals, educational, agricultural, economic, and welfare institutions as the Black Sea Mennonites. This autonomy greatly enhanced their
historical ethnoreligious cohesiveness and created a state within a
state, what historian David G. Rempel refers to as a "Mennonite Commonwealth."[31]

Self-rule was unfamiliar to most Mennonites. Neither in Danzig,
West Prussia, nor in Poland had they been accorded citizenship status.
During the first decade in Russia the governing functions in the colonies

were carried on by an official appointed by the national government.[32]
This was not satisfactory and in 1801 a new system was devised under
which each colony formed a separate unit of government consisting of
a Mennonite village assembly and Mennonite mayor (Schulze). The Schulze
was the key organizational figure of local government. The powers vested
in him ranged from insuring Sunday church attendance to a far reaching
authority over agriculture, commerce, and industry. Along with his two
assistants (Beisitzer) the Schulze was elected every two years by the
village assembly. Although he had the potential to become a village
dictator by virtue of his right to interfere in every sphere of the
settlers' private lives, he was usually held in check by the village
assembly.[33] The relationship between the Schulze and the church elders
was generally intimate and cooperative. There were instances when either
the church or the secular authorities seemed to dominate colony leadership but usually their relationship was harmonious.[34] Several colonies
were grouped together to compose a district or volost. The district
office was presided over by an Oberschulze who exercised police powers
in the district and imposed sentences with the consent of the local
Schulze.

     Self-government was both a blessing and a burden to Russian
Mennonites. While it allowed for complete local autonomy and a subsequent
lack of interference from the outside world, it thoroughly tested the
Mennonite concept of non-resistance. When it came to the matter of
punishing offenders, Mennonites could no longer wash their hands and
refer punitive action to a "worldly" authority. The ecclesiastical
power structure of the elder-led congregation was also challenged by a
local government headed by a Schulze. In Prussia the elder was the sole

leader of the congregation since secular officials had no concern for the church attendance activities or the moral demeanor of Mennonites. In Russia, however, the Schulze had complete right of supervision over the lives of the colonists and for the first time the elder was forced to share his authority with a Mennonite civil official.

Ultimately the burdens of self-government were equaled by blessings. Through self-rule Mennonites in Russia gained a separation from the world that could not be achieved in Holland, Prussia, or Poland. The likelihood of intermarriage with Russian peasants or other non-Mennonite colonists was practically non-existent. Until 1870 Russification was not a threat to Mennonites. The Anabaptist principles for which they had previously suffered could now be implemented without interference. Even though the Schulze was a secular official he was also in every case a Mennonite and henceforth subject to the same guidelines of lifestyle prescribed by the church for all colonists. Thus, self-rule allowed the local congregation to gain an even stronger hold on the life of the individual and strengthen the ethnoreligious cohesiveness of the church.

Economic Development

Prosperity was not immediately realized by the Mennonites in New Russia. The first years, especially in the Chortitza settlement, were filled with hardships. The extremely hot, dry summers and cold, windy winters of the Russian steppes were often accompanied by plagues of locusts, gophers, and drought. These conditions, coupled with an isolation from markets, forced colonists to turn from crop raising to stock farming, particularly sheep. Marino sheep managed well on the grassy areas of the Taurida and Crimea regions.[35] Later Mennonite

settlers imported a sturdy breed of Frisian cattle which also
flourished on the steppes.

Sheep rearing reached its peak in Russia in the 1840s and
gradually began to decline due to competition of fine wool overseas.
At the same time Britain repealed her Corn Laws (1846) and Russian
export of Ukrainian wheat rose sharply. Mennonite colonists in the
1840s made the shift from stockraising to grain production, particularly wheat, but also rye, barley, and oats. In the 1850s, the
black earth belt of the steppes became Russia's grainary, producing
70 per cent of the country's cereals.[36] From 1865 to 1875 the average
cropland per farm grew from 25 dessiatine (67.5 acres) to 34 dessiatine
(113.8 acres).[37]

The real turning point in their economic development came when
a Mennonite by the name of Johann Cornies was made president of the
Molotschna branch of the Agricultural Association in 1830. Over the
next eighteen years Cornies would become the most famous Mennonite in
Russia.[38] He was given a free hand and endowed with unlimited powers
to develop the agricultural economy of the Mennonite colonies. The
results of Cornies' efforts were impressive. By means of summer fallow
productivity of the soil drought was overcome. Breeds of sheep and cattle
in the colonies were considerably improved. Orchards and groves were
planted under the supervision of the Agricultural Association so that by
1850 the forty-seven villages of the Molotschna settlement could boast of
5 million trees. For a period of time silk production became a major
source of income for the colonists. All of this resulted from the
effort of Cornies' leadership of the Agricultural Association.[39]

Education

Just as the colonists had suffered economically during the
first decades in Russia, they also experienced a poverty of education.
During the first half of the nineteenth century schools remained under
the supervision of church elders. Often the village school was conducted in the private home of a teacher who was inadequately educated.
Emphasis was placed upon memorization and the Bible served as a textbook.
Other textbooks were in the German language but the classroom language
was usually Low German. Corporal punishment was common.[40] In 1843
when the Agricultural Association assumed jurisdiction over the educational interests of the colonies, a new day dawned for Mennonite schools
of Russia. Cornies headed the reform of school which included an
expanded curriculum, improved relationships between students and
teachers, restrictions on corporal punishment, standardized textbooks,
special exams for teachers, and a building code for school buildings.
No teacher could be hired or fired without the consent of Cornies.
Inspectors periodically visited each school to insure quality education.
Each village maintained its own school and attendance was compulsory.
Illiteracy did not occur.[41] Secondary schools (Zentral-Schulen) were
founded to prepare qualified teachers for elementary schools.

Many of Cornies' educational reforms met with resistance,
especially from amongst the clergy. Heinrich Heese, a pioneer
of the Zentralschule, sensed this same opposition when local authorities expressed the notion that "the more you learn, the more mixed up
you get."[42] However, many of the teachers in the newly reformed
schools of the late nineteenth century were ordained Mennonite ministers.

The church continued to have a strong influence over the education of the colonists until the twentieth century.

The Church

The first group of settlers in Chortitza in 1789 did not contain a single elder. This was probably due to the fact that the first contingent of 228 families was poor and Mennonite elders were traditionally chosen from amongst the wealthy. Five years later the congregations in Prussia sent an elder with instructions to unite the Flemish and the Frisian into one congregation. This was never realized. When the Flemish settlers arrived in the Molotschna area in 1804 they were accompanied by ministers. One Jakob Enns was ordained and installed as the elder of the Molotschna settlement in 1805.

The Mennonite Church in Russia encountered three major difficulties in the nineteenth century. The first resulted from congregational mixing. Although some congregations had been transplanted en masse from Prussia to Russia, settlement on the steppes resulted in the mixing of different groups. Agreement on the fundamentals of Mennonite belief did not guarantee complete conformity on all issues. Two hundred years in Prussia with very little contact between individual Mennonite churches had produced congregational distinctives in customs and practice. Some Mennonites had been influenced by a wave of pietistic revivals in Prussia during the early nineteenth century. European Pietism was a product of the late seventeenth century. It emphasized a "heartfelt" religion based on an emotionally experienced conversion stressing good works, nonconformity, and the second coming

of Christ. The Moravian Brethren under Count Nicholas Ludwig von Zinzendorf
(1700-70) gave Pietism an emotional, missions orientation. Moravian literature was widely circulated amongst Prussian Mennonites in the early nineteenth century. The greatest impact of Pietism among Prussian Mennonites
was to occur later in Russia during the middle of the nineteenth century.
However, the first settlers of New Russia displayed varying degrees of
pietistic influence which in turn was a source of contention in local
congregations.[43]

The second difficulty facing the church in Russia was the new
administrative structure of the colonies. As previously mentioned,
the leader in each settlement was the Schulze. He was a Mennonite
but not a minister. Mennonites were not used to having one of their
own as a civil authority and had subsequently looked to the congregational elder exclusively for leadership. Self-rule in Russia, however, necessitated the Schulze. The result was a period of adjustment
characterized by an occasional power struggle between the elder and
the Schulze producing an atmosphere conducive to church schisms.
In Prussia excommunication by an elder not only meant expulsion from
the congregation but also implied a more complete severance of Mennonite ties. In Russia, under a system which placed the Schulze as the
settlement leader, the elder did not have the legal power for complete
severance through excommunication. Thus, Mennonite schisms resulted
producing officially recognized branches of the Mennonite church.
Such was the case with the Kleine Gemeinde (1814), the Mennonite
Brethren (1860), and the Krimmer Mennonite Brethren (1869).

Klaas Reimer was the founder of the Kleine Gemeinde in the
Molotschna settlement in 1814. Reimer's objection to what he perceived

as a relaxed church discipline, low moral standards, and worldly compromise
caused him to take issue with the Molotschna Mennonite elder, Jacob Enns,
and leave the church, establishing his own following. The Kleine Gemeinde
remained small but continued to exist, due in part to a strong resistance
from the "grosse Gemeinde" (big church). In 1843 Johann Cornies intervened and the elders of the Mennonite church were compelled by civil
authorities to recognize the Kleine Gemeinde as a valid denomination.[44]

The founding of the Mennonite Brethren in 1860 represented a
greater impact upon the Mennonite experience in Russia than that of
the Kleine Gemeinde. The creation of the Mennonite Brethren was the
result of pietistic revivals which had earlier influenced some of the
Mennonites in Prussia. In 1835 a group from Brenkenhoffswalde, who
had come in contact with the Moravian Brethren, founded the village
of Gnadenfeld, Molotschna. This settlement later became the center
of Pietistic revivals in New Russia. In 1845 a pietistic Lutheran
pastor, Edward Wuerst, located in a Lutheran colony south of the
Molotschna settlement. Wuerst was a dynamic speaker and a powerful
personality and had a remarkable influence upon the Molotschna Mennonites, whom he occasionally visited as a guest speaker. His messages
stressed repentance, conversion and a life consistent with an enthusiastic faith. The Pietistic Movement was met with both reception and
resistance amongst Black Sea Mennonites. It represents the most important religious awakening in the history of Mennonites in Russia. In
some congregations the revival fires were received warmly and no schisms
occurred. In other congregations there was resistance to the pietistic
notion of an emotional salvation experience, an eschatological emphasis,
and baptism by immersion. In these churches splits took place, the

first on January 6, 1860 in the village of Elisabeththal. The withdrawal of eighteen men marked the beginning of the Mennonite Brethren
Church. Adding a newly acquired pietistic emphasis to their long held
Anabaptist distinctives, the Mennonite Brethren appealed to St. Petersburg
for official recognition and legal status. They received such by 1862.[45]

The Krimmer Mennonite Brethren (1869) were originally from the
Molotschna settlement. In 1860 a group established a village in the
Crimea named Annafeld. Shortly thereafter a spontaneous revival unrelated
to the Pietist Movement but similar in nature occurred. The leader of the
group, Jacob A. Wiebe, became acquainted with the Kleine Gemeinde and for
a short time affiliated with them. In 1869 when a disagreement arose concerning mode of baptism, the Krimmer Mennonite Brethren Church was founded.
The group was never large in Russia (twenty families) and, with the exception
of three families, emigrated in 1874. Eventually the KMB merged with the
Mennonite Brethren in North America.[46] There were other schisms in the
Mennonite Church in Russia but the Kleine Gemeinde, Mennonite Brethren, and
the Krimmer Mennonite Brethren represent the major fractures which resulted
from internal strife, outside revival influences, and an administrative
structure that limited the authority of elders.

The third difficulty confronted by the Mennonite Church in
Russia was the development of a landless Mennonite proletariat referred
to as Anwohner. For the most part Mennonite families were large and
government regulations prohibited the subdivision of standard farms.
Surplus lands gradually had been settled or were no longer used for
their intended purposes and additional industries remained undeveloped
by 1860. By this time nearly two-thirds of the Molotschna families
belonged to the Anwohner class.[47]

There were those numbered amongst the landless who were successfully engaged in business and had no desire to own colony land. The
majority of Anwohners, however, were either hired farm laborers or land
renters and were by no means satisfied with their plight. Since they were
voteless in village assemblies (only farm owners were represented on these
assemblies) they carried their grievances to the church. This turned out
to be a fruitless venture since the elders were non-salaried and elected
by the village congregation, which was virtually identical to the village
assembly. Furthermore, the elders of the church were usually elected
from the wealthy farming class and thus were generally sympathetic with
the landowners. Ultimately the landless accused the landowners and
elders of growing cold and possessing a "Sunday" religion that was
dead in form.[48] The Chortitza settlement experienced the same Anwohner
problem but not to the extent of the Molotschna settlement. Chortitza
Mennonites never reached as high a degree of prosperity as Molotschna
landowners and consequently the gulf between the Anwohner and the
landowner was not as great.

By 1860 the Anwohner crisis had intensified. When the pietistic
revivals of the 1850s swept across southern Russia there was a significant
response from the landless. Many of the converts of the Pietist Movement
were those who had previously threatened to leave the church over the land
issue. In 1860 their threats became reality as the Bruedergemeinde
(Brethren Church) was established. The elders, who previously had sided
with the landowners against the Anwohner, were surprised as they realized
government agencies no longer sided with them in Mennonite disputes.

When the government recognized the Mennonite Brethren as
an independent religious body in 1862 with all rights and privileges

pertaining to the Mennonite church, the church leaders finally expressed
their willingness to make concessions to the Anwohner. This settlement
took place in 1866 and granted lands to the Anwohner by means of dividing
full farms, distribution of surplus lands, and purchase of new settlements
(daughter colonies).[49] In many cases, however, the Anwohner had to migrate
to the Caucasus and beyond to establish farms. Thus the wheels of migration
were set in motion for the mass immigration of the 1870s to North America.

By 1874 the division between the Flemish and Frisian factions were
beginning to disappear although some distinctive practices were still in
the local church early in the twentieth century. However, intermarriage
between Flemish and Frisian congregations produced a generation in the
late nineteenth century ignorant of the old schism. In some respect the
schisms in the nineteenth century had drawn away from the ancient
Frisian-Flemish conflict.

The Mennonite church in 1870, with the exception of the Mennonite
Brethren, was in many respects the same as the Prussian church a century
earlier. The elder stood at the head of the church and was ordained by
the laying on of hands. He was elected from amongst the ministers of a
local congregation and alone exercised discipline, baptism, dispensed
the Lord's Supper, and commissioned other elders, teachers, and deacons.
He was assisted in his duties by other preachers, teachers, assistants,
and deacons. The three levels of church leadership--elder, minister,
deacon--were maintained in Russia. Ministers were commissioned by
elders to preach, marry, and bury but not to perform baptism or communion.
The deacon assisted at baptisms and communion services and oversaw the
church property as well as the care of the poor. The elder, ministers,

and deacons made up the church council (Lehrdienst) while the brotherhood (Bruederschaft) consisted of all adult male members of the local
congregation. By majority vote the brotherhood made final decisions on
financial matters, excommunication of erring and readmission of penitent
members, matters of dogma and church governance, and the acceptance or
rejection of all other various church council decisions.[50] Every
congregation, along with its council, constituted an autonomous religious
community. A regional council of church leaders met for a time in the
Molotschna settlement but any resolutions were accepted as recommendations
by the local congregation.

An elder nearly always was chosen from within the congregation and
had no formal preparation for his ministry. A general theological
knowledge was obtained through listening to years of sermons. Beyond
that he might read on his own but few did extensively. Elders ranged
from competent spiritual leaders to inadequately prepared tyrants. Few
were of the latter category and most were in the middle range of ability.
Regardless of an individual's ability or incompetence, the congregation
maintained a deep reverence for the position of elder. He was addressed
as Ohm or Onkel (Uncle), a title of affectionate regard for church leaders,
or as Prediger (preacher) or the more official title, Aeltester (elder).[51]
Outwardly the Mennonite clergy led an honorable Christian life and displayed
a solid knowledge of the Bible.[52] Sermons written by early Prussian Mennonites were usually read and sometimes repeated on an annual basis.

Mennonite church services in nineteenth century Russia were similar
in nature to the buildings in which they were held--simple and functionable.
Men and women sat segregated from each other facing a raised pulpit from
which sermons were delivered. The Vorsaenger (songleader) had his own

special elevated seat at the front of the congregation. He was chosen
by a secret ballot usually for life and was held in high esteem by the
congregation. As a rule there were several Vorsaengers in one congregation and they entered the church before the ministers. In the absence
of musical instruments the Vorsaenger started each song by singing the
first line. The hymnals up to 1860 had no notes and contained lengthy
hymns. Church choirs did not become commonplace in Russia until the 1890s.
Singing was by ear, out of memory, and in unison.[53]   Congregations in nineteenth century Russia held one service a week on Sunday morning.

Communion services were usually held four times a year. The common
cup containing wine was passed from member to member and bread was placed
into a hand-held handkerchief until eaten in unison. In many of the more
conservative Flemish congregations communion was followed by footwashing.
Although it was not universally practiced in Russia, footwashing was far
more common than elsewhere among Mennonites in Europe and America at the
time.[54]

The spiritual development of the Russian Mennonites in the
nineteenth century was hard pressed to keep pace with their material
success. As they approached the second half of the nineteenth century
Mennonites in Russia experienced the economic benefits of a "Golden
Age." At the same time the spiritual life of the colonists by 1850
was generally at a low ebb. Robert Kreider points out that the
Mennonite Church in the Russian Mennonite environment moved in the
direction and exhibited many of the characters of the Volkskirche, or
what the English call the 'parish pattern of the church.'[55]   John A. Toews
observes that in the Russian Mennonite Church by mid-century there was a
lack of strong spiritual leadership, a loss of the Biblical church concept,

a loss of consistent church discipline, and widespread secularism among the laity.[56] Church membership, which was necessary for Mennonites who desired to enjoy privileges and exemptions in the Empire, came to be regarded as a matter of course no longer based on actual conversion. Mennonite historian C. Henry Smith reports that "everybody joined the church at a certain age."[57] When a strong Pietistic movement swept through the colonies in the 1860s the Russian Mennonites were ripe for a revival which prompted an Anabaptist awakening. Thus by 1874 the condition of the church had improved so that Smith could report:

> Mennonites of all shades of belief remained staunch defenders
> of the fundamental principles of non-resistance, opposition to
> the oath, opposition to war, and the demand for consistent
> living, even though they found it difficult sometimes to enforce
> their doctrines and beliefs.[58]

One thing is certain about the Mennonite Church in Russia in 1874: it had remained separated from Russian culture. In spite of all its internal conflicts and spiritual dimensions, the Mennonite Church had managed over eight decades in Russia to avoid Russification. The German language and distinctive culture had produced an ethnoreligious, cohesive Mennonite community maintained through granted privileges under the czar. James Urry contends that historically Mennonites required a hostile host society to strengthen the cohesive nature of community. Without outside opposition Mennonites tended to seek out an enemy within:

> Schisms and virulent discord marked such periods. Hell
> has no fury like a Mennonite community which sees its
> principles at risk, and Satan's hosts are not equal to
> Mennonite set against Mennonite![59]

In 1870 the privileged status of Mennonites in Russia came to a sudden end. The crisis demanded a cooperative spirit amongst the brethren dealing with a challenge to their faith and the prospect of emigration.

Fig. 2-2. European location of thirty-two Kansas General Conference Mennonite Congregations prior to migration.

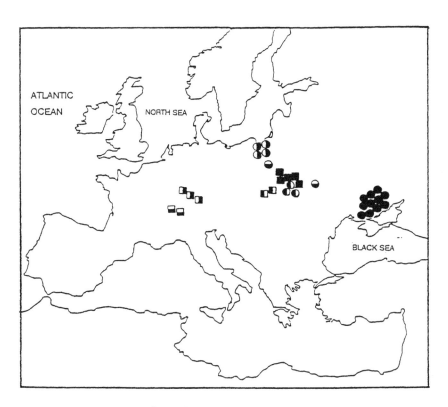

●Dutch-Prussian in South Russia

◑Dutch in West Prussia

◓Dutch-Prussian in Volhynia

◐Dutch-Prussian in Polish Russia

■Swiss in Volhynia

◻Swiss in South Germany

◩Swiss in Galacia

▣Swiss in Switzerland

CHAPTER II - ENDNOTES

1. Harold S. Bender and C. Henry Smith, <u>Mennonites and Their Heritage</u> (Scottdale, Pennsylvania: Herald Press, 1964), p. 26; Cornelius J. Dyck, ed., <u>An Introduction to Mennonite History</u> (Scottdale, Pennsylvania: Herald Press, 1981), p. 50. For a complete study of Anabaptism see William R. Estep, <u>The Anabaptist Story</u>(Grand Rapids, Michigan: William B. Eerdmans Publishing Company, 1975); Walter Klaassen, <u>Anabaptism: Neither Catholic nor Protestant</u> (Waterloo, Ontario: Conrad Press, 1973); Franklin H. Littell, <u>The Anabaptist View of the Church</u> (Boston: Star King Press, 1958); George H. Williams, <u>The Radical Reformation</u> (Philadelphia: Westminster Press, 1967).

2. C. Henry Smith, <u>The Story of the Mennonites</u> (Newton, Kansas: Faith and Life Press, 1981), pp. 72-73.

3. Ibid., pp. 3-73.

4. Bender and Smith, p. 49.

5. Smith, <u>The Story of the Mennonites</u>, pp. 208-09.

6. Ibid., p. 168.

7. C. Henry Smith, <u>The Coming of the Russian Mennonites</u> (Berne, Indiana: Mennonite Book Concern, 1927), pp. 16-17.

8. See Horst Penner, "West Prussian Mennonites through Four Centuries," <u>Mennonite Quarterly Review</u> 23 (October 1949): 232-45; Benjamin H. Unruh, "Dutch Background of the Mennonite Migration of the Sixteenth Century to Prussia," <u>Mennonite Quarterly Review</u> 10 (July 1936): 173-81; John Horsch, <u>Mennonites in Europe</u> (Scottdale, Pennsylvania: Mennonite Publishing House, 1942), pp. 227-32, 271-89.

9. <u>Mennonite Encyclopedia</u>, s.v. "Migrations of Mennonites," by Cornelius Krahn and Harold S. Bender.

10. David G. Rempel, "The Mennonite Commonwealth in Russia: a Sketch of its Founding and Endurance, 1789-1919," <u>Mennonite Quarterly Review</u> 47 (October 1973): 261.

11. Ibid., p. 262.

12. The term "Gemeindechristentum" was used by Mennonite historian C. H. Wedel extensively in his four volume history of the Mennonites; C. H. Wedel, <u>Bilder aus der Kirchengeschichte fur Mennonitische Gemeindeschulen</u>, rev. Cornelius Krahn (7th ed.;

Newton, Kansas: Harold Book and Printing Co., 1951). Wedel picked
up the term from Ludwig Keller who used it to describe the Walden-
sians in Die Reformation und die Aelteren Reformparteien (Leipzig:
S. Hirzel, 1885). Wedel expanded upon Keller's application of
the term to emphasize the difference between the "gemeindechristentum" and both the Protestant State-church and the Catholic Priest-
church. In Wedel's version "Gemeindechristentum" provided distinctive patterns of worship, conflict resolution, intergenerational
relationships, leadership recruitment, and church discipline. In
this respect Wedel, one of the early leaders of the Kansas Mennonites
and first president of Bethel College, had an apostolic model in mind.
For further reference to "Gemeindechristentum" see James C. Juhnke,
"Gemeindechristentum and Bible Doctrine: Two Mennonite Visions of the
Early Twentieth Century," Mennonite Quarterly Review 57 (July 1983):
206-21.

13. Will Herberg, Protestant, Catholic, Jew: An Essay in
American Religious Sociology (Garden City, New York: Doubleday, 1955),
p. 11.

14. Cornelius Krahn, "Mennonite Church Architecture," Mennonite
Life 12 (January 1959): 22.

15. Smith, The Story of the Mennonites, p. 174.

16. Mennonite Encyclopedia, s.v. "Ban," by Christian Neff.

17. Mennonite Encyclopedia, s.v. "Flemish Mennonites," by
Christian Neff and N. van der Zijpp; "Frisian Mennonites," by Christian
Neff and N. van der Zijpp; "Waterlanders," by N. van der Zijpp; Smith,
The Story of the Mennonites, pp. 72-73, 110-12, 116, 127, 133, 135,
139, 166, 173, 175, 252, 272-75; Horsch, pp. 233-58; Smith, The Coming
of the Russian Mennonites, pp. 20-21.

18. Adam Giesinger, From Catherine to Khrushchev (Battleford,
Saskatchewan: Marian Press, 1974), pp. 1-8; James Long, "The Russian
Imperial Manifestoes of 22 July 1763 and 20 February 1804," Germans
from Russia in Colorado, ed. Sidney Heitman (Ft. Collins, Colorado:
Western Social Science Association, 1978), pp. 9-13; Rempel, "The
Mennonite Commonwealth in Russia," pp. 269-70.

19. Rempel, "The Mennonite Commonwealth in Russia," p. 272.

20. Ibid., p. 286.

21. Mennonite Encyclopedia, s.v. "Chortitza Mennonite Settlement," by Cornilius Krahn.

22. Rempel, "The Mennonite Commonwealth in Russia," pp. 291-92.

23. Ibid., p. 307.

24. Oscar Handlin, The Uprooted (Boston: Little, Brown and Co., 1951), pp. 22-24; Maldwyn A. Jones, American Immigration (Chicago: The University of Chicago Press, 1960), pp. 95-99; for a detailed account on German emigration see Mack Walker, Germany and the Emigration, 1816-1885 (Cambridge, Massachusetts: Harvard University Press, 1964).

25. Jones, p. 99.

26. Smith, The Coming of the Russian Mennonites, p. 31.

27. Mennonite Encyclopedia, s.v. "Alexander I," by Christian Neff. Legend has it that one group of Prussian Mennonites had met Alexander I enroute to their new homeland. After a friendly exchange the Mennonites were so impressed they decided to name their village after the Russian monarch. The largest segment of Kansas Mennonites came from the village of Alexanderwohl and the Alexanderwohl church to this day remains among the largest General Conference Mennonite congregations in central Kansas. See David C. Wedel, The Story of Alexanderwohl (North Newton: Mennonite Press, Inc., 1974).

28. Mary Holderness, New Russia (London: Sherwood Jones and Co., 1823), pp. 161-62.

29. H. D. Seymour, Russia on the Black Sea (London: John Murray, Albemarle Street, 1855), p. 17.

30. David G. Rempel, "The Mennonite Colonies in New Russia. A Study of Their Settlement and Economic Development from 1789 to 1914" (Ph.D. dissertation, Stanford University, 1933), pp. 36-43, 102-22. Rempel's research on Russian Mennonite history is of particular significance because of his insistence on telling the story from the vantage points of Russian civil authorities and peasants as well as from within the Mennonite world. His use of the Russian State Archives lends credibility to his findings on the economic, political, and social development of Mennonites in Russia during the nineteenth century. However, his treatment of the Mennonite church in Russia is superficial.

31. Rempel, "The Mennonite Commonwealth in Russia," pp. 9-10.

32. Ibid., p. 11.

33. Rempel, "The Mennonite Colonies in New Russia," pp. 113-22.

34. Mennonite Encyclopedia, s.v. "Government of Mennonites in Russia," by Cornelius Krahn. The first elder of the Molotschna settlement, Jakob Enns, excommunicated the Schulze of Steinbach, Klaas Weins, early in the nineteenth century. See P. M. Friesen, The Mennonite Brotherhood in Russia (1789-1910) (Fresno, California: Board of Christian Literature, General Conference of Mennonite Brethren Churches, 1978), p. 72.

35. Rempel, "The Mennonite Colonies in New Russia," p. 123.

36. Richard Pipes, Russia Under the Old Regime (New York: Charles Scribner's Sons, 1974), p. 148.

37. Rempel, "The Mennonite Colonies in New Russia," p. 243.

38. Walter Quiring, "Johann Cornies - a Great Pioneer," Mennonite Life 3 (July 1948): 30-34, 38; M. S. Harder, "A Pioneer Educator - Johann Cornies," Mennonite Life 3 (October 1948): 5-7, 44; Cornelius Krahn, From the Steppes to the Prairies (North Newton, Kansas: Mennonite Publication Office, 1949), pp. 3-4. Cornies' influence went beyond that of the Mennonite colonists. His authority was extended to the Hutterian Brethren, numerous Nogai tribes, and to the Russian sectarians, the Molokans and the Doukobors. At least on two occasions Mennonite elders were removed from their ecclesiastical offices because of opposition to the powerful Cornies. This represents a rare instance in which an elder was superceded by a Mennonite civil authority. For details of Cornies' conflict with Mennonite leaders see Cornelius Krahn, trans., "Heinrich Hesse (1787-1868)," by Heinrich Hesse, Mennonite Life 24 (April 1969): 70-71.

39. Krahn, From the Steppes to the Prairies, pp. 3-4.

40. Harder, pp. 4-5; Peter Braun, "The Educational System of the Mennonite Colonies in South Russia," Mennonite Quarterly Review 3 (July 1929): 169-73.

41. N. J. Klassen, "Mennonite Intelligensia in Russia," Mennonite Life 24 (April 1969): 52.

42. Krahn, trans., "Heinrich Hesse (1787-1868)," p. 70.

43. Mennonite Encyclopedia, s.v. "Pietism," by Cornelius Krahn. For a more detailed study of the Pietistic impact on Mennonites in Russia and the subsequent founding of the Mennonite Brethren see Goerge Eisenach, Pietism and the Russian Germans in the United States (Berne, Indiana: The Berne Publishers, 1948); Robert Friedmann, Mennonite Piety Through the Centuries (Scottdale, Pennsylvania: Herald Press, 1949); Fritz Grunsweig, Die Evangelische Bruedergemeinde Korntal: Weg, Wesen, und Werk (Metzinger, Wuerttemberg: E. Franz, 1957): F. Ernest Stoeffler, German Pietism During the Eighteenth Century (Leiden, Netherlands: E. J. Brill, 1973). For a theological treatment of Pietism see Dale Brown, Understanding Pietism (Grand Rapids, Michigan: Wm. B. Eerdmans Publishing Co., 1978).

44. Friesen, pp. 127-35.

45. The most exhaustive account of the Russian origin of the Mennonite Brethren Church is P. M. Friesen, Alt-Evangelische Mennonitsche Bruederschaft in Russland (1789-1910) (Halbstadt: Raduga, 1911). The English translation was released in 1978 and is henceforth cited as

The Mennonite Brethren in Russia (1789-1910) (Fresno, California:
Board of Christian Literature, General Conference of the Mennonite
Brethren Churches, 1978). Also see John A. Toews, A History of the
Mennonite Brethren (Hillsboro, Kansas: Mennonite Brethren Publishing
House, 1975).

46. Mennonite Encyclopedia, s.v. "Krimmer Mennonite Brethren,"
by Harold S. Bender; Albert Pantle, "Settlement of the Krimmer Mennonite Brethren at Gnadenau, Marion County," Kansas Historical Quarterly
13 (February 1945): 259-85; David V. Wiebe, They Seek a Country (Free-
man, South Dakota: Pine Hill Press, 1974), pp. 56-63.

47. Rempel, "The Mennonite Commonwealth in Russia," p. 25.

48. Ibid., p. 26; Cornelius Krahn, "Some Social Attitudes on
the Mennonites of Russia," Mennonite Quarterly Review 9 (October 1935):
173.

49. Rempel, "The Mennonite Commonwealth in Russia," pp. 27-28.

50. Friesen, p. 52. The history of Mennonites indicates that
the majority of the brotherhood usually agrees with the elder. Over-
riding the views of elders by a congregation represents the exception.

51. Mennonite Encyclopedia, s.v. "Ohm," by Cornelius Krahn;
"Preacher," by Harold S. Bender.

52. Friesen, p. 55.

53. Wesley Berg, "The Development of Choral Singing Among the
Mennonites of Russia to 1895," Mennonite Quarterly Review 55 (April
1981): 131-42. Mennonite Encyclopedia, s.v. "Chorister," by J. G.
Rempel.

54. Clarence R. Hiebert, "The History of the Ordinance of
Foot-washing in the Mennonite Churches" (S.T.B. Thesis, Biblical Seminary
in New York, 1954), pp. 70-73; Mennonite Encyclopedia, s.v. "Communion,"
by Cornelius Krahn.

55. Robert Kreider, "The Anabaptist Conception of the Church
in the Russian Mennonite Environment," Mennonite Quarterly Review 25
(January 1951): 22.

56. John A. Toews, pp. 19-25.

57. Smith, The Coming of the Russian Mennonites, p. 42.

58. Ibid., p. 43.

59. James Urry, "The Transformation and Polarization of the
Mennonites in Russia, 1789-1914." Paper presented to the 1977
Conference on Russian Mennonite History, Winnipeg, November 1977.

CHAPTER III

IMMIGRATION TO AMERICA AND SETTLEMENT IN KANSAS

It is true that the Mennonites do not Americanze as fast
as some other nations, but they have no habits or beliefs
which are anti-American, hence they make very fair citizens
at present, and will develop rapidly in the future. - McPherson
Republican, June 1, 1882.

Causes of Immigration

By 1870 rumors spread in Mennonite circles that a new military

law in Russia meant universal conscription for all colonists. A Menno-

nite deputation was quickly assembled and sent to St. Petersburg in

March, 1871 to seek out the basis for such rumors. Here they discovered

a proposed law of universal conscription that included Mennonites.[1] Non-

combatant service was a distinct likelihood. Efforts to gain an audience

with the Czar failed. Three subsequent delegations in 1872 and 1873

failed to secure desired concessions in the new military law.[2] Further-

more, Mennonites learned that Russian would be introduced into Mennonite

schools as the main language of instruction, and schools of the colonists

were to be placed under the direct control of the Russian government.[3]

Russification appeared inevitable. Together universal conscription and

a Russified education policy prompted emigration considerations.

In 1872 four young Mennonites traveled to the United States and

visited various American Mennonite communities. One of the four, Bernhard

Warkentin, remained in America and sent favorable reports back to Russia.

In the summer of 1873 a delegation of twelve men including Hutterite, Dutch and Swiss Volhynian, Prussian, and Russian Mennonite representatives, sailed for North America in search of land. Accompanied by several prominent American Mennonites and anxious railroad agents, they inspected prairie lands in Manitoba, the Dakota Territory, Nebraska, Minnesota, Kansas, and Texas. Even though the Canadian government offered more liberal military exemption terms, the delegates seemed to favor settlement in the United States. Upon their return to Russia the delegates enthusiastically reported the availability of land in North America. At this point the Russian government, reluctant to lose so many of its best farmers, made significant concessions in an effort to persuade them to stay. The most important of these concessions to the Russian Mennonites was the substitution of forestry as an alternative service to military conscription.[4] This concession along with others was accepted by the majority of Mennonites. However, for a strong minority the concessions were too few, too late. By 1874 the wheels of emigration were already irreversibly in motion. Hutterite colonists in Russia departed early en masse. Most of the Polish Russian, Swiss Volhynian, and a segment of Prussian Mennonites joined the South Russian Mennonites emigrating from 1874 to 1880.[5]

The Mennonites who left Russia during the late nineteenth century were part of a larger group of 120,000 Germans who migrated from Russia to the United States between 1870 and 1920.[6] Approximately 18,000 of the 45,000 Mennonites in Russia emigrated between 1874 and 1880 with the majority departing the first two years. Of this number 10,000 settled in the United States while the remaining 8,000 chose Manitoba.[7] The more conservative faction of the Mennonites generally settled in Canada. The largest segment of Mennonites to settle in the United States selected the state of Kansas. Approximately 5,000 Russian Mennonites

settled in a five county area of central Kansas from 1874 to 1880.[8]

Early Mennonite historians tended to emphasize the religious causes

for emigration. More recent treatment has rendered an economic inter-

pretation viewing the exodus as the result of a conflict between the

landowners and the landless.[9] By the middle of the nineteenth century

3% of the Russian Mennonite population owned 30% of the land leaving

two-thirds of the Mennonite population in the Anwohner class.[10] However,

it is impossible to separate the economic and religious causes of emigratic

since they were intricately interwoven into the fabric of Mennonite work

ethic. By virtue of two hundred years of farming experience on the

Vistula and an additional century on the Russian steppes, farming had

become a religious duty that no one could shirk. Mennonites adhered to

a literal application of the Biblical injunction, "In the sweat of thy

face shalt thou eat bread" (Genesis 3:19). The land was not simply a

means of economic survival. For Mennonites it had become a means of

ethnoreligious identity and subsequent survival. For many the Bible and

the plow (Bible und Pflug) were inseparable. The causes of emigration

may have varied for different individuals but for the most part it was

motivated by three interrelated factors; universal Russian conscription,

Russification of Mennonite education, and the growing restlessness of the

Anwohner class in Russia.

Two agencies accommodated the pull factor of land: American

Mennonites of earlier migrations and expanding railroads. The Mennonite

Board of Guardians organized in 1873 to assist Russian immigrants in their

settlement of America. Christian Krehbiel, a South German Mennonite of

Summerfield, Illinois, was elected president; John F. Funk, an Old Mennonite

from Elkhart, Indiana, was chosen treasurer; two recent Russian Mennonite
arrivals, David Goerz and Bernhard Warkentin, served as secretary and
agent respectively. Pennsylvania Mennonites formed the Mennonite Executive Aid Committee and furnished loans to assist in the establishment of
farms. Through the efforts of American Mennonites all details of the
long journey were provided for at every step of the way. Mennonite
periodicals, such as the Herald of Truth and Friedensbote, reported
progress of the migration, and financial assistance was solicited. In
all, nearly $100,000 was loaned or donated to Russian Mennonites by their
American cousins. Those destined for Canada received the assistance of
$100,000 in loans from the Canadian government.[11]

Various railroad companies were interested in Mennonite immigrants as settlers on railroad lands. The United States government had
endowed railroad companies with generous portions of land to entice
settlers westward. Alternate sections adjacent to homestead land were
available in huge chunks at reasonable rates ($2-$6 an acre). Since
earlier American pioneers had claimed the best of the homestead land
and Mennonites were naturally hesitant to receive free government land
for fear of future civil obligation, recruiting by railroad agents was
intense. In Minnesota the rivalry was between the St. Paul and Pacific
and the St. Paul and Sioux City Railroads. In the Dakota Territory the
Northern Pacific vied with the South Dakota Railroad for settlers.
Nebraska was the battleground for recruiting wars between the Union
Pacific and the Burlington and Missouri River Railroad (BMRR). The
Atchison, Topeka, and Santa Fe Railroad provided the greatest pull for
the most southern settlement of Russian Mennonites.[12]

C. B. Schmidt was responsible for securing the largest contingent

of Russian Mennonites in Kansas. Schmidt, a Prussian immigrant who
arrived in America only a decade before the Russian Mennonites, was well
qualified to serve as a railroad agent for the Santa Fe Railroad. His
familiarity with the Mennonite mother tongue won their respect during
recruiting trips to the Black Sea area. Schmidt's closest competitor
was A. F. Touzalin of the Burlington and Missouri River Railroad in
Nebraska. Touzalin had previously been employed by the Santa Fe Railroad and had made the company's initial contact with the Russian Mennonites. After Touzalin switched to the BMRR Schmidt picked up where his
predecessor left off and the two men found themselves in direct competition with each other. Touzalin managed to secure the recruiting
services of Peter Janzen, a rather cosmopolitan Mennonite who had settled
early on Burlington lands near Beatrice, Nebraska. Ultimately Schmidt
and the Santa Fe Railroad succeeded in attracting the largest contingent
of settlers for two reasons. First, they had made the earliest contacts
with Mennonites and proved to be more aggressive. Elder Isaac Peters,
who settled in Nebraska, detected this in 1875 when he wrote to a fellow
elder in Russia:

> Humanity is often compared to sheep and in the migration there
> is great similarity . . . . whichever way the first are taken
> into a certain direction, then a large part follows until another
> direction has been formed.[13]

Secondly, the Santa Fe had the good fortune of securing several Mennonite
elders to settle on Santa Fe lands. Although just two of the twelve
delegates had gone as far south in 1873 as Kansas, a number of congregational leaders led their flocks to the warmer climate of Kansas.

The railroad provided generously for the first settlers in Kansas.
Free transportation was available for the New Alexanderwohl community, not

only for the trip from Topeka to Newton, but also for themselves and
supplies for the remainder of the year. Free land for churches and
schools was included in the package and in some cases temporary housing
was provided en route and at the settlement site. A year's supply of
seed wheat was another important contribution. Railroad loans allowed
Mennonites immediately to engage in farming.[14]

Establishing New Communities

Some references to the Mennonites of central Kansas have given
the mistaken impression of an exclusive Black Sea origin.[15] In actuality
a careful examination of national origin of the early settlers reveals a
much more diverse picture (table 3-1). The dominant group was South
Russian. These settlers were of Dutch-Prussian origin who spoke Low
German (Plautdietsch) in daily conversations and used High German in
church. The vast majority were a part of the Alexanderwohl congregation
of South Russia. The Alexanderwohlers originated from the conservative
Old Flemish congregation of Przechovka along the Vistula River. They
arrived in Russia as a transplanted congregation in 1820. Fifty years
later they were again uprooted. The Mennonites of South Russia brought
with them a conservative perspective to Kansas. Originally 800 adults
and children departed the Alexanderwohl community in Russia in two
separate groups. One group led by Elder Jacob Buller arrived in Lincoln,
Nebraska in September 1874. Some thirty-five families remained in
Nebraska (Henderson) while the remainder of the group accepted C. B.
Schmidt's invitation to settle on Santa Fe Railroad lands near Newton,
Kansas. En route the Buller faction met up with the other group of
Alexanderwohlers led by Elder Dietrich Gaeddert in Topeka. However, instead

TABLE 3-1

GENERAL CONFERENCE MENNONITE CHURCHES IN CENTRAL KANSAS, 1921

	CHURCH	LOCATION	DATE ESTABLISHED	ORIGIN	ADDITIONAL INFORMATION
1.	Alexanderwohl	Goessel	1874	SR	
2.	Brudertal	Hillsboro	1874	P	also South Russia
3.	First Mennonite	Halstead	1874	SG	also South Russia
4.	Hopefield	Moundridge	1874	SV	Hoffnungsfeld
5.	Bergthal	Pawnee Rock	1875	DV	sister church to Emmanuel
6.	Bethel	Inman	1875	SR	conservative; produced Holdeman and KMB churches
7.	Canton	Moundridge	1875	DV	Emmanuel
8.	Hoffnungsau	Inman	1875	SR	part of the Alexanderwohl church in South Russia
9.	Emmaus	Whitewater	1877	P	also South Russia
10.	Gracehill	Whitewater	1877	PP	
11.	First Mennonite of Christian	Moundridge	1877	SG	also Swiss Volhynian
12.	First Mennonite	Newton	1878	P	South Russian and others
13.	Hebron	Buhler	1879	SR	from Hoffnungsau Church
14.	Johannestal	Hillsboro	1882	PP	also Prussians
15.	Zion	Elbing	1883	P	from Emmaus
16.	First Mennonite	Hillsboro	1884	M	South Russian, Polish Russian and Prussian
17.	First Mennonite	Pretty Prairie	1884	SV	
18.	Einsiedal	Hanston	1885	G	
19.	First Mennonite	Ransom	1886	S	some Lutherans joined early
20.	Garden Township	Hesston	1887	SG	also Swiss Volhynian and non-Mennonites
21.	West Zion	Moundridge	1888	SV	also South Germans
22.	Swiss	Whitewater	1890	S	
23.	Eden	Moundridge	1895	SV	from Hopefield
24.	Bethel College	North Newton	1897	M	
25.	Friedenstal	Durham	1899	DV	from Canton; also mixed
26.	Lehigh	Lehigh	1900	SB	from Alexanderwohl
27.	Arlington	Arlington	1905	G	Swiss and South German also
28.	Bethany	Kingman	1907	SV	from Pretty Prairie
29.	Burrton	Burrton	1907	SB	also mixed
30.	Tabor	Goessel	1908	SR	from Alexanderwohl
31.	First Mennonite	Hutchinson	1913	SR	mixed
32.	Buhler	Buhler	1920	SR	from Hoffnungsau Church
33.	Goessel	Goessel	1920	SR	from Alexanderwohl
34.	Inman	Inman	1921	SR	from Hoffnungsau

Dominant Groups

(SR)	Dutch-Prussian via South Russia -	11
(SV)	Swiss via Volhynea -	5
(P)	Dutch via West Prussia -	4
(SG)	Swiss via South Germany -	3
(DV)	Dutch-Prussian via Volhynia -	3
(PP)	Dutch-Prussian via Polish Russia -	2
(G)	Swiss via Galicia -	2
(S)	Swiss via Switzerland -	2
(M)	Mixed: no dominant group -	2
	total -	34

of establishing one settlement they remained divided in two congregations. Jacob Buller and his following selected land north of Newton
and founded the Alexanderwohl Mennonite Church while Gaeddert's group
settled some twenty miles west establishing the Hoffnungsau Mennonite
Church. Within four years two more congregations, Hebron and Bethel,
developed out of the Hoffnungsau church. By 1921 eleven South Russian
or South Russian "dominated" churches in central Kansas could trace
their ancestry to the Alexanderwohl community of Russia: Hoffnungsau,
Bethel, Hebron, Buhler, Inman, Alexanderwohl, Tabor, Goessel, Lehigh,
Burrton, and Hutchinson.[16]

Although the South Russian Mennonites in central Kansas were the
largest group, several other countries of origin were represented. The
partitions of Poland in 1793 and 1795 and subsequent expansion of Russian
frontiers in 1815 and 1836 brought several groups of Mennonites under
the umbrella of the Russian Empire in the late eighteenth and early nineteenth century. Such was the case of Polish Russian, Dutch and Swiss
Volhynian Mennonites. The Mennonites who immigrated to Kansas from the
area of Polish Russia were of Dutch background. They founded two congregations in central Kansas. The first was the Johannestal Mennonite Church
north of Hillsboro. Members of Johannestal arrived in small scattered
groups from two churches (Deutsch-Kasun and Deutsch-Wymysle) near Warsaw.
A second group of Polish Russians came from Michalin in the province of
Kiev and settled near Whitewater taking the name Gnadenberg (Grace Hill).
This congregation was transplanted nearly intact in 1874-75. The Polish
Russians were quite similar in religious practices and social customs to
the South Russians. Both had similar roots in the Netherlands and Prussia
and had maintained their separate communities in Russia.[17]

A third Dutch-Prussian group to immigrate to Kansas from Russia
were the Dutch Volhynians, so named to distinguish them from the Polish
Russians and the Swiss Volhynians. They had little in common with these
other groups beyond regional proximity. Seventy-five years in Volhynia
(near Ostrog) produced contact with Polish and Russian communities resulting in a significant impact on Dutch Volhynian Mennonites. Their dialect
could hardly be understood by other Low German Mennonites and they were
susceptible to outside religious influence in America. They were by far
the poorest of the Mennonite settlers in Kansas and required financial
assistance from the Mennonite Board of Guardians. Their lack of spiritual
leadership, relative inexperience at farming, and weak education emphasis
contributed to a difficult adjustment on the Kansas prairies. Initially
two congregations were founded in Kansas--the Canton Mennonite Church
(Emmanuel) and the Bergthal Mennonite Church in Pawnee Rock. In 1899
the Canton church mothered a third Dutch Volhynian congregation, Frieden-
stal north of Lehigh.[18]

The Swiss Volhynians were the fourth group to migrate to Kansas
from within the Russian borders. Not all Swiss Volhynians ended up in
Kansas; several settled in South Dakota including Andreas Schrag, the
Swiss Volhynian representative in the 1873 delegation. Swiss Volhynian
history is distinct from that of the Dutch-Prussians who settled in South
Russia. Originally from Switzerland, they migrated to Volhynia in two
groups--one via the Palatinate and Galicia and the other via France and
Poland. In Volhynia the Swiss Mennonites from Poland and Galicia merged
into one group. The Swiss Volhynians emerged out of the Amish persuasion
but during their sojourn in Volhynia they lost their Amishness due to
isolation and contact with Pietism.[19] Russification in the nineteenth

century was a particular concern of Swiss Volhynian church leaders. By
the 1860s some of the youth were already familiar with the Russian
language and Russian dress was gaining entrance into Swiss Volhynian
settlements.[20]   Although they had lost their strict Amish perspectives
in Volhynia and reflected a freer approach to form in worship, the
Swiss Volhynian Mennonites still displayed vital concern regarding worldliness and carnal pride. Thus, Russification, as a form of worldliness,
was considered a threatening force. When the rumors of military conscription reached the province of Volhynia, all four Swiss congregations
emigrated en masse.

In America the Swiss Volhynia were divided between settling in
South Dakota and Kansas. The largest group in Kansas founded the Hoffnungsfeld (Hopefield) Mennonite Church near Moundridge in 1874. In 1884 Swiss
Volhynians from South Dakota joined with some of the Hoffnungsfeld congregation and formed a second Swiss Volhynian Mennonite Church near Pretty
Prairie, Kansas. By 1921 five Swiss Volhynian Mennonite congregations
existed in central Kansas. Commonly referred to as Schweitzers, they
spoke a South German dialect. Initially they were amongst the more
conservative Mennonite groups in Kansas, inclined toward clannish behavior.
They compensated for a sense of cultural inferiority through hard work and
material success. American affluence cultivated a spirit of individualism
and independence amongst the Swiss Volhynians.[21]

Four other non-Russian groups of Mennonites completed the General
Conference Mennonite Church in Kansas: West Prussians, South Germans,
Galicians, and Swiss. The West Prussians were of Dutch ancestry and had
elected to remain in Prussia while their brethren departed for the Russian
steppes beginning in 1789. However, by 1871 a recently unified Germany

had inaugurated a system of universal military service. From 1874 to 1876 various West Prussian congregations settled in Kansas. The first church established was Brudertal founded in 1874 north of Hillsboro. Elder Wilhelm Ewert, one of the delegates of 1873, was the leader. In 1876 a second group of West Prussians arrived in America. Half chose to stay in Nebraska near Beatrice while the remainder settled in three communities in Kansas: Newton, Elbing (Zion), and Whitewater (Emmaus). The Prussions tended to be well educated and wealthy compared to other Mennonites. Many had been gentleman farmers in Prussia and maintained the Old World ways longer than other Mennonites on the Kansas prairies. Material success in Prussia may have enabled them to cling to their old social and religious customs longer than other immigrants.[22]

Another non-Russian group of General Conference Mennonites in central Kansas were the South Germans. Unlike the others, they arrived in America from 1830 to 1860 and had never lived in large villages like the South Russians. They were less isolated and tended to be more progressive. Several prominent leaders in the Kansas Conference were South Germans. Their experience in Iowa and Illinois produced a propensity to leave agriculture early for the pursuit of business interests.[23] They concentrated in an area around Halstead and closely affiliated with key leaders of the South Russians, David Goerz and Bernhard Warkentin. One of the early leaders of the Kansas Conference was a South German by the name of Christian Krehbiel. Krehbiel and his descendants played a major role in the development of General Conference churches in Kansas. South Germans first established a church in 1874 in Halstead and a second three years later near Moundridge (First Mennonite Church of Christian). In 1887 a third congregation, Garden Township, was founded in between the

56

two existing churches. In 1888 a splinter group of the First Mennonite
Church of Christian formed the West Zion Mennonite Church. However, this
congregation included Swiss Volhynians who eventually outnumbered the
South Germans.[24]

Two non-Russian groups of Mennonites arrived in central Kansas
after 1880: Galicians and the "pure" Swiss. The Galicians who came to
Kansas were Swiss who chose not to migrate to Volhynia near the end of
the eighteenth century. In the late 1880s about seventy-five families
immigrated to America with the largest portion settling near Butterfield,
Minnesota. The remaining twenty-two families migrated to Kansas and
established two congregations with the General Conference Mennonites:
Einsiedel at Hanston (1885) and Arlington Mennonite Church (1905). Their
dialect reflected a South German background and years with the Swiss
Volhynians in Galicia gave them similar cultural values.[25] The primary
impetus for immigration was the new military requirements instituted by
Austria in the late nineteenth century. The pull of American Mennonites
enhanced the Galician migration to Kansas.

The Swiss who came to Kansas in the 1880s from Switzerland via
Missouri reveal the extent of cultural distinctives acquired by the other
Mennonite groups through centuries of migrations in Eastern Europe and
Russia. Since three other Swiss Mennonite groups were already well
established in Kansas by the 1880s, it seems only logical that the Swiss
via Missouri would identify with either the Swiss Volhynians, Galicians,
or South Germans. However, the "pure" Swiss soon discovered they had
little in common with the other Swiss and formed their own congregations
in Ransom (1886) and Whitewater (1890). In fact, these two congregations
were not even related to each other. Both had lost most of their Amish

features, no longer practiced the ban, wore a head covering, or practiced
footwashing. The fact that they departed Switzerland in the nineteenth
century rather than the seventeenth century may explain why they chose
to join the General Conference rather than the Old Mennonites.[26]

Kansas Mennonite congregations of the nineteenth century were
characteristically homogenous. One exception was the First Mennonite
Church in Hillsboro (1884). Later, when the Bethel College Mennonite
Church was founded (1897) it also reflected a heterogeneous constituency.
Other congregations (Ransom and Christian) displayed some mixing in the
development stage. However, for the most part the early period (1874-
1892) reveals a homogenous congregation autonomously bound together by
family ties, a common dialect, and similar cultural experiences including
the immigration experience.[27] The homogenous nature of a congregation
was contingent upon closed settlement patterns. In Russia closed
settlements were the norm. David Rempel describes the often repeated
pattern in Russia:

> The land was assigned to each colony in the shape of a rectangle
> with the colony generally located in the center of the rectangle.
> As a rule the colonies were limited to 25 to 30 households. Each
> family received a building site of about one and one-half dessiatine
> (4 acres) in the village and a plot of several dessiatines immedi-
> ately back of its house-and-garden lot.[28]

Alexanderwohl was a typical south Russian Mennonite village (fig. 3-1).
The houses were neatly arranged in near perfect rows, all within walking
distance of each other. The church was located in the middle of the
settlement with a village schoolhouse not far away. In central Kansas
large portions of available railroad lands attracted several large congregations, like Alexanderwohl, Hoffnungsau, and Hoffnungsfeld, which brought
large compact areas for settlement. The Krimmer Mennonite Brethren attempted

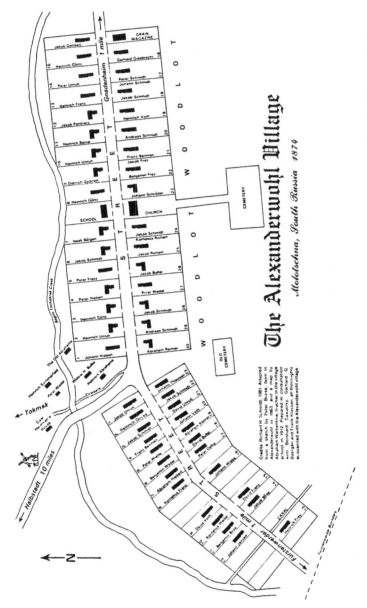

Fig. 3-1. The Alexanderwohl village, Molotschna, South Russia, 1874 (used with permission from Richard H. Schmidt, cartographer. Mennonite Library and Archives, Bethel College, North Newton, Kansas).

to duplicate the Russian village in Marion County. They established the
village of Gnadenau but after three years the Russian system proved both
inconvenient and impractical on alternate sections of railroad lands.

The Alexanderwohl congregation established a number of settlement
clusters near Goessel by 1877. Although they bore the familiar names of
Russian villages they were villages in name only. Several farm houses
were built side by side while land was divided into mile long strips of
forty to eighty acres. The Hochfeld village settlement pattern illustrates
such clustering (fig. 3-2). Hochfeld consisted of seven Alexanderwohl families who resided within one section. Five families each owned 80 acres
while the remaining two owned 120 acres apiece.[29] However, each family's
land holdings were divided into four separate acreages. This meant traveling nearly two miles to farm the farthest portion of one's land. The
Hochfeld village was gradually dissolved as farmers swapped land or sold
out in order to obtain farms with consolidated landholdings. Many times
the settlement adjustment merely entailed the division of a section into
four quartersections with farmhouses on each corner. At any rate, the
Mennonites quickly gave up the Russian village pattern but maintained
group clustering for several decades.[30] In the absence of the Russian
village, the local church maintained an important role in the persistence
of Gemeindechristentum, the basis of Mennonite ethnoreligious cohesion.
Whereas local congregations were generally homogenous, diverse national
origins produced a Mennonite polychotomy in central Kansas. Not only
were different countries represented and various dialects spoken; by
the end of the nineteenth century a number of Mennonite denominations
were also established in the region.

60

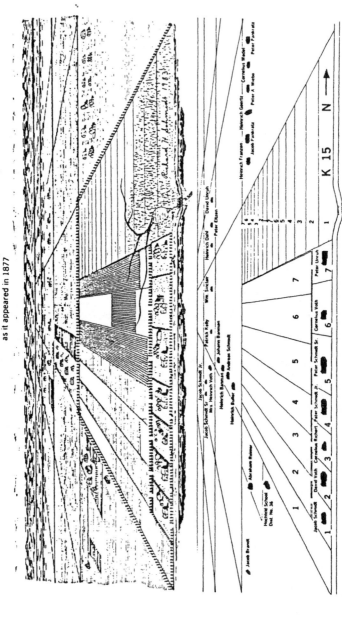

Fig. 3-2. The Hochfeld settlement in Marion County, 1877 (used with permission from Richard H. Schmidt, cartographer. Mennonite Library and Archives, Bethel College, North Newton, Kansas).

The Russian and East European Mennonites were not the first to
settle in Kansas. That distinction goes to Old Order Amish and American
(Old) Mennonites who settled in central Kansas beginning in 1870. Both
of these groups consisted of Mennonites whose ancestors had immigrated
from Switzerland in the early eighteenth century. The Amish settled in
Reno County south of Hutchinson establishing the village of Yoder in 1886
and four Amish congregations by 1918. The American (Old) Mennonites settled
in Marion, eastern McPherson, and northern Harvey counties forming a
conference in 1876 which eventually became known as the Kansas-Nebraska
Conference of the (Old) Mennonite Church. In 1908 Hesston College was
founded by the (Old) Mennonites. A third denomination of Mennonites
from eastern states were the Defenseless Mennonites who settled near
Sterling in 1880. For the most part none of these three denominations
identified with European Mennonites who settled in Kansas after 1873.[31]

The Russian and East European Mennonite settlers during the first
two decades in Kansas divided into four different Mennonite denominations:
the Mennonite Brethren (Bruedergemeinde), the Krimmer Mennonite Brethren,
the Church of God in Christ, Mennonites, and the General Conference Mennonite Church. The Mennonite Brethren (MB) Church was founded in Russia in
1860 and was still in the infant stage of development at the time of its
transfer to America in 1874. By that time the entire group numbered only
1,000. No organized congregations immigrated en masse and until the
arrival of Elder Abraham Shellenberg in 1879 organized church life was
not carried on in America. By 1900 five churches had been established
in central Kansas with Hillsboro serving as the center of denominational
leadership and site of Tabor College (1908). Mennonite Brethren Churches
were also established in Nebraska, Minnesota, South Dakota, Oklahoma, and

Canada by the turn of the century. A second wave of Russian Mennonite migration from 1922 to 1926 produced several Mennonite Brethren congregations in Canada ultimately pushing Canadian membership beyond that of America in 1948. Mennonite Brethren churches in the early years consisted primarily of converts from the Altkirchliche, a term coined by the MB for the main body of Mennonites in Russia. Tension between the Bruedergemeinde and the Altkirchliche was transferred to the American frontier where competition for church members regularly occurred between the MB and the General Conference Mennonites. Generally the Mennonite Brethren took issue with the Altkirchliche over the matter of a personal conversion experience, method of baptism (immersion vs. sprinkling or pouring), and an emphasis on personal evangelism and a Christ-centered eschatology. The Americanization of the Mennonite Brethren church merits separate treatment due to an affinity for American revivalism and a historically close association with the Baptists.[32]

A second Mennonite denomination which attracted membership from amongst the Russian Mennonites was the Krimmer Mennonite Brethren (KMB), so identified for their origin in the village of Annafeld near Simferopol, Crimea. The group actually organized in Russia in 1869 under the leadership of Elder J. A. Wiebe. The KMB consisted of thirty-five families in 1874 and emigrated en masse founding the village of Gnadenau just south of Hillsboro. The KMB differed very little from the older MB in religious belief. However, the baptismal practice of forward immersion (the MB practiced backward immersion) and a KMB emphasis on premillennialism kept the two from merging until 1960. Apart from these two technical differences and a "cultural narrowness", the development of the KMB closely parallels that of the MB. A second congregation (Zoar) was organized near Inman in 1897 and a third (Springfield) was initiated southwest of Lehigh in 1878. These three congregations represent the extent of KMB development in central Kansas by 1900.[33]

A third Mennonite denomination which gained membership from the 1874-80 immigrants was the Church of God in Christ, Mennonite (CGC). The group originated in Ohio where in 1858 John Holdeman, an (Old) Mennonite layman, responded to visions and dreams to preach without virtue of a conventional call. Holdeman proclaimed a return to the fundamentals of early conservative Mennonitism adding two distinct practices of his own--refusal to accept interest on money and the practice of "laying on of hands" after baptism. His group attracted few followers until he settled near Canton, Kansas among the economically depressed Dutch Volhynians. Leaderless, uneducated, and impoverished, the "Ostroger" of Canton immediately took to Holdeman and started the Lone Tree CGC congregation in 1878. Dutch Volhynian CGC congregations also organized in Halstead (Grace--1877) and Durham (late 1880s). Holdeman attracted South Russian Mennonites near Hillsboro (Alexanderfeld--1881) and Inman (Zion--1886). A sixth congregation in central Kansas was established from amongst American Mennonites north of Hesston (Meridan--1873). Holdeman shifted his energies to Canada in the 1880s where he established eight CGC congregations from the Kleine Gemeinde. The "Holdemans", as they were referred to by other Mennonites, maintained an emphasis on separation from the world as evidenced by bearded men, head coverings for women, and plain dress for both.[34]

The majority of Mennonites in Kansas eventually joined the General Conference Mennonite denomination (GCM). This included the majority of the Altkirchliche from Russia. By 1910 the Church of God in

Christ, Mennonite, Mennonite Brethren, Krimmer Mennonite Brethren, Old

Mennonites, and Defenseless Mennonites had a combined total of nineteen

churches in central Kansas compared to a total of twenty-three GCM

churches in the same area.[35]   The General Conference Mennonite Church

was an American denomination founded in 1860 at West Point, Iowa. The

person most responsible for its creation was John Oberholtzer, a pro-

gressive Pennsylvania Mennonite minister who advocated a more tolerant

attitude toward the non-Mennonite world. The majority decision to join

the GCM was not a foregone conclusion. Some were attracted to the (Old)

Mennonite Church. The plain appearance, strong expression of non-resistance,

rejection of many of the practices of worldliness in America, and the will-

ingness to financially assist the Russian immigration caused many of the

Russian Mennonites to look upon the (Old) Mennonite Church with favor.

However, in 1877, several congregations chose to form a separate affiliation

of churches called the Kansas Conference (Kansas Konferenz der Mennoniten).[36]

The development of the Kansas Conference from 1877 to 1892, its

eventual association with the General Conference, and the decision of a

majority of Mennonite congregations to join it can be traced to the

efforts of three persons--David Goerz, Bernhard Warkentin, and Christian

Krehbiel. Goerz had been educated in South Russia and served as secretary

in the office of the large Cornies estate. In 1873 he accepted in invi-

tation from a General Conference South German Congregation to teach at a

Mennonite school in Summerfield, Illinois. He became actively involved in

the immigration as the secretary for the Mennonite Board of Guardians and

moved to Kansas in 1875. In Kansas Goerz served as editor of an immigrant

newspaper entitled Zur Heimath which was circulated among all the new

churches. In 1877 his call for a meeting of all Mennonite teachers

indirectly resulted in the first Kansas Conference convention. Bernhard
Warkentin was the son of a wealthy wheat grower in South Russia. In 1872
he traveled to America, associated with the Summerfield Church, and later
served as a traveling agent for the Mennonite Board of Guardians, directing
many of his countrymen to Kansas where he settled in 1873. A strong pro-
moter of Russian emigration and Kansas settlement, Warkentin was also an
enthusiast for the General Conference. However, the actual link between
Goerz, Warkentin, and the General Conference was a South German Mennonite
named Krehbiel. As the head of the Summerfield congregation he had received
both Goerz and Warkentin. Christian Krehbiel had long been an advocate of a
colonization scheme by the General Conference in Kansas. With Goerz and
Warkentin as promoters, he moved to Kansas and assited early in the organization of the Kansas Conference. All three men settled near Halstead
making that community the center of activity for both the General Conference
and Kansas congregations.[37]

From the original ten churches who sent delegates to the first
meeting in 1877, the Kansas Conference expanded to include eighteen central
Kansas congregations by 1892 when it became the Western District and officially affiliated with the General Conference Mennonite Church. The church
polity of the GCM denomination was congregational. This form of church
government made a united effort possible in matters of education, missions,
and publication enterprises while preserving the individual distinctions
of worship and culture in the local congregation. In this regard the
General Conference group was the only branch of the Mennonite church able
to unite different factions of Mennonites with common goals of church
extension without destroying local autonomy and respect for the individual
conscience. Conference sessions seldom dealt with rules regarding styles

and personal habits; such matters were left up to local congregations. When occasional questions dealing with secularism would surface in conference proceedings, they were referred to a committee for study and the findings were released in the form of recommendations rather than mandates. Under this form of denominational affiliation, Swiss Volhynians, Prussians, South Russians, Galicians, Polish Russians, Dutch Volhynians, South Germans and Swiss Mennonites could associate with benefit of a unified strength but without conference encroachment upon local customs.[38] The Kansas Conference was not a union based on shared religious practice or culture. It was an alliance of local churches who shared a basic belief system and a similar religious heritage. From the beginning the largest group producing the greatest numbers of conference leaders and thereby exerting the strongest influence were the South Russians. This remained true well into the twentieth century (fig. 3-3).

The Local Church

A modern observer of an 1880 Sunday worship service in a Kansas Conference congregation would have been struck by the Old World nature of both the participants and the church service. The building was noticeably simple; it may have been an immigrant house converted into a place of worship, or it may have been a large rectangular structure constructed from native stone or whitewashed lumber. Steeples, stained glass windows, and other decorations were noticeably absent. Inside, backless benches often served as church pews. The pulpit was elevated on a platform. From this location the minister delivered his sermon, which lasted at least an hour.[39]

The seating arrangement was typically Mennonite--women sat on

Fig. 3-3. General Conference Mennonite Churches in Central Kansas, 1921.

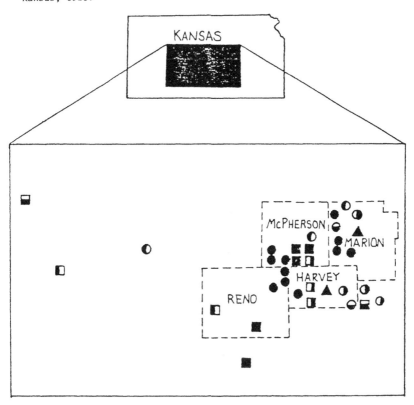

Dominant Group

- ● Dutch-Prussian via South Russia
- ◐ Dutch via West Prussia
- ◑ Dutch-Prussian via Volhynia
- ◒ Dutch-Prussian via Polish Russia
- ■ Swiss via Volhynia
- ◫ Swiss via South Germany
- ◧ Swiss via Galicia
- ⊟ Swiss via Switzerland
- ▲ Mixed: no dominant group

one side while men sat on the other with children scattered among the adults. Gender segregation actually began on the outside as some church buildings had separate entrances for men and women.[40] Women did not attend congregational meetings, vote, or speak up in services. The congregation either stood or knelt for lengthy prayers depending on the tradition of the local congregation. The entire service consisted of the sermon, prayers, scripture reading, testimonies and hymn singing. The service was conducted in the German language and, in spite of the crude surroundings, maintained an Old World formalism.

Music played an important role in the Mennonite church service. Many of the hymns could be traced back to the sixteenth century Anabaptist Movement and were cherished remnants of nostalgic Mennonite memories of a sojourn in western Europe and Russia. Hymns usually included seven or eight verses and were sung very slowly without musical instruments. A Vorsaenger (songleader) led the singing. Larger congregations had more than one Vorsaenger who alternated the leadership role for each hymn. They usually sat on the front pew with their backs toward the congregation singing loudly and occasionally reading each line of the hymn before the congregation sang it.[41]

The church leadership structure in 1880 was taken from the Old World model of elder (Aeltester), minister (Prediger), and deacon (Armendiener). Only the elder could officiate at baptisms, communion, and ordinations. Since some congregations arrived in Kansas without an elder, several elders in the Kansas Conference provided these services to a number of churches. As the congregational leader the elder was extremely important to the spiritual direction of his flock. He was an authoritarian and patriarchal figure in the local congregation and also provided leadership in the Kansas Conference. The elder was assisted by ministers whose numbers were determined by the size of the congregation. Ministers, like the elder, served without pay, preaching, marrying, and burying when needed. They were normally chosen from within a congregation, sometimes by lot, and rarely with formal preparation or training for the ministry. The deacons supervised the mutual aid within the congregation and often served on a church board which worked with the elder to provide executive leadership.[42]

An important occasion in the life of the church was the celebration of communion two to four times a year. In 1880 wine was passed amongst the members in a common cup while the elder personally broke the bread for each individual. Footwashing either preceded or followed communion in many churches although some groups never practiced this ordinance in Kansas.[43]

Even more significant for Mennonites was the universal doctrine of baptism upon the confession of faith. Church baptisms were preceded by catechism classes and were considered a major event in the life of both the church and the individual. Actually there were few events in the life of Mennonites that were not related in some way to the local church. Mate selection from within the local congregation was strongly encouraged. "Dating" was unknown to nineteenth century Mennonites. Courtship was centered around church events and family visits. However, the wedding itself was a worship service complete with a sermon from the elder, congregational singing, and attendance by the entire congregation. In some groups Thursday weddings became a tradition so that the couple could celebrate their twenty-fifth anniversary on a Sunday afternoon at the church.[44] When a death occurred, funeral preparations were cared

for by the family and the church without consultation with a funeral
director. Services were held first at the home then in the church.

In 1880 the local Mennonite church in Kansas was very much as
it had been for a century in the Old World. Some changes had crept
into the church since the seventeenth century but change had been a
gradual, lengthy process. The Mennonite immigrants felt very much at
home in their newly established church on the Kansas prairie. In spite
of all the alien aspects of a new environment, an unfamiliar language,
strange American customs and dress, and a new way of farming, at least
one facet of Old World life had been re-established in America: the
local church. Unlike most ethnic institutions, the church survived the
transition to an English-speaking society. According to Frederick
Luebke, it is difficult to overestimate the role of the immigrant church
in the settlement of the Great Plains. Of all immigrant institutions
the church was normally the first established, the most effective in its
mission, and the last to be deserted by the immigrant.[45] No immigrant
group illustrates this more than the Mennonites who settled central
Kansas in the 1870s. The church dominated their pioneer lives. It accommodated their necessary adjustment and in doing so provided the battleground
for acculturation. In the process the church underwent some major transitions
between 1874 and 1939. The story of the Americanization of the immigrant
church is the story of the immigrants themselves.

CHAPTER III - ENDNOTES

1. Sidney Harcave, <u>Russia, a History</u> (Philadelphia: J. B. Lippencott, Co., 1964), p. 292.

2. C. Henry Smith, <u>The Coming of the Russian Mennonites</u> (Berne, Indiana: Mennonite Book Concern, 1927), pp. 45-47.

3. Cornelius Krahn and John F. Schmidt, eds., <u>A Century of Witness: General Conference Mennonite Church</u> (Newton, Kansas: Mennonite Publication Office, 1959), p. 48.

4. Jacob Sudermann, "The Origin of Mennonite State Service in Russia, 1870-1880," <u>Mennonite Quarterly Review</u> 17 (January 1943): 23-46.

5. Several accounts exist of the immigration of Russian Mennonites to North America. For the best account of the delegation of twelve see Paul Tschetter, "The Diary of Paul Tschetter, 1873," trans., J. M. Hofer, <u>Mennonite Quarterly Review</u> 5 (April 1931): 112-28; (July 1931): 198-220. Also see Smith, <u>The Coming of the Russian Mennonites</u>, pp. 49-131; Krahn and Schmidt, eds., pp. 47-52; Cornelius Krahn, <u>From the Steppes to the Prairies</u> (North Newton, Kansas: Mennonite Publication Office, 1949), pp. 1-12; Adam Giesinger, "The Migration of Germans from Russia to the Americas," <u>Journal of the American Historical Society of Germans from Russia</u> 9 (October 1972): 33-40; Clarence Hiebert, ed., <u>Brothers in Deed to Brothers in Need</u> (Newton, Kansas: Faith and Life Press, 1974); George Liebbrandt, "The Immigration of the German Mennonites from Russia to the United States and Canada in 1873-1880," <u>Mennonite Quarterly Review</u> 6 (October 1932): 205-26; 7 (January 1933): 5-41; Norman E. Saul, "The Migration of the Russian Germans to Kansas," <u>Kansas Historical Quarterly</u> 40 (Spring 1974): 38-62; G. R. Gaeddert and Gustav E. Reimer, <u>Exiled by the Czar</u> (Newton, Kansas: Mennonite Publication Office, 1956).

6. Richard Sallet, <u>Russian-German Settlements in the United States</u> (Minneapolis: Lund Press, 1974), p. 6.

7. Smith, <u>The Coming of the Russian Mennonites</u>, p. 129.

8. Figures dealing with immigrant numbers vary greatly from one source to another due in part to the exaggerated reports of the railroad companies attempting to settle railroad lands. The 5,000 figure is based on census records and the report of the <u>Gazetteer</u> of Kansas. See <u>Mennonite Encyclopedia</u>, s.v. "Kansas," by Cornelius Krahn.

9. Albert P. Koop, "Some Economic Aspects of Mennonite Migration: With Special Emphasis on the 1870s Migration from Russia to North America," <u>Mennonite Quarterly Review</u> 55 (April 1981): 143-66. Also see Adolph Schock, <u>In Quest of Free Land</u> (Assen, Netherlands: Royal Vangorcum Ltd., 1964).

10. Cornelius Krahn, "Some Social Attitudes for the Mennonites of Russia," Mennonite Quarterly Review 9 (October 1935): 170-71.

11. Smith, The Coming of the Russian Mennonites, p. 111.

12. The most complete accounts of Mennonite recruitment by the railroad companies are John D. Unruh, "The Burlington and Missouri Railroad Brings the Mennonites to Nebraska, 1873-1878," Nebraska History 45 (March 1964): 3-30; (June 1964): 177-206; C. B. Schmidt, "Reminiscences of Foreign Immigration Work for Kansas," Kansas Historical Collection 9 (1905-1906): 485-497.

13. Letter from Isaac Peters to Leonhard Suderman, September 13, 1875 J. J. Friessen Collection (Mennonite Historical Library and Archives, Bethel College, North Newton, Kansas).

14. Saul, "The Migration of Russian-Germans to Kansas," pp. 55-56.

15. Nobel L. Prentis, A History of Kansas (Topeka, Kansas: Caroline Prentis, 1909), pp. 191, 193.

16. Smith, The Coming of the Russian Mennonites, pp. 138-47; David Haury, Prairie People (Newton, Kansas: Faith and Life Press, 1981), pp. 34-42.

17. Smith, The Coming of the Russian Mennonites, p. 152; Haury, pp. 44-47.

18. Smith, The Coming of the Russian Mennonites, pp. 148-52; Haury, pp. 47-51.

19. Martin H. Schrag, The European History of the Swiss Mennonites from Volhynia (North Newton, Kansas: Mennonite Press, 1974), pp. 62-66.

20. Ibid., p. 59.

21. Haury, pp. 42-44.

22. Smith, The Coming of the Russian Mennonites, pp. 153-55; Haury, pp. 29-34.

23. Haury, p. 26.

24. Ibid., pp. 25-29; Smith, The Coming of the Russian Mennonites, pp. 156-57; C. E. Krehbiel, "Historical-Sketch: First Mennonite Church, Halstead, Kansas," Mennonite Weekly Review, 5 May 1925, pp. 3-4; Christian Krehbiel, Prairie Pioneer (Newton, Kansas: Faith and Life Press, 1961).

25. Smith, The Coming of the Russian Mennonites, pp. 155-56; Haury, pp. 51-53.

26. Haury, pp. 53-56.

73

27. Cornelius C. Janzen, "The Americanization of Russian Mennonites in Central Kansas" (Masters thesis, Kansas University, 1914), p. 103.
Janzen contends that the pioneer period ended for the Mennonites by 1892
when the whole settlement was on solid footing. His evidence is the lack
of Russian farming implements, disappearance of thatched roofs, and the
conversion of sod houses to sheds. The 1890s ushered in a golden era in
the history of Russian Mennonites in central Kansas ending with World War I.

28. David G. Rempel, "The Mennonite Colonies in New Russia--A
Study of Their Settlement and Economic Development from 1789 to 1914"
(Ph.D. dissertation, Stanford University, 1933), p. 123.

29. David A. McQuillan, "Adaption of Three Immigrant Groups to
Farming in Central Kansas, 1875-1925" (Ph.D. dissertation, University of
Wisconsin-Madison, 1975), pp. 138-41. The McQuillan dissertation compares
the Americanization of Mennonite farming with that of French-Canadians and
Swedes in central Kansas. McQuillan reveals that Mennonites had the
smallest and most valuable farms and did the least amount of adapting of
the three groups. He further points out that Mennonite segregation
slowed assimilation but did not affect farm productivity.

30. Prentis, p. 159; Samuel F. Pannabecker, Open Doors: the
History of the General Conference Mennonite Church (Newton, Kansas:
Faith and Life Press, 1975), p. 118; Janzen, "Americanization of Russian
Mennonites in Central Kansas," p. 59, 99; Cornelius C. Janzen, "A Social
Study of the Mennonite Settlements in the Counties of Marion, McPherson,
Harvey, Reno, and Butler, Kansas" (Ph.D. dissertation, University of
Chicago, 1926) pp. 26-29, 33-34.

31. Emma K. Risser, History of the Pennsylvania Mennonite Church in
Kansas (Scottdale, Pennsylvania: Mennonite Publishing House, 1958), pp. 1-5;
D. H. Bender, T. M. Erb, and L. O. King, Conference Record Containing the
Proceedings of the Kansas-Nebraska Mennonite Conference, 1876-1914 (n.p., 1914
pp. 3-7; Mennonite Encyclopedia, s.v. "Yoder," by Albert Schweizer.

32. Smith, The Coming of the Russian Mennonites, pp. 254-57; John
A. Toews, A History of the Mennonite Brethren (Hillsboro, Kansas: Mennonite Brethren Publishing House, 1975), pp. 131-37, 362-74; Haury, pp. 38-40.

33. John A. Toews, A History of the Mennonite Brethren Church,
pp. 176-93; Smith, The Coming of the Russian Mennonites, pp. 250-54;
also see David V. Wiebe, Grace Meadows (Hillsboro, Kansas: Mennonite
Brethren Publishing House, 1967).

34. Clarence Hiebert, The Holdeman People (South Pasadena, California: William Carey Library, 1973), pp. 107-25; Smith, The Coming of the
Russian Mennonites, pp. 257-58.

35. Clarence Hiebert, The Holdeman People, p. 115.

36. Smith, The Coming of the Russian Mennonites, pp. 401-03;
Edmund G. Kaufman, General Conference Mennonite Pioneers (North Newton,
Kansas: Bethel College, 1973), pp. 3-17; Pannabecker, pp. 84-110; John
C. Wenger, History of the Mennonites of the Franconia Conference (Scott-
date, Pennsylvania: Mennonite Publishing House, 1938), pp. 352-59.

37. For more detailed studies of Goerz, Warkentin, and Krehbiel see David C. Wedel, "Contributions of Pioneer David Goerz," Mennonite Life 7 (October 1952): 170-75; Cornelius Krahn, "Some Letters of Bernhard Warkentin Pertaining to the Migration of 1873-1875," Mennonite Quarterly Review 24 (June 1950): 248-63; Christian Krehbiel, Prairie Pioneer (Newton, Kansas: Faith and Life Press, 1961).

38. Smith, The Coming of the Russian Mennonites, pp. 243-47.

39. Mennonite Encyclopedia, s.v. "Architecture," by Cornelius Krahn; Robert Kreider, "The Anabaptist Conception of the Church in the Russian Mennonite Environment," Mennonite Quarterly Review 25 (January 1951): 23; Gerald V. Musselman, "Architecture and Our Faith," Mennonite Life 20 (October 1965): 158-67; Cornelius Krahn, "Mennonite Church Architecture," Mennonite Life 12 (January 1959): 19-27.

40. Cornelius C. Janzen, "Americanization of Russian Mennonites in Central Kansas," pp. 88-89.

41. David C. Wedel, The Story of Alexanderwohl (North Newton, Kansas: Mennonite Press, Inc., 1974), pp. 63-64; Albert M. Gaeddert, Centennial History of Hoffnungsau Mennonite Church (North Newton, Kansas: Mennonite Press Inc., 1975), p. 67; Wesley Berg, "The Development of Choral Singing Among the Mennonites of Russia to 1895," Mennonite Quarterly Review 55 (April 1981): 131-42.

42. Cornelius Krahn, "The Office of Elder in Anabaptist Mennonite History," Mennonite Quarterly Review 30 (April 1956): 120-27.

43. Haury, p. 68.

44. Ronald Andreas, Centennial Reflections: Zion 100 (n.p., 1983), p. 15.

45. Frederick C. Luebke, "Ethnic Group Settlement on the Great Plains," Western Historical Quarterly 8 (October 1977): 411.

CHAPTER IV

THE LANGUAGE TRANSITION

To adopt English for the sake of convenience or for the sake of a few Americans seems to me to be more than risky, since we are in danger of losing more of our faithfulness to our confession than we can hope to gain in Americans.

J. S. Hirschler
Report of the Itinerant Ministers
Western District Conference Minutes, 1896

English must eventually be the language of the Conference and its publications. It is the American tongue, it is taught our children in both the East and the West, it is the medium of business intercourse . . . we must have one common language.

Silas Grubb
The Mennonite, 1899

The Role of the German Language

In his seven stages of assimilation, Milton Gordon identifies the first stage as cultural or behavioral assimilation. At the first level, immigrants simply adapted their cultural patterns to those of the host society. This did not require structural assimilation nor the abandonment of an Old World sense of peoplehood. However, for non-English speaking immigrants it meant learning a new language. For immigrant children behavioral assimilation usually resulted in the loss of the mother tongue as the dominant language of conversation.[1]

The largest group to arrive in central Kansas in the 1870s, the Black Sea Mennonites, had resisted the full impact of assimilation in Russia for nearly a century. German was the mother tongue of those who settled the Russian steppes in the late eighteenth century and was strengthened until their departure almost a hundred years later. Actually, Dutch-Prussian Mennonites adopted the German language shortly before migrating to Russia. Originally from the Netherlands in the sixteenth century, they maintained the Dutch language for two centuries in West Prussia and Danzig. By the middle of the eighteenth century, Dutch was gradually replaced by West Prussian Plautdietsch in daily conversations. The transition from Dutch to Plautdietsch preceded another language shift: Dutch to High German in Mennonite worship services. In 1757 the first German sermon was preached in West Pussia producing a mixed reaction. Twenty-five years later High German was firmly established as the official ecclesiastical language while Mennonites used Plautdietsch in daily conversations. However, Dutch still prevailed in Mennonite liturgy when the first group settled the Chortitza area of the Russian steppes in 1789. These first immigrants brought along Dutch Bibles and hymnals. Plautdietsch was the dominant language of the Chortitza Mennonites but High German remained a foreign tongue. In 1803 when more affluent Mennonites established the Molotschna settlement, High German completely replaced Dutch as the ecclesiastical language and significantly altered Plautdietsch.[2]

In Russia the Chortitza and Molotschna Mennonites mixed in secondary schools and daughter settlements producing a "more cultured" form of Plautdietsch in daily conversations. High German was used exclusively for worship. Although a few Russian loan words made their way into the Plautdietsch, Mennonites maintained German bilingualism throughout their Russian sojourn departing for America in 1874 without acquisition of the Russian language. Mennonites who remained in Prussia until the 1870s continued the shift from Plautdietsch to High German in daily use. By the time of their immigration to central Kansas, they normally conversed in High German but still knew Plautdietsch well enough to communicate with non-Mennonite servants.[3]

Language maintenance was particularly germane to the Mennonite sense of peoplehood. The retention of Dutch for nearly two centuries in Prussia contributed significantly to their ethnoreligious cohesiveness. The Dutch language served as a barrier to assimilation in Prussia and aided in the maintenance of distinctive Mennonite principles and group identity. In Russia the German language served the same purpose. E. K. Francis, the Canadian sociologist, has suggested that the retention of German by Mennonites in Russia contributed to their transition from a religious to an ethnic group. It ensured segregation from Russian society and stalled Russification for nearly a century. Maintenance of a non-Russian language enhanced nonconformity to the world and spiritual purity.[4]

When Mennonites arrived in Kansas in 1874 from Russia and eastern Europe, their use of High German as an ecclesiastical language was a common denominator. The liturgical use of German served to identify with the traditions of the past and ensured the security of Mennonite principles in a new environment. A common language contributed to a sense of unity and identity that eventually resulted in the founding of the Kansas Conference. Numerous dialects of Low German, Swiss, Palatinate, South German, along with High German, were used in daily conversations by the eight different groups of Mennonites in the Kansas Conference. However, the ecclesiastical language was the same for all Kansas Conference churches--High German. In November of 1877 several immigrant teachers and ministers met to discuss the matter of education for immigrant children. The meeting was indicative of the need by Kansas Mennonites to deal with numerous church issues from a unified perspective. The immigrant newspaper, Zur Heimath, announced the first Kansas Conference of Mennonites for December 14, 1877.

At that first Conference elder Wilhelm Ewert opened by quoting from John 17:11: "Holy Father, keep through thine own name those whom thou hast given, that they may be one, as we are." Ewert proceeded to address the Conference on unity. He noted the various European origins of the ten represented churches, acknowledging their "different practices, usages and customs" in church polity. Ewert's use of High German served to solidify the proceedings of the first Kansas Conference. The West Prussian elder encouraged the seventy representatives to set aside differences of practice and concentrate on the goal of unity.[5]

At the same Conference, representatives endorsed a resolution for teaching English in Mennonite parochial schools. The fact that after only three years Mennonites were prepared to learn the language of the host society is a bit startling in light of their refusal to learn Russian after nearly a century on the steppes. The decision maintained a two-fold justification: first, "to represent our social interests in dealing with the Americans;" and second, "to be able to be active for the kingdom of God also among the English-speaking population."[6] Mennonite settlers in Kansas recognized that the environment in America was different from what it had been in Russia. The closed Russian villages were a thing of the past. No laws forbade them from proselyting Americans. Direct contact with non-Mennonites was both more frequent and more intimate. America, with her "Christian heritage," did not pose the same threat to Mennonites as the Russian church-state. However, the recommendation to learn English by the early leaders of the 1877 Kansas Conference was not intended to encourage rapid Americanization. English acquisition was to be in addition to German, not as a replacement for the mother tongue.

Cultural linguists who suggest that the language transition was smooth and without controversy overlook its religious significance.[7] There was a fear that the use of English in worship might open the hearts and minds of Mennonite youth to non-Mennonite influences. German was a means of maintaining pure Mennonite principles and keeping young people in the fold. The use of English as proposed by the resolution of the 1877 Kansas Conference was not intended to apply to Mennonite worship. Nonetheless, Conference leaders soon recognized that English could not be neglected as Russian had been in the Old Country. From the beginning Mennonite parochial schools taught English as a second language while retaining German instruction. In 1879 at the third annual Kansas Conference, the discussion centered on the organization of an institution for training Christian workers. A resolution calling for German as the language of instruction was passed:

> Instruction in German shall also be carried on to the same
> stage, in order that students are able to render the same

work in the German domain of learning which is required in English in the district schools. A thorough religious instruction must also be given in the German language in order that in the future our churches may be able to find prepared workers along spiritual lines.[8]

For most Kansas Mennonites there were two language transitions in America: High German to English in church and Plautdietsch to English in daily conversation. Not all Kansas Mennonites spoke Plautdietsch. Prussian Mennonites had abandoned its general use for High German by the 1870s. The Swiss Volhynian spoke a Palatinate dialect; the Swiss, who came directly from Switzerland, spoke a Swiss dialect; the South Germans and Galicians spoke a South German dialect similar to that of the Swiss Volhynians. The Polish Russians, Dutch Volhynians, and South Russians all conversed in Plautdietsch and together made up the largest portion of churches in central Kansas (16 out of 34 churches by 1921).[9] Mennonite dialects persisted longer than High German. This was especially true of Plautdietsch, which in the Goessel area outlasted High German by more than a decade.[10] For most the language transition was completed in the church before it was in the home.

The language shift proceeded at a different rate in each congregation. Some heard their first regularly scheduled English sermons as early as 1900 while others had to wait until the 1940s.[11] Although the denomination (General Conference) and the district (Kansas Conference--after 1892 the Western District Conference) suggested guidelines and offered assistance, the actual process and rate of transition was strictly a congregational matter. Thus, the individual characteristics of each local church determined when to make the language shift and how to implement the process. The language transition was a delicate matter and usually occurred over an extended period of time. Numerous variables affected the rate of the language shift in the local church.

Facilitators of the Language Transition
American Mennonites

During their settlement of the Kansas prairies, the Altkirchliche Mennoniten of Russia repeatedly came in contact with American Mennonites. Mennonites in eastern states aided the immigrants with finances and temporary housing. South Germans of Summerfield, Illinois, provided leadership in the early establishment of churches in Kansas. American Mennonites followed the immigration of Russian Mennonites in church periodicals. Eventually, contacts with Americanized Mennonites in the East produced considerations of affiliation. The association of Russian Mennonites with the General Conference occurred shortly after their arrival.

The General Conference Mennonite Church organized in 1860 at West Point, Iowa, with John Oberholtzer as the early leader. Oberholtzer's progressive views on dress, church organization, and education put him at odds with the Franconia Conference (Old) Mennonites in Pennsylvania in 1847. In 1860 Mennonites from Pennsylvania, Ohio, Canada, and Iowa formed the General Conference with the intent of unifying all Mennonite churches in North America. Although they did not succeed, they managed to attract the largest number of Russian Mennonite congregations in central Kansas. By 1892 all of the Kansas Conference churches joined the General Conference to form the Western

District Conference (WDC).[12]

The language transition was just beginning in the General Conference when Russian and East European Mennonites arrived in the 1870s.
English sermons were introduced in Pennsylvania in the 1880s. In
1885 an English-language periodical, the Mennonite, was founded by
the Eastern District to reach Mennonite youth no longer familiar with
German. By 1900 English-language services were common throughout
the Eastern District and by 1920 the use of German in church services
had disappeared. The Central District followed their lead shortly
thereafter. A comparison between the eastern and western factions
of the General Conference in 1905 revealed that only four out of forty-
six General Conference churches west of the Mississippi used English
while all but four of thirty-four churches east of the Mississippi
had English-language services.[13]

At the 1896 Conference, discussion centered on the urgent
adoption by General Conference Mennonite Churches of the "language
of the nation." Proposals advocated a weekly periodical in English,
English Sunday school quarterlies, and English hymnals.[14] These progressive steps by the General Conference produced the backdrop for
a debate over the language question around the turn of the century.

Conflict between the eastern and western factions intensified
following an 1899 editorial in the Mennonite proposing English as
the official language of the General Conference. The writer, a young
Pennsylvania minister named Silas M. Grubb, believed the transition
was being unnecessarily drawn out in light of its inevitable outcome.
"But let us be done with it as soon as possible," pleaded Grubb.[15]

Grubb's plea drew an immediate response from Kansas Mennonites. David Goerz, a Russian immigrant, president of the WDC, founder of Bethel College, and editor, responded to Grubb's suggestion in a January 1900 editorial of the Bethel College periodical, School and College Journal. Goerz claimed that if the General Conference did not remain German in "language, character, and essence (wesen)," the WDC would withdraw. Goerz supported the notion of learning English but warned that a premature shift in language would be disastrous for denomination unity. Mennonites had not come to America to trade Russification for Americanization. If Kansas Mennonites had known that a language transition was to occur so early, according to Goerz, they would have joined another Mennonite conference.[16]

In the February 1900 issue of School and College Journal, Christian Krehbiel, a South German organizer of the original Kansas Conference and pastor of the Halstead congregation, supported Goerz's sentiments in an editorial entitled, "Noch einmal: 'Englisch oder Deutsch--welches?'" Krehbiel pointed to the strength of Kansas Mennonite churches who had retained the German language. He attributed their success to a strict adherence to Mennonite principles which, next to the Bible, "are resting in the Mother language in which they were first uttered."[17] Goerz and Krehbiel clearly believed in 1900 that the proposal for official recognition of English as the language of the General Conference was premature for the Western District.

The February 1900 issue of the Mennonite included two articles on the language problem. The first, by H. G. Allebach, was a response to Krehbiel's article in the School and College Journal. Allebach made certain that the English proposal was not perceived as an effort

to rid the General Conference of German. Adopting English as the
official language of the denomination was simply a natural step in
the obvious language shift of local congregations. He accused Kansas
Mennonites of remaining "studiously aloof from their American neighbors"
in their exclusive use of the mother language. Allebach further
suggested that imbedding the principles of Mennonite faith in the
German language hampered the evangelistic effort of the gospel:

> What are the points of excellence? Are they found in the
> Gospel or in the language? If in the language, why then fool
> around with the Gospel? Is the Gospel not powerful enough
> to make character, whether in a German or in a Yankee? If
> our points of excellence are centered in the Gospel, as they
> ought to be, then a change of language can't touch them.
> "The kingdom of God is not in word but in power." I Cor.
> 4:20.[18]

In an attempt to clarify the position of the eastern faction
of the General Conference, a second article appeared in the same issue
of the _Mennonite_ by the originator of the debate, Silas M. Grubb.
Grubb's article was entitled, "German or Mennonite, Which?". According
to Grubb, the Eastern District Conference Mennonite churches were
"anglicized" to the point that the mother tongue had become "useless
German." He predicted that the same would occur among Kansas Mennonites
and further resistance was wasted energy.[19] An article in the February
1900 _Review_, an English-language Mennonite newspaper published in
Newton, Kansas, by Christian Krehbiel's son, C. E. Krehbiel, called
for a peaceful solution on the language issue:

> Let us soon, yea, the sooner the better, land in the arms
> of the English language and reach a "splendid isolation" .
> . . but wherever the German language is not yet dethroned,
> it becomes the duty of parents, teachers, ministers, and
> churches to preserve it for the coming generation.[20]

There were other editorials in church periodicals that addressed the question of the language transition, but the arguments boiled down to one basic conclusion: the eastern faction of the General Conference was twenty to thirty years ahead of the Kansas Mennonites in the use of English. The association with American Mennonites via the General conference served to facilitate the language transition of Kansas Mennonites. In spite of an initial resistance to the Eastern District Conference and the Mennonite, Kansas Mennonites eventually followed the lead of brethren who, after a century and a half in this country, were less apprehensive of Americanization and more willing to embrace English as an ecclesiastical language without sacrificing Mennonite principles.

German remained the language of the General Conference sessions until after World War I. Without the influence of the Western District Conference, English would have been adopted earlier; without the lead of the Eastern District Conference, the transition would have taken place later.[21] General Conference proceedings were first held in English in 1920, years before many of the Kansas churches had introduced English sermons on a regular basis. The last German-language discussion of the Conference floor took place in 1933, just before Kansas Mennonites achieved a balance of English and German worship services.[22] In many respects, the General Conference, with its Americanized eastern churches, paved the way for the language transition of the Kansas Mennonites.

Western District Conference

The Western District Conference served as a regional rallying point for Kansas Mennonites with regard to the language issue. All of the churches of the Kansas Conference (1877-1892) used High German exclusively as a worship language. Thus, it was only natural that German serve as the conference language from its founding and eventual development into the Western District Conference in 1892. For fifty-eight years all reports to the Kansas Conference and Western District Conference sessions were given in German. In 1918 the WDC passed a resolution calling for the publication of an abbreviated English report of the WDC proceedings in church periodicals. In 1932 the opening sermon was delivered in English. In 1934 English was officially recognized as the "predominant language" of the WDS. The following year the Bethel College report was the first English report made on the conference floor. In 1941 the last German report was turned in by the Deaconness Committee.[23]

Although leaders of the Western District Conference joined forces to resist the adoption of English in 1900 as the official language of the General Conference, disagreements existed over the language issue within the WDC. The choice between public schools and parochial schools stemmed from the language issue. C. H. Wedel, in his report to the 1894 WDC on Mennonite parochial schools, emphasized the importance of German instruction:

   . . . if our young people grow up without German instruction, they are later on unable to participate in our catechetical instruction, and are compelled to turn elsewhere.[24]

To Wedel and other WDC leaders, the loss of German meant the loss of Mennonite youth. Later they came to realize that English would persist as the language of Mennonite youth and failure to provide English-language instruction and church services meant the actual loss of Mennonite young people. J. K. Penner reported for the Committee for School and Education at the 1913 WDC session that Mennonite youth had accepted English as the conversational language. The only effective strategy for retaining German was a bilingual approach. "English and the German language should not oppose each other," pleaded Penner. "A man who speaks two languages is worth two."[25] It was obvious to the WDC leaders just prior to World War I that the exclusive maintenance of the German language was no longer possible or even desirable. Penner described German-language instruction in Mennonite schools in 1913 as "merely a means to an end: the building of the kingdom of God."[26] A pragmatic attitude emerged in the thinking of WDC leaders with regard to the English language.

The 1916 WDC proceedings revealed further concern with the language transition. This was in relation to English-speaking Mennonite youth who could no longer understand sermons in churches that exclusively used German.[27] By 1917 when the Committee for School and Education reported that the war had weakened German instruction in Mennonite parochial schools, efforts had already been made to provide religious instruction in English. World War I did not initiate the use of English in Mennonite schools and churches. The prospect of losing English-speaking children first caused the church to consider the use of English as a religious instruction language. However, World War I greatly accelerated the rate of transition.

In 1919 a recommendation was passed by the WDC that religious instruction of young people be carried on in English. "We believe that in that way we are building better and more safely for the future than if we do not do this."[28] The report of the Committee for School and Education revealed that most parochial schools were already giving some instruction in English. The WDC further encouraged the churches to consider this recommendation dispassionately with a pragmatic approach. In 1923 a WDC statement reinforced a wartime position that German instruction was a means to an end: religious instruction could be carried on effectively in English. In 1924 the WDC responded affirmatively to a recommendation for an English songbook for children.[29]

The WDC was not limited to facilitating the language shift in parochial schools. The question of English-language worship services surfaced continually in the conference proceedings. Requests for English sermons filtered in from scattered congregations in western Kansas and Oklahoma during the first two decades in America. By the turn of the century the WDC regularly intervened in local conflicts over the language question. The conference accepted numerous invitations from several congregations for English preaching. However, intervention by the WDC did not guarantee an immediate remedy.

Usually no "quick fix" solutions existed for language conflicts. Yet the WDC served as a mediator when local efforts failed. In this way the WDC acted as a vehicle for the language shift. Without district involvement the transition would have encountered greater difficulty and subsequently prolonged the struggle. When conference officials recognized English as the predominant language in 1934, the WDC was years ahead of most local churches in the language transition.

Sunday School and Christian Endeavor Society

An early vehicle of the language shift in the local church was Sunday school.[30] Sunday school was an American institution generally accepted by the General Conference Mennonites before the arrival of the Russian Mennonites in central Kansas. Kansas Mennonites quickly incorporated the Sunday school concept during the first years in America. Initially, classes were organized for children and were carried on in German. As Mennonite youth began attending public schools, Sunday school gained greater significance in the local church. Without the religious education of parochial schools, Sunday schools were called upon to pick up the slack. Early in the twentieth century Kansas Mennonites recognized the need for English Sunday school classes. It is not known when the first English-speaking Sunday school occurred, but by 1911 Hoffnungsau, Inman, and Newton churches all had English-language classes. By the time of America's involvement in World War I, several churches already had English-language Sunday school classes. During the war a number of churches added them. In 1918 the Brudertal (Hillsboro) church organized an adult English-speaking class for draftees compelled to state their nonresistance convictions in English.[31] The First Mennonite Church of Christian (Moundridge) added its first English-language Sunday school class in 1919. That same year the Tabor Mennonite Church (Goessel) initiated English-language classes for children unable to read German. By 1924 English-language Sunday school classes for

children were prevalent in WDC churches.[32] The desire to educate
children in the fundamentals of Mennonite belief was often instrumental
in dispelling the lingua-phobia of parents.

Young adult English-language Sunday school classes were common
in most churches by 1930. Alexanderwohl organized an English class
in 1925 to accommodate migrant harvest hands from the Ozarks. Even
after one of the older brethren learned to his distress that the English
class had not been discontinued after the harvest, Alexanderwohl
continued to conduct English-language Sunday school classes.[33]
Alexanderwohl was one of the last churches to make the shift to English.
Ironically, Sunday school was not only a catalyst of the English
language; it usually proved to be the last vestige of German in the
local Mennonite church. German-language classes continued in some
congregations well into the 1970s, long after the disappearance of
German sermons.

Another pioneer in the language transition was the Christian
Endeavor Society.[34] Organized in 1881 as an interdenominational youth
organization, it was closely associated with the Sunday School
Movement.[35] The Mennonite counterpart of the national organization
developed rapidly. By 1896, eleven <u>Christlicher</u> <u>Jungendverein</u> had
organized in the WDC and by 1916 only a few Mennonite churches in
central Kansas were without a society.[36] Certain church leaders had
reservations about the Christian Endeavor Society because of its
non-Mennonite origins. However, as early as 1878 the Kansas Conference
recognized a need for Mennonite youth among whom "pride and luxurious
clothes are gaining ground to such an extent that the true humility

of Jesus is trampled underfoot by most of them."[37] Like Sunday school,
Christian Endeavor Societies provided an opportunity to involve
disenchanted youth in the functions of the church. By the early
twentieth century young people frequently could not understand a High
German sermon. Rather than shifting to English for the benefit of
the young and to the disdain of the elderly, several elders chose
to allow the organization of a local Christian Endeavor Society to
maintain the interest of Mennonite youth without infringing upon
traditional German-language worship. In 1916 the Committee for School
and Education reported that the language question had become a problem
in numerous Christian Endeavor Societies.[38] Mennonite young people
were more likely to use English than German in their meetings. In
1920 the committee reported: "In the Christian Endeavor work the
language transitions has perhaps progressed farthest."[39] Evidence
of the pioneering spirit of Christian Endeavor Societies in the language
shift is demonstrated in a comparison of the first English constitutions
with those of the church (table 4-1).

In each of the six churches where available records allowed
comparison, the English translation of the Christian Endeavor Society
constitution preceded that of the first English version of the church
constitution by six to nineteen years. By World War I nearly every
Mennonite church in central Kansas had a Christian Endeavor Society.
Local societies frequently used English in regular meetings. The
impact of World War I on the language transition was not nearly as
traumatic for Christian Endeavor Societies as it was for the rest
of the church.

TABLE 4-1

COMPARISON OF FIRST ENGLISH CONSTITUTIONS IN SIX CHURCHES

Church	English C. E. Constitution	English Church Constitution
Bethel College Mennonite	1912	1925
First Mennonite of Halstead	1920	1939
West Zion Mennonite	1920	1926
First Mennonite of Newton	1922	1937
Garden Township Mennonite	1927	1933
Buhler Mennonite Church	1927	1941

SOURCE: Christian Endeavor Society and Church constitution collections, Mennonite Library and Archives, Bethel College, North Newton, Kansas.

Clergy

A major factor in the language transition of a local congregation was the Mennonite elder. Upon his arrival in America he still wielded a strong hand of leadership in all church decisions. Often the personal inclinations of the elder strongly influenced the rate of language shift. He had the power to forestall English sermons or initiate them according to his desires. In most instances he took into consideration the needs and character of his congregation before making such a decision. Many of the early elders chose to maintain German-preaching simply because they had not mastered the English well enough to preach in it. Sometimes the first English sermon in a church came from a visiting speaker or on a special occasion when non-Mennonites were in attendance. The latter was the case at the Alexanderwohl Church in 1916. A funeral for a church member who did a great deal of business with non-Mennonites attracted several of his American customers. One of the sermons was in English. This marked the first English-language sermon in the church. A year later an English-speaking missionary requested permission to preach in English at Alexanderwohl. The request was granted with the provision that a German-language sermon be included.[40]

Occasional English-language sermons were an indication of future changes. A significant step toward a language transition was the decision to schedule a monthly English sermon. In 1900 a brief notice appeared in the Review:

A resolution recently adopted by the Mennonite Church at Moundridge provides that English preaching services shall be held every fourth Sunday evening. Rev. Wm. Galle is pastor of this church, and on December 2, he held his first English service under this regulation.[41]

The West Zion Mennonite Church (Moundridge) was among the first to take the bold step of scheduling English services on a monthly basis. The congregation organized in 1888 as a split from the First Mennonite Church of Christian. The split stemmed from a desire by Galle and some ninety-five charter members to extend the ministry of the church to non-Mennonites.[43] By 1900, West Zion had dropped the requirement of rebaptism for new members and added monthly English services. However, membership records from this period do not reveal a successful recruitment of non-Mennonites. The West Zion experiment with English-language services was premature; the church returned to exclusive German services until a seminary trained minister, John M. Suderman, joined the staff in 1913.[43]

Elders in three other General Conference Mennonite Churches in central Kansas conducted an English service on a monthly basis prior to America's entry in World War I. Each represented unique circumstances conducive to such a move. The Bethel College Mennonite Church was mixed according to national origin and was one of the most progressive congregations in the WDC. It consisted largely of college students and faculty members who made the language shift several years before less educated Mennonites. It rapidly became one of the most heterogeneous congregations in the conference. First Mennonite of Newton initated monthly English services in 1914 under the leadership of Elder Jacob Toews. As a town church the Newton congregation attracted a variety of Mennonite groups from the surrounding area.

As one of the earliest WDC churches of mixed background and no dominant German dialect, there was a tendency to accept English-language services at an earlier date. The First Mennonite Church of Christian (Moundridge) represented a similar situation. It consisted of South Germans and Swiss Volhynians and in 1914 conducted on English service a month.[44]

A strong force for English-language sermons in Mennonite churches was the First World War. The national mood rapidly shifted from one of pluralistic tolerance toward foreign languages to disdain for everything German. Darkened by fears and superpatriotism, stringent laws limiting the use of foreign languages were adopted.[45] Most of these were directed at schools, but the immigrant church quickly received the message: German sermons were a sign of disloyalty. On August 28, 1918, a notice was posted on the door of the First Mennonite Church of Christian. In bold letters it proclaimed: NOTICE--NO MORE GERMAN SERVICES WILL BE ALLOWED AT THIS CHURCH. The church decided not to give in to the anonymous notice and continued with its regular services inclusive of a monthly sermon in English. Most elders initially responded in a like manner to community pressure for exclusive English-language sermons during the war. However, shortly after the war the transition accelerated as a majority of WDC churches incorporated English sermons in the 1920s on a regular basis. In 1926 the First Mennonite Church of Christian added a second English-language service each month and by 1936 German sermons were limited to one each month.[46]

By 1929 twenty-one out of thirty-three (63.6%) congregations in central Kansas heard English sermons on a regular basis. Of the twenty-one, three congregations no longer used German in their church services. Two of these were Swiss churches (First Mennonite at Ransom and Swiss Mennonite at Whitewater) with a dissimilar national origin than the rest of the WDC and located on the geographical fringe of Mennonite settlements. The third congregation to abandon German language services by 1929 was the Hutchinson Mennonite Church, a recently organized, heterogeneous town church. By 1936 all of the thirty-three churches used some English, while eight (24.3%) used English exclusively (see fig. 4-1).[47]

Each elder made the language transition in a manner most suitable to his congregation. Some chose to use the Sunday evening service for English sermons; others selected one Sunday morning a month; still others followed each German sermon with a ten minute English summarization. A careful examination of one elder's sermons reveals the typical pattern of language shift.

Peter H. Richert (1871-1949) came to America from Taurida, South Russia, with his parents in 1874. He grew up near Goessel, Kansas, and attended both Halstead Seminary and Bethel College. In 1896 he was elected evangelist in his home church of Alexanderwohl and later served as a minister in this congregation. In 1908 the Tabor Mennonite Church organized as an offshoot of the Alexanderwohl congregation and ordained Richert as its elder. For the next thirty-six years he served as the leader of the Tabor congregation.

Richert was mainly an expository preacher. In 1923 he initiated a ten minute English summarization after each German sermon. This continued until 1927, the date of his first complete English sermon.

Fig. 4-1.

TRANSITION FROM GERMAN TO ENGLISH IN
WDC MENNONITE CHURCHES IN CENTRAL KANSAS

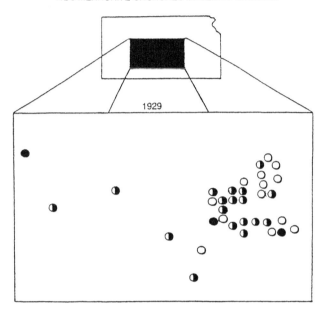

1929

OGerman language only

●English language only

◑Both Languages

1936

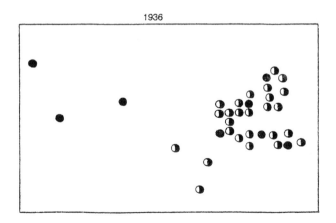

A total of 1,688 sermons is included in the Richert Collection in the Mennonite Library and Archives. Of these, 1,022 (60.5%) are in German while 666 (39.5%) are in English. Sermons from 1898 until 1927 were exclusively German. From 1928 to 1935 Richert sermons were predominantly German (407 German sermons; 48 English sermons). From 1936 to 1939 Richert reached a balance between German and English (201 German sermons; 215 English sermons). During the last six years of his ministry (1940-1946), Richert used English as the predominant preaching language (140 German sermons; 368 English sermons).

Richert's language shift was characteristic of progressive elders during the first half of the twentieth century. However, some elders who presided over Mennonite congregations during the same period were unable or unwilling to make the same language shift. The Gerhard Harms (1863-1951) and the Peter Buller (1863-1956) collections contained only German manuscripts. Both men were contemporaries of Richert.[48]

The first Mennonite clergy to grapple with the language shift in central Kansas were the itinerant ministers (Reiseprediger). Appointed by the conference, they were charged with the task of ministering to individual families isolated from the nucleus of Mennonite settlements. Occasionally they served as pulpit supply in congregations without ministers. The Reiseprediger was an evangelist and Bible teacher both inside and outside the conference. Itinerant preaching was instrumental in the development of the Western District Conference from its beginning as the Kansas Conference. Upon their arrival in Kansas in the 1870s, a portion of the Mennonite immigrants chose to settle areas isolated from major settlements; others moved

to Wichita, Hutchinson, or Emporia within a few years. Alarmed that
scattered Mennonites were joining other religious denominations, the
Kansas Conference began sending itinerant preachers, usually from
the larger churches, to minister to the needs of these scattered
sheep.[49]

The language problem was evident to itinerant preachers by
the 1890s. As the Mennonite population of central Kansas prospered
during the first two decades in America, the availability of farmland
declined. By the early 1890s, second generation immigrants once again
resettled, this time in western Kansas and the newly opened Oklahoma
Territory (1892). At the 1896 WDC session the report of the Conference
Minister reflected the widespread use of English among Mennonites
in scattered locations. Without regular German sermons and in the
absence of parochial schools to carry on German instruction, English
gradually replaced German as the conversational language. The further
Mennonites moved from the main body, the more frequent a tendency
developed to use English in church services. From the conference
minutes of 1896, it appears that one of the problems with English
services was the inavailability of English-speaking preachers.[50]

Only a few had formal training and that was usually limited
to the German language. The vast majority of itinerant preachers
in the WDC were without theological training and had little experience
in English preaching. At the same time, the reports of the Itinerant
Ministers Committee in the late 1890s contained increasing numbers
of requests for itinerant preachers capable of preaching in English.

Most requests were from western Kansas and Oklahoma, but some came from town churches in the hub of Mennonite settlements.

At the 1898 WDC session a recommendation was made for the selection of an itinerant preacher able "to carry on the work of the Lord in the German and in the English language."[51] Four years later the Itinerant Ministers Committee reported that in some of the Mennonite outposts in western Kansas, English preaching was necessary since the young people could no longer understand High German sermons.[52] One church leader summarized the frustrating circumstances of the language shift: "It seemed at times very discouraging; the results were that we had English-speaking children whom we tried to give a German religion."[53]

Reports of the Itinerant Ministers Committee from 1902 and 1918 revealed the concern of the Reiseprediger over the language problem. One itinerant pracher complained in 1914 that the young people no longer sang German hymns because their German was so poor. By 1918 the demand for English-language services still exceeded the availability of English-preaching itinerant preachers.[54]

The lack of itinerant ministers capable of English-language preaching was not the only problem plaguing the conference at this time. As more churches adopted English-language services, visiting itinerant preachers were hard pressed to keep track of the transition in each congregation. The shift to English proceeded at a different rate in each church. Various factors at the local level influenced attitudes producing a great disparity from one church to another. This posed an especially complex situation for itinerant ministers.

As they traveled into an area they were often uncertain which language to use. Often the itinerant minister inquired of another Reiseprediger as to which language a local church was using.[55] Occasionally the visiting speaker was caught in the middle of a language struggle. In such a situation he found two audiences and could not please both. Keeping abreast with the language shift in the local congregations was a perplexing task and failure to preach in the "right" language could be quite awkward.

One Reiseprediger during the period of language transition was C. E. Krehbiel, son of Kansas Conference founder, Christian Krehbiel. Young Krehbiel served the WDC in various capacities including that of itinerant minister during the 1920s. He also served as president from 1925 to 1927. In 1938 he was chosen president of the General Conference and served seven years. In 1931 he organized a Mennonite Church in Wichita and served four years. He also helped publish various Mennonite periodicals with his brother, H. P. Krehbiel. Throughout his ministry (1923-1946), C. E. Krehbiel frequently spoke in conference churches, either as Reiseprediger or in another conference capacity.[56] His sermon collection at the Mennonite Library and Archives reflects both a personal and a WDC language shift.

From 1926 to 1930 he preached a sermon on Zacchaeus in nine Mennonite churches--five times in English, four times in German. In 1927 he delivered a German sermon at the WDC session. Fourteen years later he preached the same sermon in English at the General Conference session. Fourteen wedding sermons from 1925 to 1946 were all in English.[57] Wherever he traveled, Krehbiel preached in the

language most acceptable to the local congregation. In 1929 he wrote
to a colleague inquiring which language to use:

> How is it with Ebenezer, are you English altogether now, or
> do you have preaching in both languages? And what languages
> do Sichar, Hinton, and Tologa use now? I forget these things.[58]

Even a brilliant leader of Krehbiel's stature found the language
transition perplexing for itinerant preaching.

Education

Mennonite parochial schools were an extension of the church
in the language transition.[59] German schools had two basic objectives:
teach the German language and acquaint students with the Bible. Upon
arrival in Kansas, Mennonites soon discovered that the state did not
have a well-established school system. State requirements were minimal
and school laws were lenient. Children from ages eight to fourteen
were required to attend only twelve weeks of school each year. Few
restrictions were placed on Mennonites who organized their own schools.
Lessons in private Mennonite elementary schools were taught in German,
but the first Kansas Conference session in 1877 urged schools to teach
the English language. Conference leaders assumed that Mennonite
children needed to learn English as a second language to relate socially
and spiritually to the host culture.[60]

Throughout the history of private Mennonite elementary and
secondary schools the maintenance of German remained a primary theme.
When the third annual Kansas Conference in 1879 discussed the
establishment of Halstead seminary, a resolution was passed stating:

> Instruction in German shall also be carried on to the same stage,
> in order that students are able to render the same work in the
> German domain of learning which is required in English in the

district schools. A thorough religious instruction must also
be given in the German language in order that in the future
our churches may be able to find prepared workers along spiritual
lines.[61]

The two-fold desire to maintain German for the sake of religious
instruction while incorporating English for the purpose of evangelism
and economic survival presented a paradox for Mennonite education.
Bilingualism may well have been a noble concept for educated Mennonites,
but for the vast majority it was an impractical solution. The result
was a "bilingual Mennonite family"; parents who conversed in
Plautdietsch, or one of the other German dialects, and were accustomed
to High German sermons; and children who conversed in either a
Plautdietsch-English mixture or exclusively English, and understood
little of the High German sermons in the church.

The practice of conducting German schools in the spring following
the public school year was threatened early in the twentieth century.
As the state of Kansas increased the requirements of public schools
and lengthened the existing school year from three to five months
in 1903, seven months in 1909, and eight months in 1923, little time
was left for private Mennonite schools to carry on German instruction.[62]

The shorter German school year was not the only problem
Mennonites faced in efforts to maintain German instruction in the
twentieth century. The German Teachers Association noted in 1897
that the different German dialects of students were a detriment to
learning standard German. Instead of conversing in "proper" German
while under the supervision of a teacher, they reverted to Plautdietsch
or another of the local German dialects. This was a source of

frustration for German teachers who tirelessly attempted to teach the ecclesiastical language: High German.[63]

Another condition that had an impact on the language transition in Mennonite education was the lack of teachers qualified to instruct in German. Ironically, a system which was founded to provide quality education was also responsible for producing a lack of qualified German instructors. In the first private Mennonite schools many of the teachers were ministers. Later, however, the educational standards of private Mennonite schools had improved to the point that few ministers qualified for teacher certification. At the same time, the 1916 WDC Committee for Schools and Education noted that many of the qualified Mennonite teachers chose to teach in public schools because of better pay.[64] Some parents complained that certain teachers' German language skills were so poor children were unable to learn German well enough to understand the sermons.[65]

Another aspect of the language shift in private Mennonite schools was the cost factor. Mennonite immigrants in Kansas as early as the late nineteenth century displayed a hesitancy to pay for private education when they could send their children to Mennonite-dominated public schools. The founding conference in 1877 passed a resolution supporting enrollment in those public schools under the dominant influence of Mennonite constituents. Gradually the percentage of Mennonite students in public schools increased to the point that in 1923 the Committee for School and Education noted that the transition from parochial to public school was complete. "With the transfer of the control over the system of education to the state, the influence of the Church has become weak."[66] Declining enrollment in private schools paralleled the exchange of German for English by Mennonite youth.

Still another factor in the language shift in Mennonite education was the development of higher institutions of learning. Of special significance were Halstead Seminary Preparatory School (Halstead, Kansas, 1883-1893) and Bethel College (North Newton, Kansas, 1893). With the 1878 closing of the General Conference school of theology in Ohio (Wadsworth Institute), General Conference Mennonites were left without an institution of higher learning. In 1883 the Halstead College Association, under the control of the Kansas Conference, organized the Halstead Seminary with seventy-six students during the first year. The purposes of the school were: (1) to prepare teachers for both public and parochial schools; (2) to prepare students for college entrance; (3) to offer liberal arts training to any who desired an education beyond the elementary level.[67] Halstead Seminary admitted non-German speaking students and employed an English-language teacher. In the 1884-85 school year, sixty-five students were enrolled with "forty Germans, twenty Americans, and five Indians."[68] English instruction was important to the students at Halstead. When the English teacher resigned in 1886 and the school did not hire a replacement for an extended period of time, several students left and chose to attend where they could receive English instruction.[69] Certainly the close contact with American students who spoke little German served to encourage Mennonite students to learn English. The report of the school to the WDC in 1889 noted the "preference of our young people for everything American," including the English language.[70] The seminary played a significant role in the language transition by emphasizing the importance of knowing both languges.

In 1893 Halstead Seminary closed its doors and Bethel College was organized as the denominational school of the General Conference Mennonite Church. Its aim was to "serve the Mennonite churches in the Kingdom of God by teaching the truths of the Holy Scriptures in German and English.[71] From the beginning instruction was bilingual. It was not long before English became the dominant language of instruction. In 1914 Professor J. F. Balzer responded in the college newspaper (Monatsblaetter) to the charge that Bethel took preference to the English language. Balzer acknowledged that Bethel stood accused of being responsible for the widespread use of English by Mennonite youth in central Kansas:

> To this we must say that we are living in a country where English is the language of the country. This circumstance alone is sufficient to make the problem a critical one. We are living in a country where the English language is used; the children go to the English school; at home there are English newspapers; in many cases one has English neighbors; in larger towns business is transacted in the English language. These are well known facts. Is it a wonder that we have a language question? It would be wonder if we did not have.[72]

Balzer realized that the college no longer used German instruction as frequently as in the past. This was due to the fact that a growing number of students no longer spoke German. In an attempt to accommodate both languages, the school implemented a policy under which students voluntarily agreed to pay a fine if caught using English at meal hours. Balzer recognized that this alone would not slow the language shift at Bethel. However, it represented a token response to criticism that blamed the school for being a leader in the language transition. After all, Balzer concluded, the college was under a mandate from accreditation agencies to include more English instruction. Furthermore, by using English, Bethel prepared students for a realistic ministry in the church of tomorrow. He pointed to the fate of certain Mennonite churches in Pennsylvania who refused to allow English in their worship services. "They are empty today, because the people thought the English language was not to be taken into account."[73]

From 1893 until World War I, Bethel College served as an important vehicle for the language transition of Mennonites in central Kansas. The first president of Bethel, C. H. Wedel (1893-1910), was a first-generation immigrant who attended two American institutions: McKendrie College, Lebanon, Illinois, and Bloomfield (New Jersey) Theological Seminary. He supported both the acquisition of the English language and the retention of the German. From an academic perspective, bilingualism was appropriate and defensible. However, most Mennonites were, at the least, suspicious of higher education and, at the most, disdainful of the Americanizing impact upon their young people.

The pre-World War I debate over the language question at Bethel gave way to an even greater battle during the 1920s and 1930s: modernism versus fundamentalism. Some of the same issues overlapped and many of the participants found themselves allied with familiar faces in a new debate.

The greatest impact on the language shift in Mennonite education was World War I. The trend toward English instruction was well underway by 1914. Mennonite educators were aware of the increased use of English by Mennonite youth in the two decades before World War I. At the 1913 WDC session the Committee for School and Education reported that some Mennonite parochial schools had adopted bilingual instruction. This signaled a pragmatic approach to the use of English as the conversational language of Mennonite youth. The committee urged the conference to accept the bilingual position of Mennonite parochial schools to "enlarge our field of vision, to utilize the spiritual treasures of both languages."[74] Mennonite leaders encouraged the instruction of Mennonite principles via the English language. "Mere knowledge of German is not the goal of these schools," concluded the 1913 committee report, "but merely a means to the end: the building of the kingdom of God."[75] Although this attitude gradually gained acceptance among Mennonite church leaders, it was not generally accepted by the Mennonite laity prior to World War I. Many had great difficulty perceiving God's Kingdom without virtue of the German language. Thus, World War I had the effect of accelerating what had been theoretically initiated in Mennonite education.

As a result of America's declaration of war on German in April 1917, the American Protective League and the American Defense League waged a campaign through indiscriminate attacks on German-American institutions, especially parochial schools using the German language. One of the pamphlets of the American Defense League claimed: "Any language which produces a people of ruthless conquestadors [sic] such as now exists in Germany, is not a fit language to teach clean and pure American boys and girls."[76]

Parochial schools of the Lutheran church were particularly targeted by superpatriots bent on eliminating the German language from educational institutions. The councils of defense for several Great Plains states joined in the anti-German language campaign and passed laws restricting its use. Early in 1918 the Educational Council of the Kansas State Teachers Association recommended that all instruction in elementary schools be in English.[77] In March 1919 the Kansas State Legislature passed a bill which stated bluntly: "All elementary schools in this state, whether public, private or parochial, shall use the English language exclusively as the medium of instruction."[78] The bill included a clause enabling the State Board of Education to enforce the language restriction by closing down schools that failed to comply.

Even before the language restriction was placed on the statute book, two Mennonite elders traveled to Topeka to meet with the state attorney general. Although he was hesitant to discuss a legislative act before it had been officially enacted, the attorney general admitted that German might still be taught as a foreign language and was permissible as a conversational language in class. German instruction, however, was no longer legal under the new law. The German Teachers Conference of April, 1919, discussed the recently enacted language restriction law at length. Professor Peter J. Wedel of Bethel College reflected that the options of Mennonite educators were limited. Lamenting over the issue was not the solution; neither was closing Mennonite schools. Public schools certainly could not be expected to carry on German religious instruction. Wedel called for an increase of Mennonite parochial schools with English instruction. German instruction was the responsibility of the home.[79]

The WDC Committee for School and Education monitored the language question throughout the war. The 1917 report noted that the war had weakened German language instruction in Mennonite schools. In 1919 the committee, in response to the new law restricting German instruction, recommended that all Mennonite schools carry on the religious instruction of young people in English. "We believe that in that way we are building better and more safely for the future than if we do not do this." The committee appealed to the churches and private schools to consider the recommendation with a pragmatic approach. Several parochial schools had already made the transition to religious instruction in English. Others that had closed down during the war were already re-opening in 1919, fully prepared to carry on instruction in English.[80]

The war sentiment in Newton strongly opposed the use of German in either public or private institutions. Several businesses posted signs with the inscription, "Speak the American language; if you don't know it, learn it; if you don't like it, get out." A Loyalty League was organized in Newton, directing its attention toward the department of German in the college. The Loyalty League pressed the issue in 1918 demanding that all German classes be discontinued at Bethel and that an announcement be made by the school recognizing Bethel as the first college in the state to drop German from its curriculum. In compliance with public war sentiment, President Kliewer agreed to drop German for the sake of peace but refused the latter request.

He informed the league that he considered this action a mistake from an educational standpoint, and that it was only a temporary move. Kliewer confided to the WDC his intent to introduce the study of German in the college "when conditions will again become normal." Campus organizations such as the Deutsche Verein (German Society) and the Mennonitisch Historische Verein von Bethel College (Mennonite Historical Society of Bethel College) decided to discontinue meetings during the war.[81]

The Evening Kansas Republican, a Newton daily newspaper, hailed the discontinuance of all German classes as "sweeping step" for American loyalty by both the academy and the college. The paper claimed that when the viewpoint of the community had been explained to the school's faculty, "there was not a moment's hesitance in taking of action."[82]

If Mennonite educators had hopes that the language issue would revert to its pre-war situation immediately following a cease fire, they were disappointed. In the years immediately following World War I, further steps were taken to purge the United States of "unAmerican" foreign influences. In 1923, five years after the fighting had ended, representatives from the WDC traveled to Topeka to meet with state representatives to seek permission to use German instruction in Mennonite schools. By this time the Supreme Court had overruled a Nebraska law restricting German instruction in parochial schools. With this precedent decision in mind, an agreement was reached with Kansas authorities allowing Mennonite schools once again to use German instruction.

However, the impact of the war was irreversible. The German language was no longer perceived as a prerequisite for religious education. A few months after their trip to Topeka, members of the Committee for School and Education reported to the 1923 WDC that the ultimate priority of Mennonite schools was religious instruction, not retention of the German language:

> But may we not forget that in all instruction language is only a means to an end; and if we, by using a foreign language, no matter which one it is, are perhaps weakening the interest and understanding for religious matters among our young poeple, then we are doing them an injustice.[83]

For all practical purposes, Mennonite schools never recovered the German language after World War I. In conference reports parochial schools were no longer referred to as "German schools." Instead, they were known as institutions of "religious education." The German Teachers Association changed its name to the Mennonite Teachers Association. In its 1923 report, the Committee for School and Education acknowledged that its work had been reduced significantly in recent years. For the first time the committee went to the extent of recommending public schools for Mennonite children. Without German instruction Mennonite education lost one of its distinguishing characteristics of a century and a half.

At the annual Teachers Conference of the German Teachers Association in April 1919, one of the topics of discussion was, "Are we in a transitional period with our German?" The discussion leader, C. C. Heidebrecht, summarized the issue with a direct answer:

> Yes we are. The new school laws have not caused it, but only quickened it. We have not used our opportunity as we should. We should have had longer terms. The preparatory schools had to solicit students, when they should have come voluntarily.[84]

Heidebrecht realized that in 1919 Mennonites were abandoning German for English in parochial schools, and World War I was not the sole cause. He noted the transition began in the decades before the war when Mennonite families chose to send their children to English-speaking schools rather than Mennonite schools; when parents did not encourage children to attend the German school in the spring of the year after the public school term had ended; when Mennonite school boards chose to reduce the length of the German school term to accommodate the lengthening public school year. These changes were implicit steps in the Americanization process. The language transition in Mennonite schools was in full swing by the time World War I burst upon the scene. The war served to remind Mennonites that further religious education of Mennonite youth required the English language. "We should go slowly and cautiously," stated Heidebrecht in 1919. Looking back he summarized that Mennonites should not have embodied their religious principles so thoroughly in a language; they were ashamed to speak the German language; they were ashamed of their religious principles.[85]

For Mennonite educators the German language had served its purpose during the first fifty years of Mennonite schools in America. By the 1920s the time had come to embrace English fully. Mennonite schools in central Kansas attempted to be pragmatic and accept the language transition as long as they could maintain other Mennonite distinctives. However, the loss of German instruction in Mennonite parochial schools signaled the end of an era in Mennonite education.

Periodicals

Another facilitator of the language transition was the Mennonite periodical.[86] There were three primary sources of periodicals for

Kansas Mennonites: the General Conference, the Western District
Conference, and Bethel College. Each of these three sources produced
a number of periodicals read by Mennonites in central Kansas from
1874 and 1939 (fig. 4-2). The German newspaper played an important
role in blending the secular with the sacred and the ethnic with the
American across Mennonite congregational and conference lines. Along
with English Mennonite newspapers they accommodated the language shift
of Russian and East European Mennonites in central Kansas.

The earliest source of Mennonite reading in central Kansas
was from the General Conference. David Georz left South Russia before
the main body of immigrants, arriving in Summerfield, Illinois, in
1873. In February, Georz began publishing Zur Heimath, the official
organ of the Mennonite Board of Guardians. It was distributed on
a monthly basis without charge to immigrants from Russia. In December
of 1875 Goerz moved to Halstead, Kansas, and Zur Heimath was published
as a semimonthly German periodical until 1881. From the beginning,
Zur Heimath functioned as a reporter for the immigration, sharing
news from Russia and reporting on new settlements in America. The
paper increasingly became a servant of the General Conference and
in 1882 merged with Der Mennonitische Friedensbote to form the first
official newspaper of the General Conference, Christlicher Bundesbote.
Goerz continued to serve as editor of the German weekly until 1885.
The Christlicher Bundesbote united a reading constituency of Russian
Mennonites with the more Americanized Pennsylvania-Swiss-South German
Mennonites. It later (1947) joined ranks with a Canadian Mennonite
weekly, Der Bote, and continued as a German periodical with a

Fig. 4-2

General Conference, Western District, and
Bethel College Mennonite Periodicals

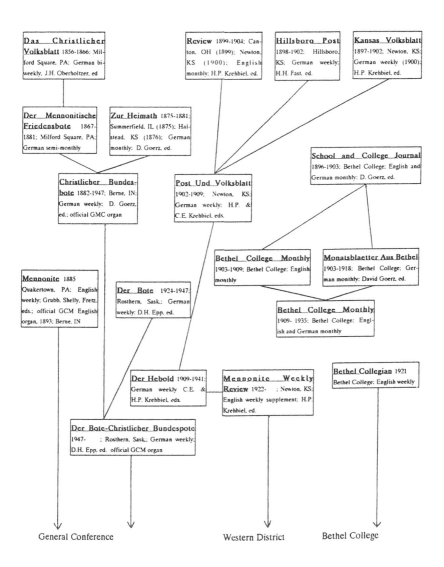

116

predominantly Canadian and South American reading constituency.[87]

The English-language organ of the General Conference was the Mennonite. Founded as an Eastern District weekly newspaper in 1885, it was published in Quakerstown, Pennsylvania, until 1902. In 1893 the General Conference adopted the Mennonite as its official English-language newspaper. From 1902 to 1937 it was published in Berne, Indiana. From the beginning the Mennonite had a distinctively progressive slant characteristic of some of the younger Eastern District ministers. It originally was founded to meet the needs of city consti- tuents and Mennonite youth, both of whom were more accustomed to English than German.[88]

The second source of reading for Mennonites of central Kansas was the local Mennonite periodical of the Western district. The best known was Der Herold (1909-1941). Three newspapers came together to form the predecessor of Der Herold, the Post und Volksblatt (1902-1909). The Hillsboro Post (1898-1902) merged with the Kansas Volksblatt (1897-1902) to form the Post und Volksblatt in 1902 with brothers H. P. and C. E. Krehbiel as editors. H. P. Krehbiel founded an English Mennonite periodical called the Review (1898-1904) while studying at Oberlin College. In 1900 he moved the Review to Newton, Kansas, and in 1904 merged it with the Post und Volksblatt. In 1909 the Post und Volksblatt became Der Herold with C. E. and H. P. Kreihbiel alternately serving as editors until 1935. In 1922 Der Herold added an English weekly supplement called the Mennonite Weekly Review. Both were published in Newton and combined secular news with local Mennonite news. In 1923 the Mennonite Weekly Review became independent of Der Herold maintaining a circulation of 1,000-1,200 subscribers until 1935. In the meantime, the circulation of Der Herold peaked in the mid 1930s with 2,800 subscribers. In 1935 the Mennonite Weekly Review expanded its scope of interests to include Mennonites throughout North America. By the late 1930s it surpassed Der Herold in circulation and in 1945 had nearly 8,000 subscribers.[89]

A third source of Mennonite reading in central Kansas was Bethel College. Although the constituency of college-related periodicals was restricted to pastors, students, and alumni, Bethel publications reflected the thinking of progressive WDC leaders on the language question. The college published its first catalog in German in 1893 with some English course descriptions. From 1894 to 1912 the school published two catalogs: an English-language edition and a German-language version. In 1912 the German version was dropped and only an English catalog was published thereafter. In 1913 the Bethel College Bulletin began publication as a German-language quarterly report of course offerings and financial status. At first it contained only an English preface but after 1918 entirely abandoned the German language.

In January 1896 the School and College Journal began publication as a monthly newspaper at Bethel. Initially, it was bilingual and kept Bethel alumni and college constituents informed about the work of the school. David Goerz, the first editor, recognized that even after two decades in America, many Russian and East European Mennonites were still uncomfortable with the English language. However, Goerz defended the bilingual school newspaper with an editorial in the first issue:

> We know, some of these are not yet thoroughly at home in the
> English, still we hope, they will not frown at the English
> columns of our paper, but acknowledge the necessity, practical
> value and mental profit of the cultivation of English. English
> is the language of this country that we are privileged to
> call our home; our young people acquire it readily and our
> "old folks" may follows. It will bring them profit.[90]

Goerz's apologetic defense of the English reflects both the
conservative position of the WDC churches as well as his own convictions
regarding the retention of the German language in Kansas Mennonite
churches. In the second issue of the school newspaper, Goerz encouraged
the retention of German for Mennonites who wished to pass on a precious
legacy of "self-respect and national instinct." Goerz perceived
bilingualism as the product of a gradual, healthy assimilation. He
illustrated his point by referring to the Galatians who migrated from
the banks of the Moselle and settled in Greece. Here they retained
their German language for centuries even though they learned Greek
fluently.[91]

In 1903 the School and College Journal began producing both
a German and an English edition. In 1909 the Monatsblaetter aus Bethel
College merged with the Bethel College Monthly to once again form
a bilingual periodical. In 1918 the paper dropped the Monatsblaetter
aus Bethel College maintaining both English and German sections until
the paper ceased publication in 1935. In 1921 a weekly student
newspaper was published entirely in English.

As mentioned earlier, Mennonite newspapers served as the format
for debate on the language question. The English-language Mennonite
revealed its preference by reporting the first English services in
local congregations. Editors of the Kansas-dominated Review, School

and College Journal, and Christlicher Bundesbote reacted with responses
that ranged from threats to withdraw from the General Conference to
pleas for bilingualism and locally autonomous solutions to the language
question. Attempts to "unruffle the feathers" on both sides brought
no immediate remedy. It was obvious that the varying convictions
of Mennonites on the language issue were deeply imbedded.[92] Mennonites
in central Kansas were more likely to subscribe to German-language
newspapers rather than the Mennonite. However, as an official organ
of the General Conference Mennonite Church, the Mennonite had a
far-reaching impact on Russian Mennonites on the Great Plains. In
a report of the 1908 General Conference session held at a WDC church
in Beatrice, Nebraska, the Mennonite noted "a spirit of greater
liberality on the language question." Although the people of the
Western District held to the German language more closely than the
rest of the General Conference, editor I. A. Sommer remarked: "Our
people are roused to a realization that there is a great deal more
to do than to quibble about which language one should serve and praise
God in." The Mennonite concluded that the language question in 1908
was "a dead issue."[93]

Certainly the Mennonite was premature in its pronouncement
on the language question. It was far from settled in central Kansas
in 1908. However, both sides had learned something from the debate
of 1900. All the arguments of Mennonite periodicals further verified
that an immediate solution leasing to everyone was unlikely. Time
was on both sides. Both German and English advocates learned to be
sensitive to the position of each other. In the years after World

War I when thousands of Russian Mennonites settled in Canada, the Western District ironically found itself advocating the use of English while their Canadian brethren clung to the mother tongue.

A more likely choice of reading for central Kansas Mennonites was Der Herold (1909-1941). Der Herold was the most widely circulated Kansas-based, German-Language, Mennonite newspaper. In 1910 Der Herold was exclusively German with the exception of an occasional English-language advertisement. These English-language advertisements became more frequent until by 1916 each edition included two or three. The frequency of English-language advertisements in Der Herold reflected the general rate of the language transition among Mennonites in central Kansas. In the June 14, 1917 issue there were five; in the March 28, 1918 issue six English-language advertisements appeared; and in the December 1917 edition seven were included. The English language was not restricted to advertisements in Der Herold. English articles featuring local news in the Nesston and Bethel College communities appeared in 1916. Hesston was the settlement center of the (Old) Mennonite Church in Kansas; English was commonly used in the daily conversations of these "American" Mennonites. English was likewise common on the campus of Bethel College. Occasional English-language articles summarizing recent college activities frequently appeared in the 1916 Der Herold. The May 16, 1916 edition featured an English article entitled, "Christ and War."

In 1916 a total of twelve English-language articles appeared in Der Herold.[94] With America's entry into World War I, the number of English-language articles in Der Herold increased to thirty. Many of these were published letters to and from congressmen regarding military exemption. In 1918 over 203 English-language articles appeared in Der Herold. A regular English Bible study appeared on the front page of each edition. By the middle of 1918 Der Herold took the appearance of a bilingual newspaper with thirty English-language articles in the month of June. In May 1919, Der Herold announced it would expand its English articles to an entire page. Finally in 1922 the Mennonite Weekly Review was introduced as an English supplement and Der Herold once again reverted to a German-language newspaper with only English-language advertisements.[95]

World War I disrupted what had been a relatively smooth language transition for Kansas Mennonites. For over a decade there had been little open dispute over the language question between the Kansas Mennonites and their American cousins in the East. The war reopened the debate. In the October 11, 1917 edition of the Mennonite, Silas M. Grubb, now editor, noted that the General Conference session was to be held in Pennsylvania for the first time since 1899. Under the cloud of war, Grubb claimed the language question was a non-issue for General Conference Mennonites, even in the Western District Conference. For Kansas Mennonites, who had not yet realized the full impact of the war by the fall of 1917, the language question was far from being a non-issue.[96]

Kansas Mennonites were torn between the desire to retain the German language with its implications of ethnoreligious identity and the desire to be viewed as loyal Americans. The Mennonite distinctive of nonresistance further complicated matters. The First World War was a traumatic conflict of conscience and loyalty for all Mennonites but especially difficult for Kansas Mennonites because of their continued use of the German language. The 1918 _Der Herold_ illustrates this conflict. In the April 4, 1918 edition, a full page of English advertisements summoned financial assistance for the war effort. Restricted by conviction from bearing arms, _Der Herold_ called upon Mennonites to aid the war effort through the purchase of Liberty Bonds and the enactment of conservation policies. Mennonites were admonished to "eat more corn," "cultivate the soil," "feed our soldiers," and "save liberty in America--buy now Liberty Bonds." In a May 23, 1918 English editorial, C. E. Krehbiel cleverly argued that World War I was being fought to preserve the freedom of languages. America had "always permitted her alien immigrants to speak, write, and read in any language." Krehbiel pointed to Mennonite patriotism as a prime example of this pluralist linguistic policy:

> We Americans insist that disloyalty cannot be cured by suppressing the tongue in which it finds expression. We have never questioned the right of a government to teach the dominant language in its state schools and to require it in official business, but we have already condemned any government which attempts to prevent the free use of other languages in conversation, newspapers, churches, public meetings and private schools.[97]

Krehbiel's argument for the retention of German-language newspapers was thoroughly cloaked in American patriotism and cleverly written in the English language. At the same time he did not depart from Mennonite principles to champion Mennonite support of the war. It was the goal of the war, not the means of warfare, that Krehbiel claimed Mennonites could support.

In spite of their many attempts to justify the continued use of the German language, Mennonite periodicals were forced to accelerate the language transition as the result of World War I. The creation of the English-language Mennonite Weekly Review in 1922 was a byproduct of war. As a result of World War I, Kansas Mennonites recognized a need for an English-language periodical. The decision by Bethel College to publish an exclusive English-language weekly student newspaper in 1921, further revealed the impact of the war on the language shift. The action of the college in 1918 to abandon German instruction completely and temporarily terminate the German language department was the most dramatic step in the transition.

Evidence of Transition

One evidence of the language shift in the church was the translation of the church constitution from German to English (table 4-2). Only two WDC churches in central Kansas had English constitutions before World War I. Four more published an English constitution in the 1920s; ten churches added English versions in the 1930s; and four churches did not have an English constitution until the 1940s. The Goessel Mennonite Church did not publish an English version until 1952. The bulk of Mennonite churches in central Kansas translated German constitutions between 1920 and 1940.

Another indication of the language transition was the first English-language church yearbook. Not all of the churches published an annual report, but a tally of those that did indicates the varying transition rates in local congregations (table 4-3). The first

TABLE 4-2

FIRST ENGLISH CONSTITUTIONS IN CENTRAL KANSAS
GENERAL CONFERENCE MENNONITE CHURCHES

Year	Church	Year	Church
1898	Grace Hill Mennonite	1937	Burrton Mennonite
1908	Tabor Mennonite	1937	First Mennonite of Newton
1922	First Mennonite of Hutchinson	1938	First Mennonite of Pretty
1925	Bethel College Mennonite		Prairie
1926	West Zion Mennonite	1939	First Mennonite of Halstead
1927	Hebron Mennonite	1939	First Mennonite of Hillsboro
1931	First Mennonite of Christian	1941	Johanhestal Mennonite
1932	Inman Mennonite	1941	Buhler Mennonite
1933	Eden Mennonite	1942	Emmaus Mennonite
1933	Garden Township Mennonite	1947	Alexanderwohl Mennonite
1935	Eisiedal Mennonite	1952	Goessel Mennonite

SOURCE: Compiled from the collection of church constitutions at the Mennonite Library and Archives, Bethel College, North Newton, Kansas.

TABLE 4-3

FIRST ENGLISH YEARBOOKS IN CENTRAL KANSAS
GENERAL CONFERENCE MENNONITE CHURCHES

Year	Church	Year	Church
1918	First Mennonite of Christian	1937	Alexanderwohl Mennonite
1922	Bethel College Mennonite	1939	Hebron Mennonite
1923	West Zion Mennonite	1940	Johannestal Mennonite
1933	First Mennonite of Newton	1941	Hoffnungsau Mennonite
1936	Buhler Mennonite	1941	Emmaus Mennonite
1936	Goessel Mennonite	1941	First Mennonite of Pretty
1937	First Mennonite of Hillsboro		Prairie
		1942	Inman Mennonite

SOURCE: Compiled from the collection of church yearbooks at the Mennonite Library and Archives, Bethel College, North Newton, Kansas.

TABLE 4-4

COMMON NAMES IN THE TABOR MENNONITE CHURCH
FAMILY RECORDS, 1875-1945

Name	Number born before 1875	Number born 1875-1900	Number born 1901-1925	Number born 1926-1945
Maria	52	24	10	0
Heinrich	45	10	3*	0
Helena	40	18	4**	0
Jacob	40	23	5	0
Peter	38	20	3	0
Anna	28	24	0	2
Eva	25	10	2	0
Sara(h)	16	15	1	0
Johann	15	15***	4****	0
David	14	12	1	0

*   Henry
**   Helen
*** John twelve times, Johann three times.
**** John three times, Johann once.

SOURCE: "Family Records of the Tabor Mennonite Church," Mennonite Library and Archives, Bethel College, North Newton, Kansas.

Mennonite Church of Christian published an English-language yearbook during the war years (1918-1919) but reverted back to a German version until 1927. The Bethel College Church and West Zion followed with English-language yearbooks in 1922 and 1923. These three congregatinos represented the progressive churches of central Kansas. The bulk of the churches did not publish an English-language yearbook until the years 1933-1942.

Another evidence of the language shift was the departure of traditional German first names for Mennonite offspring. An examination of the family records of one congregation illustrates this (table 4-4). The Tabor Mennonite Church (Goessel) organized in 1908 as a daughter church of the Alexanderwohl congregation. The records of those Dutch-Russian immigrants who transferred to the Tabor Church are included in the church records. Some 420 persons born in Russia before 1875 had a total of only thirty-six different names. All were traditional German names. Over one-half (215 or 51.2%) had one of five popular names--Maria (52 or 12.4%), Heinrich (45 or 10.7%), Helena (40 or 9.5%), Jacob (40 or 9.5%), and Peter (38 or 9.1%).

Those born in America between 1875 and 1900 constituted a total of 370 persons in the Tabor family records. There were twice as many different names (79), far fewer traditional names, and several which did not appear in the pre-1875 records. Johannes became John, Franz became Frank, Wilhelm changed to William, and Susanna changed to Susie. The five most common names made up a total of 29.5% (109) of all persons in this period.

From 1901 to 1925, 357 persons were added to the Tabor family records with 174 different names. There was a radical departure from traditional German names. The five most common names made up only 10.9% (39) of all the individuals born in this period. Noticeably absent were traditional favorites such as Heinrich, Helena, and Anna.

In the period of 1926-1945, 171 persons were added to the Tabor family records with a total of 122 names. The five most common names (LeRoy, Raymond, Arthur, Darlene, and Gladys) made up a total of 9.4% of all names selected in this era. Of the ten most common German names in 1875, only one (Anna) was repeated by those born in the 1926-1945 period.

The replacement of traditional German names of the nineteenth century by contemporary American names of the twentieth century is further evidence of the language transition of Mennonites in central Kansas. An American name usually indicated the acceptance of the English language.

The language transition occurred more rapidly for both town churches and those isolated from the hub of Mennonite settlements. For many there were two language shifts: High German to English (or a Plautdietsch-English combination), and local dialect (Low German, Swiss, etc.) to English. High German lost out to English first; Plautdietsch and other dialects were replaced later. In other words, the language shift occurred for most in the church before the home. Local dialects actually hindered the continued use of standard German in worship services. The transition from Plautdietsch to English occurred last among the Dutch-Russian Mennonites in the Goessel area.[98] Linguist J. Neale Carman discovered that the critical year for Low German transition in central Kansas was 1935. In the Goessel area it was 1950. The loss of Low German by Dutch-Russian Mennonites had an even greater impact upon group identity than loss of the Swiss or South German dialect among the other Mennonites in central Kansas.[99]

Comparatively speaking, Mennonites maintained High German along with local dialects longer than other German settlements on the Great Plains. The Lutheran Church--Missouri Synod, a conservative German immigrant church, experienced a similar language transition. English had been introduced in the Synod before 1900, but by the First World War German was still the dominant church language. However, by 1919 English achieved dominance over German in almost every aspect of Synodical life.[100] Mennonites in central Kansas were slightly more successful in maintaining High German. English was introduced into worship services around 1900. Four churches had regular English services before America's entry into the First World War. By 1936 English-language services were common to all but one congregation; one-fourth of the WDC churches in central Kansas exclusively used English. By the Second World War, English had achieved dominance in nearly all WDC congregations, a decade after the Lutheran Church--Missouri Synod.

Conclusion

For centuries the German language served as a distinction of Mennonite ethnoreligious cohesiveness in the Old World. It was particularly important to those Mennonites from Russia who settled in central Kansas in an attempt to maintain a position of nonconformity. In the absence of any distinctive religious costume such as was common to the (Old) Mennonite Church, the German language served to separate Mennonites from an English-speaking secular society. As long as the church retained its German-language tradition, there was little threat of an infiltration from non-Mennonite sources. From 1874 until the First World War, language functioned as the "dress code" for Russian and East European Mennonites in central Kansas. The gradual transition from German to the English language marked the loss of an important means of retaining their ethnoreligious identity. Without the retention of the mother tongue, Mennonites were vulnerable to further levels of what Gordon refers to as behavioral assimilation and eventually structural assimilation.

The reference of David Goerz to the German language as reflecting the "character and essence (Wesen)" of Mennonite existence reveals the real importance of the language issue.[101] Goerz and other WDC leaders perceived the German language as more than a means of maintaining a religious heritage. They saw German as integral to a sense of Mennonite peoplehood or Wesen. When the 1919 WDC acknowledged the German language as "merely a means to an end," the church unwittingly conceded something that was critical to Mennonite identity.[102]

Various elements accommodated Kansas Mennonites in the language shift. Contact with American Mennonites who had experienced nearly two centuries of acculturation encouraged the language transition. Both the General Conference (1920) and the Western District Conference (1934) made English the official language years ahead of many local congregations. Sunday schools and Christian Endeavor Societies led the way to local churches. The <u>Reiseprediger</u> was among the first to preach English sermons in central Kansas. In many congregations the elder determined the rate of transition.

Mennonite parochial schools, especially those of higher education, served as agencies of the language shift. Halstead Seminary and Bethel College both provided bilingual instruction and brought Mennonites into close contact with English-speaking non-Mennonites. Mennonite periodicals served as a format for the language conflict. German-language newspaper in the WDC gradually took on a bilingual appearance and by 1941 were replaced by English-language periodicals.

The language shift in the church stemmed largely from a desire to retain Mennonite youth. English-language Sunday schools, Christian Endeavor Societies, and regular English services were evidence of a relatively smooth transition prior to World War I. The war interrupted a gradual, delicate process and abruptly accelerated the inevitable shift. Mennonites were unprepared for a change in the national mood which by 1917 no longer tolerated a pluralistic approach to the language question. The war shifted the focus of the language issue from an internal struggle to an external conflict of loyalty and patriotism.

In 1946 Walter H. Hohmann, professor at Bethel College, reflected on the language transition.

> In these transition periods it seems that very often one may find a lowering of standards of quality. Many congregations in changing from one language to another experience a loss of spiritual power.[103]

Hohmann's observations appeared to be the fulfillment of a prophetic warning by J. S. Hirschler some fifty years earlier at the 1896 Western District Conference session:

> To adopt English for the sake of convenience or for the sake of a few Americans seems to me to be more than risky, since we are in danger of losing more of our faithfulness to our confession than we can hope to gain in Americans.[108]

The language transition was both a gain and a loss for Mennonites in central Kansas. Gone was the language of the past, the language so closely associated with Mennonite traditions in Russia, eastern Europe, and nineteenth century Kansas. With the acquisition of the English language, the Mennonites lost an important essence of Mennonite peoplehood and a barrier to worldly conformity. The mother tongue, which had ensured the maintenance of Mennonite ethnoreligious identity in the Old World for nearly a century, was purposefully replaced in America by the English language in a briefer period and with less government pressure. At the same time, the language transition encouraged Mennonites in central Kansas to make major strides in education.

CHAPTER IV - ENDNOTES

1. Milton M. Gordon, Human Nature, Class, and Ethnicity (New York: Oxford University Press, 1978), pp. 166-80.

2. Mennonite Encyclopedia, s.v. "Plattdeutsch (Plautdietsch)," by Cornelius Krahn; Jakob A. Duerksen, "Transition to German in West Prussia," Mennonite Life 22 (July 1967): 107-09; Robert H. Buchheit, "Mennonite 'Plautdietsch': a Phonological and Morphological Description of a Settlement Dialect in York and Hamilton Counties, Nebraska" (Ph.D. dissertation, University of Nebraska, 1978), pp. 8-16; Jakob W. Goerzen, "A Study of 'Plautdietsch' as Spoken by Mennonite Immigrants from Russia" (Ph.D. dissertation, University of Toronto, 1952), pp. 20-32; Mennonite Encyclopedia, s.v. "Language Problem," by Harold S. Bender; Walter H. Hohmann, "Transition in Worship," Mennonite Life 1 (January 1946): 8.

3. Mennonite Encyclopedia, s.v. "Plattdeutsch (Plautdietsch)," by Cornelius Krahn.

4. Mennonite Encyclopedia, s.v. "Language Problem," by Harold S. Bender: E. K. Francis, "The Russian Mennonites: From Religious to Ethnic Group," American Journal of Sociology 54 (September 1948): 101-07.

5. Minutes of the Kansas Conference (hereafter referred to as Minutes), 14 December 1877, Mennonite Library and Archives, Bethel College, North Newton, Kansas (transcript, English translation).

6. Ibid.

7. Robert H. Buchheit, "Language Maintenance and Shift Among Mennonites in South-Central Kansas," Yearbook of German-American Studies, Vol. 17 (Lawrence, Kansas: The Society for German-American Studies).

8. Minutes, 27-29 October 1879.

9. Buchheit, "Language Maintenance," pp. 111-18; David Haury, Prairie People (Newton, Kansas: Faith and Life Press, 1981), pp. 132-57; C. Henry Smith, The Coming of the Russian Mennonites (Berne, Indiana: Mennonite Book Concern, 1927), pp. 132-57.

10. J. Neale Carman, "Language Transition Amongst Kansas Mennonites," (unpublished paper, Mennonite Library and Archives, Bethel College, North Newton, Kansas, n.d.), p. 23.

11. The First Church of Christian (Moundridge) passed a resolution to begin services once a month in English in 1900. By contrast, the Bethel Mennonite Church did not introduce regular English sermons until 1942. "Minutes--Congregational Meetings, First Mennonite

133

Church of Christian, 1876-1956," at the First Mennonite Church of Christian, Moundridge, Kansas; "Minutes--Bethel Mennonite Church, 1926-1952," at Bethel Mennonite Church, Inman, Kansas.

12. Haury, pp. 72-77; Samuel F. Pannabecker, Open Doors: the History of the General Conference Mennonite Church (Newton, Kansas: Faith and Life Press, 1975), pp. 16-26, 96-103.

13. Pannabecker, Open Doors, pp. 170-72.

14. Henry P. Krehbiel, The History of the Mennonite General Conference, Vol. II (Newton, Kansas: Herald Publishing Co., 1938).

15. Mennonite, November 1899, p. 12

16. School and College Journal, January 1900, pp. 4-5.

17. School and College Journal, February 1900, pp. 12-13.

18. Mennonite, February 1900, p. 34.

19. Ibid., p. 37.

20. Review, February 1900, pp. 3, 5.

21. Pannabecker, Open Doors, p. 116.

22. Buchheit, "Language Maintenance," p. 119; Carman, "Language Transitions," p. 23.

23. Minutes, 12 November 1918; 19-20 October 1932; 24-25 October 1934; 23-25 October 1935; 22-23 October 1941.

24. Minutes, 7-9 November 1894.

25. Minutes, 8-11 October 1913.

26. Ibid.

27. Minutes, 4-5 October 1916.

28. Minutes, 5-7 November 1919.

29. Minutes, 17-18 October 1923; 21-23 October 1925; 19-20 October 1927.

30. Otto D. Unruh, "Schism of the Russian Mennonites of Harvey, McPherson, and Reno Counties, Kansas" (Ph.D. dissertation, University of Kansas, 1939), p. 99. Chapter V deals extensively with the complete Americanizing impact of Sunday schools upon Kansas Mennonites.

31. Ray N. Funk, Brudertal, 1873-1964 (North Newton, Kansas: Mennonite Press, 1964), p. 31.

32. Abraham Albrecht, "Mennonite Settlements in Kansas" (M.A. thesis, University of Kansas, 1924), p. 29.

33. Interview with Richard H. Schmidt, Bethel College, North Newton, Kansas, 20 July 1 984.

34. Otto D. Unruh, p. 99; for further discussion on the Christian Endeavor Society, see Chapter V.

35. Paul M. Lederach, "The History of the Young People's Bible Meeting in the Mennonite Church," Mennonite Quarterly Review 26 (July 1952): 216-31.

36. Haury, Prairie People, pp. 283-87.

37. Minutes, 12 November 1878.

38. Minutes, 4-5 October 1916.

39. Minutes, 20-22 October 1920.

40. Interview with Richard H. Schmidt, Bethel College, North Newton, Kansas, 20 July 1984.

41. Review, December 1900, p. 6.

42. Haury, pp. 172-73.

43. In an interview with the wife of Rev. William Galle in 1950, Mrs. Galle contended that her husband preached exclusively in German throughout his lifetime. He died in 1920. Apparently Galle returned to exclusive German preaching after a brief experiment to attract non-Mennonites in 1900. Jacob Fransen, "Survey of the West Zion Mennonite Church, Moundridge, Kansas" (unpublished paper, Mennonite Library and Archives, Bethel College, North Newton, Kansas, 1950), p. 12; "John M. Suderman," Mennonite Library and Archives, Manuscript-94, Boxes 4-10.

44. P. S. Goerz and Harley J. Stuckey, Our Church Past and Present (North Newton, Kansas: Mennonite Press, 1954), p. 12; Mennon Schrag, First Mennonite Church (n.p., 1978), p. 12; n.a., Centennial Chronicle: First Mennonite Church of Christian (n.p., 1978), p. 46.

45. Frederick C. Luebke, "Legal Restrictions on Foreign Languages in the Great Plains," in Languages in Conflict, ed. Paul Schach (Lincoln: University of Nebraska Press, 1980), pp. 8-16; Alan Niehaus Graebner, "The Acculturation of an Immigrant Lutheran Church:

(Ph.D. dissertation, Columbia University, 1965), pp. 94-161; James C. Juhnke, A People of Two Kingdoms (Newton, Kansas: Faith and Life Press, 1975), pp. 104-106; Frederick C. Luebke, Bonds of Loyalty (Dekalb, Illinois: Northern Illinois University Press, 1974), pp. 233-34, 250-54, 314-15.

46. P. P. Wedel, Church Chronicle of the First Mennonite Church of Christian, Kansas (Published by the author, 1957), p. 31.

47. Minutes, 16-17 October 1929; 21-23 October 1936.

48. "P. H. Richert," Mennonite Library and Archives, Manuscript-16-boxes 25-27; Ruby Funk, Peace, Progress, Promise: A 75th Anniversary History of the Tabor Mennonite Church (North Newton, Kansas: Mennonite Press, 1983), pp. 153-158.

49. A more detailed examination of the role of the Reiseprediger in the Americanization process is given in Chapter VII. Haury, pp. 110-22; Mennonite Encyclopedia, s.v. "Reiseprediger," by Harold S. Bender; Lois Barrett, The Vision and the Reality (Newton, Kansas: Faith and Life Press, 1938), pp. 7-14; Pannabecker, Open Doors, pp. 52-54.

50. Minutes, 14-15 October 1896.

51. Minutes, 1-2 November 1898.

52. Minutes, 8-9 October 1902.

53. David C. Wedel, The Story of Alexanderwohl (North Newton, Kansas: Mennonite Press, 1974), p. 14.

54. Minutes, 28-30 October 1914.

54. Minutes, 21-23 October 1925.

56. Edmund G. Kaufman, ed., General Conference Mennonite Pioneers (North Newton, Kansas: Bethel College, 1973), pp. 365-71.

57. "C. E. Krehbiel," Mennonite Library and Archives, Manuscript-II-boxes 9, 10.

58. C. E. Krehbiel to H. H. Wedel, 18 December 1929, Mennonite Library and Archives, Manuscript-II-3-b, box 1, folder 3.

59. A more detailed examination of the role of education in the Americanization of the Mennonite churches in central Kansas is given in Chapter V.

60. Minutes, 15 November 1877.

61. Minutes, 27-29 October 1879.

62. Cornelius C. Janzen, "A Social Study of the Mennonite Settlements in the counties of Marion, McPherson, Harvey, Reno, and Butler, Kansas" (Ph.D. dissertation, University of Chicago, 1926), pp. 101-103.

63. H. P. Peters, "History and Development of Education Among the Mennonites in Kansas" (M.A. thesis, Bluffton College, 1925), pp. 197-99.

64. Minutes, 4-5 October 1916.

65. Minutes, 28-30 October 1914.

66. Minutes, 17-18 October 1923.

67. Mennonite Encyclopedia, s.v. "Halstead Seminary," by Edmund G. Kaufman; James C. Juhnks, "Except the Lord Build the House: Halstead Seminary Centennial," Mennonite Life 38 (December 1983): 4-7.

68. Minutes, 12-14 October 1885.

69. Minutes, 3-5 October 1887.

70. Minutes, 5-6 November 1889.

71. Peter J. Wedel, The Story of Bethel College (North Newton, Kansas: Bethel College, 1954), pp. 41-50; Minutes, 14-15 October 1896.

72. Monatsblaetter (Bethel College Monthly), September 1914, pp. 4-6; October 1914, pp. 4-5.

73. Ibid.

74. Minutes, 9-11 October 1913.

75. Ibid.

76. Quoted in Wallace Henry Moore, "The Conflict Concerning the German Language and German Propaganda in the Public Secondary Schools of the United States" (Ph.D. dissertation, Stanford University, 1937), p. 33.

77. Luebke, "Legal Restrictions on Foreign Languages," p. 7; P. J. Wedel, p. 237.

78. H. P. Peters, pp. 204-05.

79. Ibid.

80. Minutes, 24-25 October 1917; 5-7 November 1919.

81.   P. J. Wedel, pp. 236-37; Minutes, 12 November 1918.

82.   Evening Kansas Republican, 16 September 1918.

83.   Minutes, 17-18 October 1923.

84.   Quoted in H. P. Peters, pp. 210-11.

85.   Ibid.

86.   For a complete treatment of German-language newspapers see Cal Wittke, The German-language Press in America (Lexington, Kentucky: University of Kentucky Press, 1957). With special reference to Mennonite newspapers see Harold S. Bender, Two Centuries of American Mennonite Literature (Goshen, Indiana: Mennonite Historical Society, 1929). For Kansas newspapers see William E. Connelly, History of Kansas Newspapers (Topeka: Kansas State Printing Plant, 1916).

87.   Mennonite Encyclopedia, s.v. "Zur Heimath," by Harold S. Bender; "Christlicher Bundesbote," by Cornelius Krahn; B. Bargen, "General Conference Mennonite Press," Mennonite Life 1 (January 1951): 35-37, 48.

88.   Mennonite Encylopedia, s.v. "The Mennonite," by J. N. Schmuker; Bargen, pp. 35-36.

89.   Mennonite Encyclopedia, s.v. "Der Herold," by Harold S. Bender; "The Review," by Cornelius Krahn; "Post und Volksblatt," by John F. Schmidt; "Mennonite Weekly Review," by Menno Schrag; Connelly, p. 204; interview with Menno Schrag, former editor of Mennonite Weekly Review, Newton, Kansas, 30 July 1984.

90.   School and College Journal, January 1896, p. 1.

91.   School and College Journal, February 1896, p. 9.

92.   Mennonite, November 1899, p. 12; Christlicher Bundesbote, 11 January 1900, pp. 2-3; School and College Journal, January 1900, pp. 4-5 and February 1900, pp. 12-13; Review, February 1900, pp. 3, 5; Mennonite, February 1900, pp. 34, 37.

93.   Mennonite, 17 September 1908, p. 4.

94.   Der Herold, 1 January 1916; 14 June 1917; 28 March 1918; 5 December 1918; 16 March 1916, p. 6.

95.   Der Herold, 1 May 1919, p. 4.

96.   Mennonite, 11 October 1917, p. 4.

97.   Der Herold, 23 May 1918, p. 5.

98. Carman, "Language Transition," p. 23.

99. Buchheit, "Language Maintenance," p. 119.

100. Graebner, pp. 94-161.

101. School and College Journal, January 1900, pp. 4-5.

102. Minutes, 5-7 November 1919.

103. Hohmann, p. 8.

104. Minutes, 14-15 October 1896.

CHAPTER V

THE AMERICANIZATION OF MENNONITE EDUCATION

Teachers are servants of the churches, serving for the same
aim as the churches of the Conference in general, namely as
laborers in the vineyard of the Lord, in building up and extend-
ing the Kingdom of God . . . .

> Peter Balzer
> Western District Conference
> October 15, 1896

The Immigrant School

The education of immigrants was an important aspect of the

Americanization process. Progress in education was a definite sign

of assimilation to local reporters who recorded in detail the placement

of virtually every plank and stone in each schoolhouse. For the immi-

grant, education was more than simply another means of displaying

a new national identity.

The parochial school was one of a variety of responses of immi-

grant groups to the impact of Americanization. It was especially

characteristic of immigrants bent on preserving their Old World iden-

tity. In both rural and urban areas, immigrant groups threatened

by the insensitivity of public schools organized their own educational

institutions. Slow assimilators, in particular, were suspicious of

American public schools that took little account of the cultural back-

ground of students. For church-minded immigrants concentrated in isolated areas, there was no better means of maintaining ethnoreligious cohesion amongst their children than the parochial school. They were most common in Lutheran and Catholic churches. Roman Catholic parochial schools differed from Lutheran and other Protestant parish schools in that the typical Catholic parish was a polyglot institution which might include Irish, Poles, French-Canadians, and Germans, along with native Americans. In such heterogeneous situations where English was a necessary medium of instruction, parochial schools had a minimal influence in slowing the Americanization process. Among German Lutherans, parochial schools functioned more effectively as a conservator of an ethnoreligious heritage.[1]

W. Lloyd Warner claimed that immigrant parochial schools served three basic functions: the retention of the mother tongue, perpetuation of religious symbols, and perpetuation of national symbols. Since worship services were conducted in the language of the immigrant, religious instruction required the use of the mother tongue. Parochial schools served to train children for entrance into the church. Many of the teachers were sacerdotal personalities, either priests, nuns, or ministers. At the same time, it was the responsibility of the church to instill a sense of national pride based on an Old World identity. Warner pointed out that as immigrant youth Americanized, a second type of parochial school emerged. He referred to this as the "ethnic folk school." The ethnic folk school emphasized language first, nationality second, and religion third. Usually students attended public schools along with ethnic folk schools. This second form of parochial school recognized Americanization as inevitable.

Thus, the ethnic folk school served to link ethnic and American values without forcing the student into the dilemma of choosing one over the other.[2]

Mennonite Parochial Schools

Mennonite parochial schools had their roots in Russia. When Prussian Mennonites first settled the area around the Black Sea, a developed Russian school system did not exist. One of the rights granted by the Russian crown was the management of their own school system. From the beginning of their sojourn in Russia, Mennonites established autonomous schools without government involvement. The first schools were relatively primitive and most teachers had only an elementary education. Each village had its own school. Instruction was given in reading, writing, arithmetic, and religion. Of the four topics, religion was deemed most important. Schools usually came under the supervision of elders and church leaders. In 1843 all Mennonite schools were placed under the supervision of the Agricultural Association headed by Johann Cornies, a Mennonite. Significant improvements were made under Cornies' leadership. In 1869 the Molotschna Mennonite School Board was organized and replaced the Agricultural Association as protector of the Mennonite educational system. Further progressive strides were taken under the board's leadership. In 1881 the educational system of Mennonites was placed under the Russian imperial department of education. This marked the beginning of a rigorous program of Russification initiated by the government in 1871. The government decision to nationalize education was a major impetus for Mennonite emigration in the 1870s. The earliest arrivals in central Kansas knew only the threat rather than the actual experience of Russified schools.[3]

After maintaining an autonomous education system for nearly a century, it was natural for the Russian and East European Mennonites to establish their own schools in central Kansas. The state school laws of Kansas in 1874 were lenient and the educational system undeveloped. Children between the ages of eight and fourteen were required to attend a minimum of twelve weeks a year. Teachers merely had to be "competent" rather than formally trained. All Kansas Mennonite settlements in 1874 were located in one huge school district, 31,734 square miles in size, or roughly three-eighths of the entire area of the state. State legislators were obviously more interested in attracting productive settlers to the Kansas prairies than developing an effective educational system.[4]

The American educational environment differed significantly from that in Russia. The public school system of American was available to both native-born and immigrant residents of Kansas. Maintaining autonomous schools was not as easy in their new homeland. However, Mennonites brought a suspicious attitude toward public schools with them from Russia. Parents were hesitant to entrust their children to educational institutions that taught neither the mother tongue nor religious values of the Mennonite faith. Only Mennonite schools could be completely trusted as the conservators of a precious ethno-religious heritage.

The Mennonite response to the American educational environment was far from uniform. From the beginning, some Mennonite children

attended public schools. In areas where a church could not afford
a school or a qualified teacher was unavailable, parents were forced
to send their children to district schools. In other school districts
where the Mennonite population was dominant, public schools were organized with Mennonite board members, schools teachers, students, and
German-language instruction. This arrangement technically was illegal
since an 1877 Kansas law required English-language instruction in
public schools. However, the state raised few objections in the early
years. Some parents sent their children to public schools one year
and private schools the next. This proved to be unsatisfactory.
Other students attended public schools in the winter months and Mennonite schools in the spring or fall. This became the most common practice
among Mennonites in central Kansas during the first four decades.
Another response was exclusive attendance at a Mennonite school that
operated in the winter. Only a few congregations were able to offer
such an opportunity.[5]

There are a variety of terms used in conjunction with Mennonite
education. Various references to private schools, parochial schools,
academies, Fortbildungsschule, preparatory schools, Zentralschule,
and German schools at times become confusing. Without suitable defini-
tions of these various terms, a proper understanding is not possible.
All Mennonite schools were technically parochial schools, sometimes
referred to as German schools because of their use of German-language
instruction. However, not all parochial schools were operated by
a congregation--some were privately run by individual teachers. Initially, the majority of Mennonite parochial schools were privately oper-

ated by individuals. Thus, elementary schools were referred to as German schools, parochial schools, private schools, or simply Mennonite schools. Secondary schools were referred to as Zentralschule, Fortbildungsschule, academies, and preparatory schools according to specific goals. Most maintained a two-year curriculum with German-language instruction and an emphasis on religious studies. Although the students' ages varied greatly, these schools generally served as a link between elementary schools and colleges or seminaries.[6]

The first Mennonite schools were organized in 1874 shortly after their arrival in central Kansas. The earliest parochial institutions were elementary schools. Most were organized by an individual teacher who often served as a minister as well. Usually these private schools began in homes of the teachers. The relationship of the parochial schools to the church was one of cooperation and mutual trust. According to David Goerz, the school was the servant of the church.[7] Teachers were regarded as leaders and had the full confidence of the church. Several problems plagued the church schools during the 1874-77 period. One severe need was for qualified teachers. Too few had come from Russia and those who made the trip needed further theological training that could not be easily obtained in their new environment. Compensation for teaching was minimal; some served without pay. Facilities and equipment were inadequate. Parochial schools rapidly outgrew the private homes of teachers. However, Mennonites were too involved in the construction of farms and churches to build school buildings in the first years. Overcrowding made the learning process difficult at best. The curriculum was severely limited. Textbooks were rare and usually outdated. On top of all this, Mennonites were concerned lest parochial schools be perceived by the host society as a competitor with the public schools.[8]

On August 15, 1877, Zur Heimath, the unofficial newspaper of Kansas immigrants, called for a meeting of all Mennonite teachers to discuss the problems of Mennonite parochial schools. On November 15, 1877, a group of interested teachers, elders, and ministers met at the district schoolhouse near Alexanderwohl. This marked the first attempt to unify the work of a dozen or so Mennonite schools in central Kansas. In his opening address, elder Wilhelm Ewert pointed to a lack of education as a source of conflicts and divisions in the church. Mennonite education was a necessary support for the work of the church. It was the responsibility of Mennonites to possess "better knowledge and more thorough information." The group proceeded to draw up several resolutions which were passed on to the First Kansas Conference in December of 1877. These resolutions included a recommendation that in areas where Mennonites were able to exert a controlling influence, they were advised to organize public schools. In other areas where Mennonites did not exercise a controlling influence on existing school districts, they were encouraged to establish Mennonite parochial schools. The teachers' meeting endorsed the acquisition of English as a second language for the purpose of engaging in both business interests and evangelism with an English-speaking population. A list of textbooks and a uniform daily schedule of study was proposed. The group also recommended a teacher training school.[9]

The recommendations of the November meeting served as the agenda for the first session of the Kansas Conference on December 14, 1877. The conference accepted the curriculum and list of textbooks and approved the English language proposal. They further endorsed establishment of parochial schools. However, a disagreement resulted from the recommendation endorsing public schools in areas of Mennonite dominance. The process of setting up public school districts required public elections and the completion of first citizenship papers for prospective school board members. Some Mennonites felt it wise to wait before initiating such a serious step. The 1877 Kansas Conference left the matter of citizenship to the discretion of each congregation but endorsed participation in public school districts.[10]

During the next twenty years parochial schools of Mennonite immigrants in central Kansas increased from a dozen in 1877 to forty-two in 1898. The Kansas Conference and, after 1892, the Western District Conference, enthusiastically promoted the school cause. A report of the Education Committee in 1898 summarized the importance of parochial schools:

> They are absolutely necessary in order to preserve the young people for our denomination (Gemeindeschaft), not only outwardly, but to link them to us inwardly with a deeper understanding of our faith, and with cords of love to our arrangements handed down to us by our fathers . . . .[11]

Most of the forty-two schools in the WDC met annually for two or three months in the spring. They supplemented the secular instruction of public schools with religious instruction in German. The earliest schools had no textbooks other than the Bible and were usually taught by ministers. Actual statistics of Mennonite parochial education

were difficult to maintain due to the very nature of the schools.
Fluctuating attendance, shifting locations, and the lack of teachers
produced unpredictable circumstances that eluded the statistical surveys
of the WDC Education Committee. Only four actual statistical reports
can be gleaned from the WDC minutes.

TABLE 5-1

NUMBER OF MENNONITE PAROCHIAL SCHOOLS
IN THE WESTERN DISTRICT CONFERENCE

Year	Number of Schools
1877	11
1898	42
1904	56 (39 private; 17 church)
1915	60

SOURCE: Minutes of the Kansas Conference, 14 December 1877;
1-2 November 1898; 19-21 October 1904; 20-21 October 1915, Mennonite
Library and Archives, Bethel College, North Newton, Kansas (transcript,
English translation).

The peak of Mennonite parochial schools was 1915 when sixty existed
within the WDC.

The growth of Mennonite schools in central Kansas from 1874
to 1916 was due in part to promotion by the Kansas and Western District
Conferences. One widely known champion of the German parochial school
was C. H. Wedel. The first president of Bethel College, Wedel was
active in the early development of German parochial schools. In 1894
he reported to the WDC for the Education Committee, calling for the
upgrading of teaching requirements in Mennonite schools. Wedel was
responsible for the WDC role as mediator between hiring parochial

school boards and applying Mennonite teachers. The autonomous nature of Mennonite church polity was a negative factor in the random development of Mennonite schools. Wedel called for a larger role by the WDC in the education of Mennonite youth. Local congregations required centralized leadership in the establishment and development of local parochial schools. Wedel urged the 1894 WDC to follow the leadership of other American denominations in establishing guidelines in the hiring of teachers, development of curriculum, and publications of textbooks.[12]

The emergence of Wedel as an early leader of Mennonite education had a significant impact on the development of German parochial schools. Born in south Russia in 1860, Wedel was one of the few Kansas Mennonites in the 19th century to receive an American seminary education. He attended and later taught at the Presbyterian seminary in Bloomfield, New Jersey. He was a scholar who combined contemporary intellectualism with traditionalism to produce a progressive philosophy of education for the Mennonite church. Wedel's idea of an educational setup for Kansas Mennonites included three aspects: (1) parochial schools of at least three months' duration each year in all Mennonite congregations for children to age fourteen; (2) Mennonite-educated teachers whose preparation was equal to that of public school teachers; and (3) a secondary educational institution that would serve as a college preparatory school for teacher-candidates.[13]

The development of secondary education among Kansas Mennonites was directly related to the need for teachers in elementary parochial schools. The early immigrants did not hold education beyond elementary

years in high esteem. They perceived higher education more as a luxury
than a necessity. Interest in elementary education was rooted primarily
in the religious life of the people, and they looked upon those who
received a degree from an institution of higher learning with suspicion.[14] This is illustrated in Who Needs an Oil Well?, a novel by
Ruth Unrau. Young Matt Rempel, a Mennonite teenager whose parents
migrated to Oklahoma from Goessel, Kansas, in the early twentieth
century, longed for a formal education beyond the eighth grade.

> Mama said gently, "Do you need schooling to be a farmer?"
> "Yes, Mama. I would like to have schooling before I am any-
> thing. I would like to read all the books and work all the
> problems and do all the experiments. I don't know if I will
> be a farmer. I don't know what I will be."
> Mr. Rempel spoke up sharply. "And I suppose you would
> like to play all of the basketball games, go to all the parties,
> and court all the English girls."
> Matt watched as his mother took careful stitches in an
> overall patch. "Not if you say not to."
> His father's voice softened. "We Mennonites are a people
> of one Book. If you want to read, there is the Bible. Every-
> thing has been said there. We are afraid you won't be inter-
> ested in the church after you get educated. You would marry
> outside and move away."[15]

Such attitudes were common among those who traditionally viewed higher
education as an encroachment upon Mennonite nonconformity and a threat
to their sense of peoplehood.

The growth of Mennonite elementary schools on the Kansas prairies
necessitated a teacher training school. The original meetings of
educational leaders in 1877 adopted a resolution favoring the establishment of a Zentralschule for the preparation of German-language teachers.
Meanwhile, two events occurred that were significant in the development
of Mennonite higher education. The only General Conference institute
of higher learning which was located in Wadsworth, Ohio, closed down

in 1878 leaving Mennonite youth without any opportunity for advanced training in a college of their own denomination. The second event took place in 1879 when a private preparatory school was organized by Peter Balzer near Goessel. Balzer was one of the few educated teachers to accompany the immigrants to Kansas. He accepted the challenge of the Kansas Conference to organize a Zentralschule, or Fortbildungsschule, for the training of teachers. The Peter Balzer school served as a temporary solution. Meanwhile the Kansas Conference continued its plans for a district-sponsored institution that would prepare both ministers and teachers. In 1882 such a school was organized ten miles north of Newton, Kansas, called the Emmatal School. This marked the beginning of Mennonite higher education in Kansas.[16]

After a year at Emmatal the school was moved to Halstead, Kansas, and in 1883 became known as the Halstead Mennonite Seminary. The name was somewhat misleading since the school was in reality a preparatory school (Fortbildungsschule), not an actual seminary. The label "seminary" indicated the school's religious emphasis. All classes were divided between the German and English departments with an instructor heading each department. Halstead Seminary came under the close supervision of the Kansas Conference and was directly responsible to its Education Committee. For ten years Halstead functioned as the official preparatory school of the Kansas Conference and was the most important secondary education venture prior to the founding of Bethel college in 1893. Halstead Seminary also marked an important step in the Americanization of Mennonite education. The report of the Education Committee revealed four "American students" in 1883.

151

Women were initially admitted on a trial basis and in subsequent years achieved regular status. An English-language instructor was secured to teach some Bible lessons, arithmetic, grammar, reading, United States history, penmanship, and geography. Students were required to receive instruction in German only if their parents were German-speaking. During the 1884-85 academic year the committee reported sixty-five students enrolled: "forty German, twenty Americans, and five Indians." It is unclear whether the twenty Americans were non-Mennonites from the Halstead area or American Mennonites from the East. Later evidence is explicit. In 1888 the Education Committee reported an enrollment of forty-eight students, including seventeen from "outside our denomination" (Gemeindeschaft). Moreover, records for tuition and lodging at Halstead Seminary included seventeen non-Mennonite names, some of which were common in Newton and Halstead. The 1888 report of the Education Committee further stated that all but three of the American students took some instruction in German.

In 1886 a resolution was passed by the Kansas Conference calling for mandatory church attendance by students on Sunday. A reference to non-Mennonite students at Halstead Seminary stated:

". . . it is expected of such students of other confessions who have no opportunity to attend worship services in their own denominations, that they attend worship service of that denomination under whose leadership the Continuation School stands."[17]

The admission of non-Mennonites to a Mennonite institution of higher learning in 1883 was a notable departure from a century of restricted denominational contact in Russia. The fact that most of the students at the Halstead Seminary were housed on campus and

lived in close confines further accentuated the level of social interaction between Mennonite youth and non-Mennonite American students.
Surely the school produced a broadened experience for these immigrant
offspring by virtue of daily contacts with American-born students.

Suspicions of higher education continued to plague the Kansas
Conference throughout the existence of Halstead Seminary. The school's
endless financial woes reflected a lack of support for higher education
in the Kansas Conference. Even the principal of the school, H. H.
Ewert, was fearful that graduates would be tempted to forsake teaching
jobs in Mennonite schools for secular job.[18] Ewert's fears ran even
deeper than this; he openly admitted that the school might someday
be capable of undermining the influence of the church. He encouraged
the Kansas Conference to maintain in the future careful leadership
of Halstead Seminary.

In 1889 when the attendance dropped to an all-time low of thirty-
five, the Education Committee blamed the declining enrollment on a
preference of Mennonite youth "for everything American." Some students
who transferred elsewhere or dropped out of school altogether considered
obligatory religious courses and German-language instruction unnecessary. The committee also blamed declining enrollment on "various
prejudices in our church against a higher education in general."[19]
The immigrant church was well aware of the assimilating tendencies
of higher education, even in a conference-directed Mennonite
institution.

Conference leaders made numerous attempts to bridge the gap
between the local church and higher education. In 1890 a resolution

TABLE 5-2

MENNONITE PREPARATORY SCHOOLS IN KANSAS, 1874-1939

Name of School	Location	Founded	Closed
Peter Balzer's School	Near Goessel	1879	188?
Emmatal Fortbildungsschule	Near Goessel	1882	1883
Halstead Seminary	Halstead	1883	1893
Buhler Vereins Schule*	Buhler	1889	1902
Bethel Academy	North Newton	1893	1927
Hillsboro Preparatory School	Hillsboro	1897	1935
Whitewater Bible School	Whitewater	1900	1915
Goessel Preparatory School	Goessel	1906	1925
Hoffnungsau Bible School	Inman	1907	1927
Moundridge Bible School	Moundridge	1908	1918
Zoar Bible School**	Inman	1915	1946

 * In conjunction with Mennonite Brethren and General Conference
   Mennonites.
** Krimmer Mennonite Brethren.

SOURCE: Mennonite Encyclopedia, s.v. "Bible Schools," by Harold S. Bender.

was passed calling for the urgent support of Halstead Seminary by
the Kansas Conference churches.[20] There were frequent resolution
at the Kansas Conference sessions for unity and cooperation in regard
to higher education. However, entire congregations retained suspicions
of higher education and were skeptical of Bethel College following
its founding in 1893.[21]

The termination of Halstead Seminary in the spring of 1893
was not the end of Mennonite preparatory schools in central Kansas.
From the organization of Peter Balzer's school in 1879, eleven Mennonite
preparatory schools existed at one time or another before World War
I in Kansas (table 5-2). One was organized by the Krimmer Mennonite
Brethren near Inman, Kansas. The other ten were either run by, or
in conjunction with, the churches of the Kansas and Western District
Conferences.

In 1897 a preparatory school was organized in Hillsboro
by a former instructor at Bethel College, H. D. Penner. Penner
perceived a lack of public high schools in the area and responded
with his own private preparatory school to serve as a bridge between
Mennonite elementary schools and Bethel College. In 1913 Penner left
and the school came under the control of Brudertal, Johannestal, and
the First Mennonite churches of Hillsboro. In 1927 it took on the
title of Bible Academy even though the curriculum remained the same.
In 1936 the school closed due to a lack of students. Penner's school
served as a model for later preparatory schools in central Kansas.
From the beginning, English was taught at the Hillsboro Preparatory
School although German-language instruction was carried on until the
First World War.[22]

In the Buhler area a preparatory school served both Mennonite Brethren and General Conference Mennonite students from 1889 to 1902. A preparatory school opened in 1893 in conjunction with Bethel College. In fact, the Bethel Academy actually held classes earlier than the college and for years maintained a larger enrollment. In 1909 it reorganized on the plan of a four-year public high school. In 1927 the Bethel Academy was discontinued due to the financial inability to compete with public schools. Four more WDC preparatory schools were organized in the twentieth century: Whitewater Bible School (1900-1915), Goessel Preparatory school (1906-1925), Hoffnungsau Preparatory School (1907-1927), and Moundridge Bible School (1908-1918). Several Bethel College students came directly from these preparatory schools.

In 1886 the German Teachers' Association was organized for the purpose of promoting Mennonite parochial schools in the Kansas Conference. The association met twice a year in an attempt to standardize curriculum and update methodology. In 1894 the association conducted a two week seminar for all Mennonite instructors. This became known as the German Teachers' Institute and functioned as advanced teacher training for Mennonite educators for the next two decades. The German Teachers' Association perceived itself as the guardian of Mennonite religious and cultural traditions.[23] In 1910 the name was changed to Mennonite Teachers' Association.

The Americanization of Mennonite Schools

Three factors influenced the Americanization of Mennonite education--public schools, Bethel College, and World War I. The first public schools in central Kansas during the 1870s were so poorly organized that they either offered no threat to Mennonite education, or they soon came under the complete dominance of Mennonite settlers. The first Mennonite immigrants in central Kansas were encouraged by the 1877 Kansas Conference to set up public schools in areas where they constituted a majority. A few concurred. Almost all nineteenth century Mennonite young people attended both public and private schools. A public school year usually consisted of only three winter months and thus left sufficient opportunity for parochial schools to operate in the spring or fall. A three month public-school term followed by a three-month parochial-school term was the most common arrangement from 1874 to 1903. When a Kansas law extended the school year in 1903 to five months, parochial schools were correspondingly reduced in length. In 1909 an additional law lengthened the public school term to seven months causing competition to become intense. Most Mennonite youth worked on the family farm and the 1909 law forced some to drop out of German schools during the planting months. In 1912 a survey by the Education Committee revealed that approximately 15% of Mennonite children no longer attended a German elementary school. The causes for declining attendance reportedly included indifference, insufficient appreciation for religious education, and a lack of interest in the German language. Furthermore, the survey showed that nearly half of the German schools had reduced their terms to two months. In the same survey, school board members complained of competition with public schools, the summer heat that accommodated the German school term, and a lack of competent teachers.[24]

A 1912 survey and subsequent report of the Education Committee in 1916 revealed the impact of public schools on Mennonite parochial education. More Mennonite youth attended public high schools (17.7%) than preparatory schools (15%). The lengthened public school term left an insufficient amount of time to teach the rudiments of the German language. Too few Mennonite teachers met the rising standards of certification, and those who did were often attracted to other areas of the state by more lucrative salaries. The Education Committee initiated aggressive teacher recruitment tactics. They sought out Mennonite students at Bethel College who majored in teacher education and tried to induce them to teach in German schools. Most refused because of weak German-language skills or an inability for religious instruction. This frustrated the recruiting efforts of the Education Committee, which reported that "Our young people are thronging out; they no longer ask whether it is a Mennonite school or not."[25] The decision by the 1877 Kansas Conference to sanction public schools in areas of Mennonite dominance further hastened acculturation. Four decades after arrival in America, church leaders recognized they could no longer compete with public schools. The committee reported in 1922: "With the transfer of the control over the system of education to the state, the influence of the Church had become weak."[26] The best they could hope for was some level of accommodation within the public school system.

In the 1920s Mennonite strategy for education made an important transition from championing parochial schools to recognizing public schools as inevitable and acceptable. Gone were the days of the four month German school term. The 1923 report of the Education Committee indicated that its workload had been noticeably reduced in recent years due to the increased role of public schools in Mennonite education. A suggestion for the introduction of religious instruction in public schools was under investigation by the committee. At one point in the 1923 report there was actually an attempt to promote public schools. The committee stated that public schools afforded Mennonite youth the opportunity to discover "Many a truth founded on the Bible, which will be of greatest importance to them later in life." The report went on to list the opportunities for moral and ethical development in public schools according to a recently released course of study for the 1922-1927 time period. The virtues of Biblical principles, obedience to God, parents, teachers, government, and conscience were all identified with the public school philosophy of education. Of particular importance to the committee was the fact that public schools placed "love of God" above patriotism. Reference was further made to a recent resolution passed by the South Dakota state legislature to restore a balance between "spiritual and material matters" in the public schools system.[27]

The 1923 report of the Education Committee reflected a pragmatic attempt by Mennonites in central Kansas to accommodate the transition from parochial to public schools. Any attempt by the church to discredit public education was a lost cause. By the mid-1920s, Americanization of Mennonite education had reached a point of no return. The most church leaders could hope for was a strong Mennonite influence in public schools.

In 1925 the Education Committee followed through with its earlier suggestion to promote religious education in public schools. Five district school superintendents responded to a questionnaire sent by the committee. The survey included three questions.

1. Would you object to three twenty minute periods of religious education a week?
2. Would you object to religious instruction before or after school?
3. Would you object to a public school teacher who administered religious instruction in either of the above situations?

None of the five superintendents objected to any of the three questions. One agreed to twenty minute periods of religious education provided it was in English. Another qualified his consent with the stipulation that instruction "follow the Bible rather than creed." The same survey was sent to the state superintendent of schools. At this point the Mennonite proposal for religious instruction in public schools encountered some difficulties. Although he was not personally opposed to religious education, the state superintendent replied that when carried on during school hours and financed by public funds, religious instruction violated existing laws.[28] Apparently state school laws were not consistently enforced. In 1927 the Education Committee reported that teachers and ministers had been permitted to give religious instruction during the school hours in public schools at Goessel, Moundridge, Inman, Buhler, Halstead, and Newton. All of these towns were located in the center of Mennonite settlements. In 1928 the committee reported that additional public school systems permitted religious instruction on school time.[29]

The incorporation of religious education in the public schools had a negative impact on preparatory schools. From 1925 to 1927 three of the four remaining WDC preparatory schools were discontinued. The 1929 report of the Education Committee listed competition from public high schools as the primary cause for school closings. The termination of the Hillsboro Preparatory School in 1935 marked an end of an era for Mennonites in central Kansas.[30]

Kansas Mennonites did not embrace public schools without reservations. Public schools were at various times referred to as a poor substitute for Mennonite German schools, a direct threat to the perpetuation of Mennonite identity, and a necessary evil in communities that could not support a parochial school. As late as 1930 a comparison of public high schools and Mennonite preparatory schools noted that the former emphasized the "spirit of sport and frivolity" which was not evident in the latter.[31] Any notion that a resurgence of Mennonite parochial education loomed on the horizon was shattered by the advent of the Great Depression. At the 1931 WDC sessions, the Education Committee had little to report due to a "scarcity of means" among Mennonite constituents. "There is everywhere a lack of courage for beginning new undertakings; we do not wish to burden our people with still more cares."[32] Mennonites simply could not afford the luxury of funding two educational system, one public and one private. The transition from private to public schools was accompanied by a warning from the Western District Conference:

> But even though it may be welcomed by us with joy, that more
> and more Bible and religious instruction is being introduced
> in our public schools, we must nevertheless tell ourselves,
> that this arrangement too does not yet produce the results
> which thorough and systematic religious instruction aspires
> to; at least not yet to the desired degree.[33]

A second factor in the Americanization of Mennonite education was Bethel College. Founded in 1893, the same year Halstead Seminary closed its doors, Bethel was more than a mere continuation of previous efforts in secondary education. While Halstead Seminary served as both a preparatory school and a ministerial and missionary training institute, Bethel College sought to offer a more advanced and diversified program.

When an offer of $100,000 was made in 1887 by a group of local citizens for the organization of a Mennonite college in Newton, Kansas conference leaders were faced with an important decision. Were the Mennonites of central Kansas prepared to take such a bold step just over a decade after their arrival on the Great Plains? Was a second conference school financially feasible? What advantages did a college education have to offer these immigrants? Even the most progressive Mennonite educators and ministers seldom sought a liberal arts degree. They might benefit from a seminary training or a preparatory school experience, but how could liberal arts courses such as biology, geology, and accounting prepare students to serve the church?

From the very inception of the college concept, two sides emerged among the immigrants. One group perceived any notion of a liberal arts education as a threat to Mennonite values and sense of peoplehood. The only secondary education effort worthy of church support was one for the exclusive training of ministers and parochial school teachers. Support for the college concept came from a progressive element consisting of educators, ministers, and a few established Mennonite businessmen. Two of the most prominent proponents were David Goerz and

162

Bernard Warkentin. Goerz was a leading official in the Kansas Conference and greatly respected for his promotion of numerous Mennonite
efforts. Warkentin was a prominent businessman in Newton who was
well known for his assistance in the immigration of the 1870s. Along
with some of the other leaders of the Kansas Conference, Goerz and
Warkentin felt the $100,000 offer by the Newton community was too
good to pass up. They foresaw the day when a college education would
become more common among Mennonite youth. Failure to establish a
church school could result in the loss of the brightest Mennonite
young people.[34]

Goerz managed to convince the Kansas Conference to approve
the formation of a private corporation which would accept the Newton
offer and finance and maintain a college without any risk to the conference. In 1887 the Bethel College Corporation was organized, but it
was another six years before the school actually opened its doors.
During this period the debate over the need for a Mennonite college
continued. Opponents generally cast their support behind the existing
Halstead Seminary, claiming that a more advanced level of education
was unnecessary. Proponents of the college replied that the desire
to know was God-given; Mennonite youth were destined to turn to state
colleges if their own denomination failed to provide a college; the
church could only be strengthened by the existence of a church college.

Although the struggle over the college concept was of a complex
nature, there were overtones of a debate between the Americanizing
and anti-Americanizing factions. Supporters of the college represented
the most progressive element of Mennonites in central Kansas. When

faced with resistance from those who feared the impact of a liberal arts education, they turned to the East to solicit support from American Mennonites in Ohio and Pennsylvania. Visits by Goerz and others proved successful and created a means of soliciting financial aid for the college fund.[35] Goerz realized that Americanized congregations in the East had fewer reservations about a church college than conservative Russian and East European Mennonites in central Kansas. However, the Bethel proponents were cautiously progressive and willing to make necessary concessions in an attempt to achieve their goals. As a result, the college was organized in 1893, not as a WDC school but rather as an auxiliary institution of the conference operated by a private association. A description of the school in the 1895 Mennonite Yearbook and Almanac sounded similar to that of the Halstead Seminary ten years earlier:

> The aim of the school is to prepare teachers for our district schools, our parochial schools, and our Sunday schools, and to prepare laborers for our missions whether at home or abroad.[36]

Initially, Bethel was limited to operating a preparatory department for teacher training and an academy which offered a college preparation course. The collegiate department did not open until 1895. In 1896 a Bible Institute was established as a modest effort to assist duly certified candidates for the ministry.

Even with these modifications the school was forced to walk a fine line between the progressive and conservative elements of the Western District Conference. President C. H. Wedel recognized this in his 1901 report to the WDC stating that the very existence of Bethel

College might be perceived as a threat to the local church. Wedel noted that the school was pulled in two directions, "ready and willing to meet the imperative needs of the time," yet hesitant not to go "faster than the churches also must go."[37] This situation continued well into the twentieth century.

There can be no doubt that Bethel College served as an agent of Americanization. Many students went on from Bethel to other institutions of higher learning. Bethel grads attended graduate schools at the University of Kansas and University of Chicago; others went onto seminary training at Bloomfield Seminary and Oberlin College. As early as 1896 the Education Committee expressed concerns over the dangers of non-Mennonite upper education--"doctrinal heresies, confusion, and Darwinism."[38] Mennonite youth were encouraged to restrict their college aspirations to Bethel. However, the college served to open the floodgates to other American secular institutions and non-Mennonite seminaries. Once the WDC officially approved of a college education, it was impossible to keep Mennonite youth from seeking college degrees in non-Mennonite schools as well. In 1910 the Education Committee reflected on the problem:

> What can be done to keep our young people who are desirous of learning in our schools, in order that they need not go to other schools to seek that which our schools are not yet able to offer them? From Mennonite circles in Kansas alone, twenty young peole have gone to other colleges and universities this fall in order to get their education. On the one hand that is gratifying, but on the other hand it is also to be regretted that such young people who are looking for a complete theological education must do this in non-Mennonite colleges.[39]

Bethel College not only encouraged the general pursuit of higher education among Kansas Mennonites; it also helped broaden the occupational pursuits of second generation immigrants. Traditionally, Mennonite higher education was intended for those studying for either the ministry or teaching in parochial schools. Education beyond the basics was considered unnecessary for agrarian Mennonites. However, the liberal arts program of Bethel served to encourage occupational pursuits beyond that of ministry and parochial education. In 1899 the Education Committee noted this shift in the educational aspirations of Mennonite students at Bethel. Fewer attended college for the pursuit of religious studies than before, and an increasing number sought higher education for the purpose of professional preparation and subsequent material gain.[40]

In 1915 the Education Committee lodged a complaint with the WDC that Mennonite young people enrolled at Bethel with the wrong motives. Students attended Bethel and other colleges based on what the school could furnish professionally, rather than for its distinctive emphasis on Mennonite values. In the first eight years of its existence, Bethel produced a total of eighteen evangelists out of an enrollment of 510 students. Less than 25% of all students in this period became ministers, missionaries, and teachers.[41] In a 1926 dissertation dealing with the sociological changes of Mennonites in central Kansas, Cornelius Janzen noted that the children of immigrants were abandoning farming for teaching, business, industry, medicine, and law. Janzen credited Bethel College for playing an important role in this transition.[42]

The relationship between Bethel and the Newton community from the beginning was cordial and beneficial to both. The Kansas Conference had originally been invited to organize a Mennonite college in Newton by a group of local businessmen. Although several Mennonite settlements existed in the Newton area, the town never boasted a Mennonite dominance. As late as 1924, Mennonites controlled only 5% of the Newton businesses.[43] Like many growing frontier communities, Newton desired the prestige of a college to lend credibility to its development. Non-Mennonites from Newton enrolled early in Bethel's history. Baptist, Methodist, Evangelical, Presbyterian, Catholic, Lutheran, and Congregational students were numbered, along with those of no church affiliation, in the 1894 enrollment. In the annual report of the college to the WDC, the school acknowledged that various non-Mennonite churches were entering into a closer relationship with Bethel. Local pastors shared in chapel services. The Bethel representative reported that "on the whole, the non-Mennonite neighborhood is learning to appreciate this institution." The fact that Mennonite youth at Bethel regularly rubbed shoulders with non-Mennonites was further evidence of Americanization.[44]

From 1874 until World War I, public schools and Bethel College combined to Americanize Mennonite education at a gradual pace. When America entered the First World War in 1917, the comparatively smooth and uneventful process of Americanization was interrupted. As a third factor in the acculturation of Mennonite education, World War I accelerated what public schools and Bethel College initiated. The impact of the First World War meant more than the loss of German-language instruction. A 1919 Kansas law that required exclusive English instruction took additional steps to speed up the Americanization of German-Americans in Kansas. Schools were legally required to provide a course of instruction on "patriotism and the duties of a citizen." The war brought Mennonite schools under the scrutiny of loyalty leagues and forced them to make certain accommodations to demonstrate their patriotic support of the war effort.[45]

The Education Committee reported in 1918 that the war had affected all aspects of Mennonite education, not just the language question. The future status of parochial schools was so questionable that the committee pronounced Mennonite education "in a state of liquidity." The work of the committee came to a near standstill by November 1918. Church leaders were indecisive and confused regarding further developments in parochial schools. At the 1919 WDC sessions the conference encouraged other means of educating Mennonite youth beyond existing Mennonite schools. They recommended Sunday schools, Christian Endeavor Societies, vacation Bible schools, night schools, public schools that provided religious instruction, and urged parents to provide regular religious instruction at home in German.[46]

World War I seriously affected the already depleted ranks of Mennonite school teachers. Parochial schools were perpetually in need of quality teachers capable of German-language religious instruction. The outbreak of war heightened the teacher shortage crisis. Several teachers and prospective teachers were drafted and a number of schools were forced to close until replacements could be found. Bethel College, the major supplier of parochial school teachers, reported in 1918 a decreased male enrollment as reflected in a two to one ratio of female to male students. Although women had been considered suitable teachers by the WDC as early as the 1890s, Mennonite parochial schools were still dominated by male teachers by World War I.[47]

Problems related to the First World War continued to affect parochial schools in subsequent years. The abrupt termination of German instruction left many schools without suitable English-language textbooks to carry on religious education.[48] "German schools" were replaced by "Bible schools." The loss of a distinctive German character resulted in a decreased enrollment. Those who remained in parochial schools during the 1920s were strapped with a heavy financial burden. The Education Committee reported in 1924 that a number of schools were closing due to financial difficulties and a lack of teachers. Teacher applications for positions in Mennonite schools after 1920 were rare.

The First World War reduced Mennonite education from a strong priority of the church at the end of the nineteenth century to a feeble remnant by the 1920s. The days of German-language instruction, segregation from non-Mennonites, and four months of religious training each year were mere memories for most Mennonites after World War I. By the 1920s, most Mennonite children attended public schools exclusively. Several district schools had Mennonite teachers and were dominated by Mennonite students. However, Mennonite education was no longer under the dictates of the church. The educational efforts of the church were limited to Sunday school, Christian Endeavor work, and daily vacation Bible school.[49]

The Response of the Church to Public Schools

With the transition from Mennonite parochial schools to public schools by the 1920s, the church was forced to reconsider its strategy for religious instruction. Unlike Mennonites in Saskatchewan whose resistance to mandatory public school attendance resulted in over 5,000 prosecutions from 1918 to 1925, Kansas Mennonites readily accepted the idea of sending their children to public schools.[50] This was due to the development of three educational agencies of the church: Sunday school, Christian Endeavor Society, and vacation Bible school. The first two existed in most Mennonite churches by the First World War and, as noted in chapter IV, facilitated the language transition in the church. Vacation Bible school served to accommodate the educational transition after the war. All three were important to the continuance of religious instruction in the church.

Sunday schools were an American innovation. When the first Mennonites arrived in Kansas from East Europe and Russia, they knew nothing of Sunday schools. Religious instruction was the sole responsibility of parochial schools in Russia. In America religious instruction was first carried on in day schools. As more Mennonite students entered the public school and state laws lengthened the school year, religious instruction was greatly threatened and Mennonite Sunday schools were organized.[51]

American Mennonites encountered the Sunday school concept three decades before the East European and Russian Mennonites arrived in Kansas. The first Mennonite Sunday school as organized in 1842 in Fayette County, Pennsylvania.[52] From the beginning opposition existed.

Some felt Sunday schools overemphasized the social aspects of the church. Others felt they were too progressive. Sunday schools were accused of promoting the four-part harmony of hymn singing, unholy pride through competitive scripture memorization, and at times functioning without the supervision of an elder or bishop. Occasionally, devisive issues slipped into the church through the use of non-Mennonite curriculum.

In 1857 one of the early founders of the General Conference Mennonite Church, John H. Oberholtzer, organized a Sunday school at the West Swamp Mennonite Church in Pennsylvania. The actual Mennonite leader in the Sunday school movement was John F. Funk of the (Old) Mennonite Church. Funk attended a union Sunday school as early as 1846 and later taught Sunday school classes in Chicago with Dwight L. Moody. As editor of the Herald of Truth, Funk promoted Sunday school among Mennonites long before its general acceptance. His efforts to publish Mennonite Sunday school curriculum near the end of the nineteenth century were not widely received, an indication that Funk was ahead of his time.[53]

The first contacts with American Sunday schools by Kansas Mennonites came from three different sources: the (Old) Mennonite Church, General Conference Mennonites in the East, and non-Mennonite denominations. In 1874 the first immigrant Sunday school in Kansas was organized by the Brudertal congregation near Hillsboro. Upon their arrival from West Prussia in 1873, the members of the Brudertal Church worshipped with American Mennonites in a nearby schoolhouse. These (Old) Mennonites had organized a Sunday school before the arrival

of their Prussian brethren and when Brudertal founded their separate
congregation in 1874, the Prussians began a Sunday school of their
own. Shortly thereafter, South Germans at Halstead organized a Sunday
school in 1876. These General Conference Mennonites came in contact
with the Sunday school concept during their previous sojourns in Summerfield, Illinois, and Donnellson, Iowa. Later classes were organized
as Mennonites observed the growth of American denominational Sunday
schools. Mennonite Brethren maintained close contacts with various
Baptist groups and subsequently incorporated the Sunday school concept,
which in turn made its way into the churches of the early Kansas
Conference.[54]

There were two stages in the development of Sunday schools
among Russian and East European Mennonites in central Kansas. During
the first stage, classes were held in schoolhouses or private homes
without official sanction from the local church or elder. Most often
Sunday school was conducted on Sunday afternoon and was intended for
children. The development of Sunday school as a separate entity
resulted both from a hesitancy to incorporate any non-Mennonite concept
as well as the possible threat it may have had to the exclusive
authority of the elder.

In the second stage of development, Sunday schools were recognized as an essential work of the church in the religious education
of young people. Classes were generally held in the church in conjunction with the morning services and gradually expanded to include adults.
During the early years classes consisted of scripture memorization,
Bible study, and catechism instruction. Graded lessons were scarce

and seldom used during the first fifty years.[55]

In spite of Mennonite suspicion, the American concept of Sunday school gradually gained acceptance in the churches of the Kansas Conference (Table 5-3). By 1904 thirty-three of the thirty-seven Western District Conference churches had Sunday schools. By 1916 all churches in the WDC had organized at least one Sunday school. In 1898 thirteen Sunday schools were conducted along within the Alexanderwohl community.[56]

The Mennonite adoption of Sunday schools served several purposes. Most classes were initially organized for children. For centuries in Russia and Prussia, Mennonite children sat through adult worship services without religious instruction geared to their level. In America the educational system reduced the impact of parochial schools. As public schools gradually outdrew Mennonite schools, the responsibility of religious instruction shifted to the Sunday schools. One of the last churches to incorporate Sunday schools within the church, Hoffnungsau, did so in 1900 because of the "inadequate religious instruction of the public school."[57]

Sunday school was also a response to discontented Mennonite youth. By the turn of the century, American-educated children of immigrants were no longer satisfied with German-language worship services. They clamored for something of interest and relevance. Some attended interdenominational Sunday schools conducted by the American Sunday School Union in local schoolhouses. The Kansas Conference soon realized that failure to organize Mennonite Sunday schools meant the loss of Mennonite youth to American churches with English-language classes. In churches without a presiding elder, Sunday schools were held weekly to compensate for the lack of a preaching service. The Committee for Itinerant Preaching reported in 1893 that the Sunday school was vital to the life of scattered congregations without elders.[58]

TABLE 5-3

FIRST SUNDAY SCHOOLS IN KANSAS CONFERENCE -
WESTERN DISTRICT CONFERENCE CHURCHES

Year	Church
1874	Brudertal Mennonite
1876	First Mennonite of Halstead
	Hopefield Mennonite
1877	First Mennonite of Christian
1879	Grace Hill Mennonite
1881	First Mennonite of Newton
1884	Johannestal Mennonite
	First Mennonite of Pretty Prairie
1885	Bergthal Mennonite
1888	Zion Mennonite
	West Zion Mennonite
1893	Bethel College Mennonite*
1900	Hoffnungsau Mennonite**
1901	Emmaus Mennonite
1902	Alexanderwohl Mennonite**
1908	Tabor Mennonite

* Sunday school was organized before the church.
** Sunday school classes were conducted as early as 1877 but were
   not officially organized in the church until later.

    SOURCE: Compiled from the church records of the WDC, Mennonite
Library and Archives, Bethel College, North Newton, Kansas.

    In 1884, after a mere decade in America, the churches of the Kansas Conference held their first annual district Sunday School Convention. The purpose of the convention was the promotion of Sunday schools. Annual meetings addressed the topics of teacher training, curriculum development, and the improvement of catechetical instruction. In 1895 the Sunday School Convention was recognized as an auxiliary organization of the Western District Conference.[59]

As an American institution, Sunday school served as a vehicle of Americanization in the Mennonite churches. Sunday schools were often the first agency to use the English language in the local church. Newspapers recognized the organization of Mennonite Sunday schools as an Americanizing phenomenon. The McPherson Republican reported in 1882 that a Sunday school organized by the First Mennonite Church of Christian (Moundridge) in 1877 had increased its enrollment to 242, making it the largest in the county. The newspaper further noted that the Moundridge church was using the International Sunday School Series, a non-Mennonite source of lessons.[60]

Sunday schools continually brought Mennonites in contact with American denominations. A report at the 1898 WDC sessions revealed that Kansas Mennonites borrowed heavily from the curriculum of other denominations. The most commonly used Sunday school material was produced by David C. Cook, Sunday School Times, and International Sunday School Literature. The WDC expressed concern over the widespread use of non-Mennonite material and passed a resolution requesting General Conference publication of Sunday school lessons. However, when the General Conference finally published the requested material, local churches continued to use non-Mennonite curriculum. As late as 1924, the churches of the WDC were using material from at least seven different publishing firms. In 1894 a question was submitted to the WDC concerning cooperative ventures with the American Sunday School Union. Although the WDC did not forbid such an effort, the reply stated, "We are and want to be a Sunday school union ourselves." This did not prevent local churches from occasionally working closely with the American Sunday School Union. During the 1920s the conference affiliated with the Kansas Sunday School Association and in 1926 sponsored a seminar at Bethel College featuring Rev. Frank Richard, the KSSA executive secretary.[61]

The influence of the Sunday school movement was not limited to the progressive churches of the WDC. Even though the Swiss Volhynians were recognized by some as a very traditional group, they were among the first to embrace the Sunday school concept at Hopefield in 1876. Both Alexanderwohl and Hoffnungsau had Sunday schools as early as 1877, although they were not incorporated within the church until the turn of the century.[62] Nevertheless, the more conservative churches had reservations about Sunday schools. The report of the Sunday School Convention at the 1895 WDC recognized these reservations:

> Thus the Sunday school and so many other things have at one time been something new in the activity of the Christian community, but they have been called into existence by peculiar circumstances and needs; and hardly any Christian still takes offence at Sunday schools today.

The report acknowledged that the Sunday school was perceived at times as "a bit bold." An effort was made to portray the Mennonite adoption of Sunday school as a response to a need rather than the result of Americanization. "It is therefore conscious of its position and knows its right as an heir." With the dawn of the twentieth century and the increase of Mennonites in public schools, the Mennonite churches in central Kansas embraced Sunday schools enthusiastically as a substitute for fading parochial schools.[63]

If Sunday school was a response by the Mennonite church to the acculturation of immigrant children, then the Christian Endeavor Society was the response of the church to the needs of young people. No segment of the Mennonite population faced the pressures of Americanization on a regular basis more than the youth. At the 1878 Kansas Conference sessions, concern was expressed regarding Mennonite young people in the Canton area. Reports had come to the attention of conference leaders that "pride and luxurious clothes are gaining ground to such an extent that the true humility of Jesus is trampled underfoot by most of them." There was particular alarm in reference to the past harvest season when young people of both sexes took jobs and reportedly indulged "in carnal lusts of all kinds." The report concluded that after a mere four years in America, Mennonite young people could no longer be distinguished from non-Mennonite youth.[64]

Russian and East European Mennonites were not unaccustomed to an occasional act of youthful rebellion in the Old Country. However, the glitter of the world was not nearly as attractive in Russia as it was in their new homeland. Close contact with non-Mennonites rarely occurred on the Russian steppes. The Kansas prairie with its American farmers, public schools, and established towns afforded interaction previously unknown to Mennonite youth. Sunday school had its greatest impact on the children. However, it was the responsibility of another American agency to accommodate assimilating Mennonite young people - the Christian Endeavor Society.

The Christian Endeavor movement was launched in 1881 by Frances E. Clark as an interdenominational organization for the promotion of religious education. Devotional in nature, regularly scheduled meetings involved Bible studies, an interest in missions, and made contributions of money, Bibles, and clothing to the mission cause. Ten years later 14,000 delegates met in Minneapolis for the annual Christian Endeavor Convention. The successful growth of the Christian Endeavor work was largely associated with the Sunday school movement.[65]

The first Mennonite Christian Endeavor Societies functioned without the full support of the local congregations. There was a great deal of reservation on the part of older church members. Various members of the Hoffnungsau church feared that the presence of any sanctioned youth organization within the church could result in a takeover of leadership by the young people.[66] Others were concerned lest any association with an American organization might encroach upon Mennonite values. In 1895 the Western District Conference received the first report of the Konvention der Mennonitischen Jugendvereine (Christian Endeavor Society Convention). The report turned out to be a defense of the Christian Endeavor Society. "Offense may perhaps be taken on account of these endeavors for the reason that it is a new thing and the Kingdom of God always remains the same . . . ." The report heralded the development of societies as a response to modernization, secret societies, and the evils of society. Apparently the report "rang the bell" for the conference voted to endorse the Christian Endeavor Society Convention which had been meeting annually since 1893. However, a warning to regard invitations from non-Mennonite societies "with prudence" accompanied the endorsement. The 1896 report of the Christian Endeavor Society Convention made clear that local societies were the "wards of the church" and should in no way subvert the authority of local congregations. The 1898 conference again cautioned Christian Endeavor leaders against fraternizing with non-Mennonite societies. Individual members were at liberty to attend "English C. E. Societies," but were not encouraged to do so.[67]

The first Mennonite Christian Endeavor societies in the Western District Conference were organized in the late 1880s at Hillsboro and Halstead (table 5-4). The first convention in 1893 and a conference endorsement in 1895 encouraged the organization of Christian Endeavor Societies in central Kansas Mennonite churches. By 1896 eleven societies existed in the Western District. In 1904 twenty-one of the thirty-five WDC churches had societies. By 1916 only four of the fifty-three WDC churches did not have a local Christian Endeavor Society. In 1897, 1,200 young people rallied to attend the Christian Endeavor Society Convention at the West Zion Church. That same year the General Conference Mennonite Church was represented by several local societies at the International Christian Endeavor Society Convention in Washington, D.C.[68]

The Christian Endeavor work in the WDC was an obvious attempt by Mennonite leaders to use an American innovation to keep Mennonite youth in the fold. Societies served local churches and the conference in an attempt to curb a spirit of restlessness among Mennonite young people. At the same time, the Christian Endeavor work encouraged mixing between Swiss Volhynian, Russian, South German, Polish, and Prussian Mennonite youth. Interaction did not end at this level. Mennonite societies adopted the slogans, objectives, and programs of the international Christian Endeavor Movements. For some, Christian Endeavor

TABLE 5-4

FIRST CHRISTIAN ENDEAVOR SOCIETIES IN KANSAS CONFERENCE -
WESTERN DISTRICT CONFERENCE CHURCHES

Year	Church
1889	First Mennonite of Hillsboro
1891	West Zion Mennonite
1893	Bethel College Mennonite*
1894	First Mennonite of Halstead**
	First Mennonite of Pretty Prairie
	Grace Hill Mennonite
1895	First Mennonite of Christian
1897	Zion Mennonite
1898	First Mennonite of Newton
1901	Hoffnungsau Mennonite
1906	Eden Mennonite
	Tabor Mennonite*
1908	Emmanuel Mennonite
1909	Emmaus Mennonite
	Johannestal Mennonite
1914	Brudertal Mennonite

* A Christian Endeavor Society was founded before the church was organized.
** Functioned a number of years unofficially before 1894.

SOURCE: Compiled from the church records of the WDC, Mennonite Library and Archives, Bethel College, North Newton, Kansas.

was an introduction to later affiliations with such interdenominational organizations as the YMCA and the Federal Council of Churches. This had the effect of expanding the concept of a community of believers from the local Mennonite congregation to a much broader body of Protestant Christianity.

Sunday schools and Christian Endeavor Societies were well entrenched in the Mennonite churches of central Kansas by the First World War. Along with the German school session each spring, societies served to instill a sense of peoplehood in second and third generation immigrant children. With America's entry into World War I, parochial schools faced unexpected opposition from a superpatriotic society bent on removing foreign elements from its midst. The abandoment of German-language instruction left Mennonite schools without one of the vital basic support mechanisms. After the war the WDC attempted to regroup and promote Mennonite parochial schools, but the loss of the mother tongue combined with a general acceptance of public schools prevented a return to the days of church controlled schools. Neither the Sunday school nor the Christian Endeavor work made up for the lack of religious instruction created by the closing of German schools. Mennonite leaders realized it was unwise strategy to promote Mennonite schools and subsequently force families into the dilemma of choosing between a weakened Mennonite school and a developing public school. It was under these circumstances that the Mennonite version of vacation Bible school developed in the 1920s.

At the 1920 Western District Conference sessions, a recommendation was offered by the Education Committee signaling the transition from

German schools to vacation Bible schools. The committee recommended that in light of teacher shortages, a lack of interest in German, and a lengthened public school year, churches should organize their own daily vacation Bible schools. This way teachers could be selected within the local congregation without adhering to strict state require- ments. English was the medium of instruction and religious education was the sole objective. Classes were held in the churches during the summer months.

Throughout the 1920s the Education Committee increasingly promoted a three-fold means of religious education in the local church as a response to widespread acceptance of public schools--Sunday school, Christian Endeavor Society, and vacation Bible school. The committee frequently referred to the success of vacation Bible school in other denominations in an attempt to encourage Mennonite churches to pattern after the American model. In 1930 the committee stepped up its promotion of vacation Bible school suggesting that every WDC church organize classes each spring with six to eight weeks of "strong religious instruction." No mention of German-language instruction was included, indicating that English was most commonly used.[69]

Conclusion

The Mennonite parochial school in Russia and eastern Europe was an extension of the church. Clerical personalities often served as teachers and education centered on a study of the Bible. Schools were autonomously conducted by each village without the interference of government officials. Following their settlement in central Kansas, Russian and East European Mennonites attempted to reestablish parochial schools on the Great Plains. This was an obvious attempt to duplicate the Old World experience and subsequently perpetuate a Mennonite sense of ethnoreligious cohesiveness in a strange land. Mennonites soon realized that the educational environment in America differed substantially from that of Russia and eastern Europe. The checkerboard effect of homestead and railroad lands prohibited the reconstruction of the closed Russian village with its centrally located church and schoolhouse. In America, public schools were available for both native-born and immigrant students. The development of public schools in Kansas from 1874 to the First World War gradually drew Mennonite children into district schools. Parochial schools simply could not keep pace with the development of public schools.

Public schools were not the only factor in the Americanization of Mennonite education. The pursuit of higher education accounted for repeated contacts with the outside world. Beginning with the Emmatal school in 1882, continuing with Halstead seminary in 1883, and resulting in the founding of Bethel College in 1893, Mennonites in central Kansas sought an advanced level of education that was rare in the Old World. At Bethel, Mennonite youth rubbed shoulders with American students, developed an appreciation for a liberal arts curriculum, and mastered the complexities of the English language. The college prepared them for nonagrarian occupations in a secular society. Even those who pursued more traditional Mennonite occupations such as teaching often landed jobs in public schools. For others, Bethel was a catalyst for advanced studies at seminaries and graduate schools.

Whereas public schools and higher education gradually facilitated the Americanization of Mennonite education, World War I radically altered its course. The loss of German-language instruction during the war was the death knell of Mennonite schools. The First World War complicated all previous problems of the parochial school. After the war efforts to revive English-language Mennonite schools with a greater emphasis on religious instruction were largely unsuccessful.

The church responded to the Americanization of Mennonite education with three concepts--Sunday school, Christian Endeavor Society, and vacation Bible school. All three were borrowed from American Protestant Christianity, but each was customized to promote Mennonite distinctiveness. All three were efforts to retain Mennonite youth.

By 1939 the last preparatory school of the WDC churches in central Kansas had closed its doors. Elementary parochial school terms were replaced by a few weeks of vacation Bible school each year. Mennonite young people regularly attended public schools. Only Bethel College remained to remind the church of a day when education was the exclusive responsibility of the local congregation. Even Bethel had changed since its founding. Organized as a response to the need for educated ministers, teachers in German schools, and prepared missionaries, by 1939 the school had developed into a liberal arts college with a broader perspective of education than even the most progressive leader in the Kansas Conference could have imagined.

Two of the three basic functions of the immigrant parochial school, as described by W. Lloyd Warner, were lost in the Americanization process - the retention of the mother tongue and the perpetuation of national symbols.[70] The Mennonite experience no longer required either a comprehensive understanding of High German nor a sense of German ethnocentrism. The third function of the parochial school, the perpetuation of religious symbols, shifted the responsibility of religious instruction to Sunday schools, Christian Endeavor Societies, and vacation Bible schools. However, as we shall see in chapter VI, even the religious symbols of the church experienced significant acculturation by 1939.

CHAPTER V - ENDNOTES

1. Frederick C. Luebke, "German Immigrants and Parochial Schools," Issues 2 (Spring 1967): 11-18; Andrew M. Greeley and Peter H. Rossi, The Education of American Catholics (Chicago: Aldine Publishing Co., 1966); Bernard J. Weiss, ed., American Education and the European Immigrant, 1840-1940 (Champaign, Illinois: University of Illinois Press, 1982).

2. Leo Srole and W. Lloyd Warner, The Social Systems of American Ethnic Groups (New Haven: Yale University Press, 1945), pp. 236-53.

3. Peter Braun, "The Educational System of the Mennonite Colonies in South Russia," Mennonite Quarterly Review 3 (July 1929): 169-82; Mennonite Encyclopedia, s.v. "Education Among the Mennonites in Russia," by Peter Braun; David G. Rempel, "The Mennonite Commonwealth in Russia," Mennonite Quarterly Review 48 (January 1948): 26-28.

4. H. P. Peters, "History and Development of Education Among Mennonites in Kansas" (M.A. thesis, Bluffton College, 1925), pp. 11-14.

5. Ibid.

6. John E. Hartzler, Education Among the Mennonites of America (Danvers, Illinois: Central Mennonite Publishing Board, 1925), pp. 109-16; John J. Voth, "Religious Education in the Mennonite Churches Comprising the Western District Conference" (M.T. dissertation, Witmarsum Theological Seminary, 1922), pp. 11-20; David C. Wedel, "The Contribution of C. H. Wedel to the Mennonite Church Through Education" (Ph.D. dissertation, Iliff School of Theology, 1952), pp. 29-32.

7. David A. Haury, Prairie People (Newton, Kansas: Faith and Life Press, 1981), p. 81.

8. H. P. Peters, pp. 23-42.

9. Minutes of the Kansas Conference (hereafter referred to as Minutes) 15 November 1877, Mennonite Library and Archives, Bethel College, North Newton, Kansas (transcript, English translation).

10. Minutes, 14 December 1877; Haury, pp. 84-87; James C. Juhnke, "Freedom for Reluctant Citizens," Mennonite Life 29 (January 1974): 30-31.

11. Minutes, 1-2 November 1898.

12. Minutes, 7-9 November 1894.

13. Peter J. Wedel, The Story of Bethel College (North Newton, Kansas: Bethel College, 1954), pp. 81-83; David C. Wedel, "The Contribution of C. H. Wedel."

14. Peter J. Wedel, "Beginnings of Secondary Education in Kansas," Mennonite Life 3 (October 1948): 14.

15. Ruth Unrau, Who Needs an Oil Well? (New York: Abingdon Press, 1968), p. 114.

16. Peter J. Wedel, "Beginnings of Secondary Education in Kansas," pp. 15-16.

17. Minutes, 16-17 October 1883; 29-30 September 1884; 12-14 October 1885; 11-13 October 1886; 15-16 October 1888; Halstead Mennonite Seminary Reports and Accounts, Mennonite Library and Archives, Bethel College, North Newton, Kansas.

18. Minutes, 3-5 October 1887.

19. Minutes, 5-6 November 1889.

20. Minutes, 2-4 October 1890.

21. Haury, pp. 89-94.

22. H. P. Peters, p. 153; Mennonite Encyclopedia, s.v. "Hillsboro Preparatory School," by Cornelius Krahn; Jan Niles, "H. D. Penner and the Hillsboro Preparatory School" (Unpublished paper, Mennonite Library and Archives, Bethel College, North Newton, Kansas, 1978), pp. 6-7.

23. H. P. Peters, pp. 81-99.

24. Minutes, 23-24 October 1912.

25. Minutes, 20-21 October 1915.

26. Minutes, 18-20 October 1922.

27. Minutes, 17-18 October 1923.

28. Minutes, 21-23 October 1925.

29. Minutes, 19-20 October 1927; 17-18 October 1928.

30. Minutes, 16-17 October 1929.

31. Minutes, 22-23 October 1930.

32. Minutes, 21-22 October 1931.

33. Minutes, 16-17 October 1929.

34. Haury, pp. 94-98; Peter J. Wedel, The Story of Bethel College, pp. 45-79.

35. Peter J. Wedel, The Story of Bethel College, pp. 68-72.

187

36. C. H. Wedel, "Bethel College," Mennonite Yearbook and Almanac (Quakertown, Pennsylvania: U.S. Stauffer, 1895), p. 28.

37. Minutes, 24-26 October 1901.

38. Minutes, 14-15 October 1896.

39. Minutes, 19-21 October 1910.

40. Minutes, 2-3 October 1899.

41. Minutes, 24-26 October 1901; 20-21 October 1915.

42. Cornelius Janzen, "A Social Study of the Mennonite Settlements in the Counties of Marion, McPherson, Harvey, Reno, and Butler, Kansas" (Ph.D. dissertation, University of Chicago, 1926), p. 156.

43. Ibid., p. 50.

44. Peter J. Wedel, The Story of Bethel College, p. 96; Minutes, 7-9 November 1894.

45. H. P. Peters, pp. 203-04.

46. Minutes, 12 November 1918; 5-7 November 1919.

47. Minutes, 12 November 1918.

48. Minutes, 20-22 October 1920.

49. Minutes, 29-31 October 1924; 20-22 October 1920.

50. Adolf Ens, "The Public School Crisis Among Mennonites in Saskatchewan 1916-25," in Mennonite Images, ed. Harry Loewen (Winnipeg: Hyperion Press, 1980), pp. 73-82.

51. Hartzler, pp. 91-99; John J. Voth, pp. 45-60.

52. John Umble, "Early Mennonite Sunday School Lesson Helps," Mennonite Quarterly Review 2 (April 1938): 98-107, and "Seventy Years of Progress in Sunday School Work Among the Mennonites of the Middle West," Mennonite Quarterly Review 8 (October 1934): 166-79; Hartzler, pp. 91-92.

53. Silas Hertzler, "Early Mennonite Sunday Schools," Mennonite Quarterly Review 2 (April 1928): 123-24.

54. John J. Voth, pp. 44-46; John A. Toews, A History of the Mennonite Brethren Church (Fresno, California: Board of Christian Literature, General Conference of Mennonite Brethren Churches, 1975), pp. 217, 367; Menno Kaufman, The Challenging Faith (Newton, Kansas: United Printing, 1975), p. 34.

55. Hartzler, pp. 95-97.

56. Minutes, 19-21 October 1904; 4-5 October 1916; David C. Wedel, The Story of Alexanderwohl (North Newton, Kansas: Mennonite Press, 1974), pp. 65-66.

57. Albert M. Gaeddert, Centennial History of Hoffnungsau Mennonite Church (North Newton, Kansas: Mennonite Press, 1975), p. 70.

58. Minutes, 11-13 October 1893.

59. Minutes, 29-31 October 1895.

60. McPherson Republican, 27 July 1882, p. 4.

61. Minutes, 12 November 1898; 29-31 October 1924; 7-9 November 1894; 20-22 October 1926.

62. Samuel F. Pannabecker, Open Doors (Newton, Kansas: Faith and Life Press, 1975), p. 102.

63. Minutes, 29-31 October 1895.

64. Minutes, 6-7 November 1878.

65. Paul M. Lederach, "The History of the Young People's Bible Meeting in the Mennonite Church," Mennonite Quarterly Review 26 (July 1952): 216.

66. Albert M. Gaeddert, p. 70.

67. Minutes, 29-31 October 1895; 14-15 October 1896; 1-2 November 1898.

68. Haury, pp. 283-84; Minutes, 14-15 October 1896; 19-21 October 1904; 4-5 October 1916; Mennonite Yearbook and Almanac for 1897 (Quakertown, Pennsylvania: U.S. Stauffer, 1897), p. 26.

69. Minutes, 20-22 October 1920; 22-23 October 1930.

70. Srole and Warner, pp. 236-53.

CHAPTER VI

THE IMPACT OF AMERICAN REVIVALISM, MODERNISM, AND SECULARISM

Likewise, Mennonites have come to worship bigness or size
in membership in contrast to quality, just like the rest of
Protestantism which is so often accused of being secularized.
It seems to me that the amount of "dead timber" that is in
a church increases in proportion to the size of its membership.
At any rate, the modern Mennonite Church stands in sharp
contrast to the apostolic churches who were characterized
by their ardor and fervent zeal for evangelism among lay
members.

J. Winfield Fretz
75th Anniversary of the Swiss Mennonites
September 5, 1949

Mennonites arriving in America in the late nineteenth century

encountered a religious atmosphere completely alien from their European

experience. American religion from the beginning had been pluralistic,

not monolithic; America was a denominational society even before it

became a country. Unlike nineteenth century Europe, America did not

have a single established church. Mennonites in central Kansas soon

discovered that the American religious environment abounded with

variety, diversity, plurality, and paradox. Above all, American

religion was strongly individualistic.[1]

The impact of American religion on Russian and East European

Mennonites in central Kansas was both pronounced and complex. No

single theme dominated America's denominational society. In the new

environment, Mennonite congregations encountered modernism, fundamen-

talism, secularism, liberalism, Calvinism, Arminianism, individualism, humanism, and a host of other "isms" not central to their Anabaptist heritage. The impact of these various aspects of American religion was evident in Mennonite churches in central Kansas from 1874 to 1939. A careful examination of three aspects of American religion - revivalism (and fundamentalism in the twentieth century), modernism, and secularism - reveals the full impact of Americanization.

American Revivalism

No other religious phenomena had a greater impact on the Mennonite experience than American revivalism. Although several factors accounted for the acculturation of Kansas Mennonite churches, none produced a response comparable to revivalism.

Revivalism was no stranger to Kansas Mennonites. They encountered various waves of pietistic revivals in Europe during the eighteenth and nineteenth centuries. Moravian pietists visited Mennonites in West Prussia and Poland in the early nineteenth century. By the middle of the same century, pietistic revivals spread to southern Russia. In 1860, Mennonites most affected by pietism formed the Mennonite Brethren Church.[2]

Eighteenth century European pietism emphasized an emotional, "heartfelt" religion resulting in good works and various forms of nonconformity. Its adherents also emphasized the second coming of Christ. Nineteenth century American pietism differed significantly. It was grounded in Arminianism and centered on the individual as an autonomous, rational creature. By the end of the nineteenth century, American revivalism was enveloped within the Holiness Movement which brought the Christian to a "higher life" subsequent to salvation.

This second blessing was referred to as "entire sanctification" or "perfectionism."[3]

American revivalism has been a recurring theme in American religious history. Beginning with the Great Awakening in the early eighteenth century, revivalism played an important role in the formation of the American religious character. The second Great Awakening (1793-1810), the Charles G. Finney revival of 1824-1827, the revival of 1853, and the D. L. Moody revival of 1879-1890 firmly entrenched revivalism as a strong force within American Protestantism.

Russian and East European Mennonites arriving in North America during the 1870s were immediately confronted with American revivalism. In the twentieth century revivalism took on the form of fundamentalism in response to a modernist trend in American mainline churches. Once again American revivalism confronted Mennonites in a new form.[4] Their response was an important aspect of Mennonite Americanization.

Revivalism crept into Mennonite groups from various sources. Some congregations retained certain aspects of European pietism. Furthermore, Anabaptism itself had been born in a revival spirit and periodic renewals were not uncommon. Resistance to revival movements usually resulted from the use of non-Mennonite methods or the incorporation of doctrine contrary to the Anabaptist experience. Revivalism, as a means of renewing the original Anabaptist vision, was a part of Mennonite tradition. However, most Kansas Mennonites did not perceive American revivalism in this way. For the most part, it came from outside sources and seldom drew them to their Anabaptist roots.

American revivalism was characterized by protracted meetings, emotional salvation experiences, a strong emphasis on evangelism and missions, the growth of Bible institutes, an intense interest in the second coming of Christ, and support for the temperance movement. Certain doctrinal positions, such as Wesleyanism in the nineteenth century and Calvinism in the twentieth century, further characterized revivalism in America.

Protracted Meetings

One visible aspect of American revivalism in the late nineteenth century was the protracted meeting or revival service. Finney, Moody, and several other revivalists gained fame through their use. Camp meetings, tent revivals, and nightly church services were common in late nineteenth century frontier communities.

Mennonites of North America were not untouched by rapidly spreading revival services. In Pennsylvania, Ontario, and Indiana a few (Old) Mennonite Church elders conducted protracted meetings, often in violation of conference rulings. Even conservative Amish experienced their impact. By 1900 the Mennonite Brethren and (Old) Mennonite churches accepted the revival service as a means of awakening the church and renewing the Anabaptist vision. A number of smaller Mennonite groups developed as offshoots from the main bodies such as the Missionary Church Association, Defenseless Mennonites, Evangelical Mennonite Brethren, and Mennonite Brethren in Christ. Initially, they incorporated revivalism while maintaining the major tenets of Anabaptism.[5]

Whereas American revivalism for the Mennonite Brethren and the (Old) Mennonite Church was a return to Anabaptist roots, for the General Conference Mennonites it had a splintering, individualistic effect. The presence of protracted meetings amongst nineteenth century Kansas Mennonites was at times an indication of an impending schism. It was only in the twentieth century that protracted meetings gained a level of respectability in WDC churches. However, by then they were less like revival services and more akin to scholarly Bible lectures in most churches.

Various reports of revivals surfaced at WDC sessions in the nineteenth century. Most of these were conducted by non-Mennonites in Mennonite communities: "sanctified holy" revival services drew in Ransom Mennonites; Methodists in western Kansas made inroads in outlying Mennonite groups via revival services; Mennonites in the Elbing-Whitewater area attended protracted meetings conducted by the Missionary Church Association; and (Old) Mennonite Church schism pro-duced an annual campmeeting that attracted WDC Mennonites in the Hesston area.[6]

Finally in 1897 the WDC accepted protracted meetings for Kansas Mennonite churches. However, they played down their emotional appeal and required that they be conducted by sanctioned ministers "from within our Conference." In 1910 the Itinerant Preaching Committee recorded the first reference of "protracted meetings" (verlaengerte Versammlungen) in its report to the WDC. As Mennonites migrated from central Kansas to Oklahoma, western Kansas, and urban centers around the turn of the century, the WDC perceived protracted meetings as a means of drawing wandering sheep back into the fold. In 1914 the Itinerant Preaching Committee recommended a "series of meetings" in the Hutchinson and Wichita area in an effort to attract Mennonites who had left the farm for the city. These meetings were originally intended to draw Mennonites. When the committee proposed using them to win "other hungry souls," this signaled the use of revivalistic methods both to strengthen the Mennonite church and evangelize non-Mennonites. The latter objective met with little success.[7]

The use of special services among Kansas Mennonites is muddled by the diversity of local congregations. Although most churches in the early twentieth century held some type of "special services" on a nightly basis, they varied greatly in both objective and content. For some, special meetings were scholarly Bible lectures conducted by an outside speaker. In other congregations, special meetings followed catechism classes and usually resulted in an invitation to all catechetical candidates to join the church. In still other churches, special meetings took on the characteristics of American revivalism. A talented, powerful speaker was invited to preach for the purpose of conversions. The First Mennonite Church of Pretty Prairie held this type of protracted meeting with regularity. In the 1920s the Home Missions Committee (formerly the Itinerant Preaching Committee) used gospel singers to accompany speakers in revival services.[8]

In his 1926 report to the General Conference Mennonite Church, field secretary C. E. Krehbiel summarized the different Mennonite views of protracted meetings:

> There are those who think little of catechism and stress revivals, and there are those who deplore revivals and stress catechism. How shall souls be won?[9]

However, the Itinerant Preaching Committee concluded in 1919 that a series of special meetings continually proved to be "a good means

for revival and strengthening the faith."[10] The adoption of protracted
meetings even in a modified form reflected the inroads of American
revivalism.

Prohibition

Mennonite involvement in the temperance movement and eventual
support for prohibition was an additional sign of acculturation.
American Mennonites from 1683 to 1873 generally had no scruples against
moderate drinking. European Mennonites likewise permitted moderate
drinking. Some Russian Mennonite villages had drinking houses and
breweries. Wine was used for communion services by all Kansas
Conference churches in the nineteenth century.

Immigrants arriving in America during the 1870s were greeted
by a strong temperance movement closely associated with American revivalism. Not all temperance organizations stemmed from American revivalism; however, nearly all revival elements supported temperance as
a reform movement. Baptists and Methodists in particular backed the
efforts of the American Temperance Movement (1833) and later the Women's
Christian Temperance Union (1874) and the Anti-Saloon League (1895).[11]

Initially, Kansas Mennonites continued alcohol consumption
for both festive and communion purposes. At many of the early weddings,
wine, whiskey, and schnapps were served. Some of the settlers planted
vineyards for winemaking in their new homeland. Mennonites commonly
treated visitors to a friendly glass of wine. Carolers on Christmas
night in the Alexanderwohl community might expect to receive as a
rare treat a glass of wine.[12]

The alcohol question immediately challenged the drinking habits of Kansas Mennonites. During the 1870s the temperance movement in Kansas gained strength through cohesive organization. Protestant churches held temperance revivals and nationally recognized lecturers addressed Kansas audiences on the evils of liquor. In 1874 the Republican platform endorsed temperance principles. With the support of Governor John P. St. John, Kansas adopted a prohibition amendment in 1880.[13]

In 1879 the third annual Kansas Conference responded to the pressure of the temperance movement. A question surfaced during the sessions regarding the Mennonite stand on temperance societies. The reply stated that Mennonites should seek "right moderation" rendering support for temperance societies unnecessary.[14] This statement best reflected the Old World stance of Kansas Mennonites. They were careful not to offend their host society; at the same time they did give in to popular sentiment.

After Kansas adopted a prohibition amendment in 1880, the alcohol question involved a legal consideration. With regard to serving wine at communion services, the 1881 Kansas Conference generally agreed to disregard the new law since permits could easily be obtained. In 1883 the Kansas Conference again addressed the issue of the temperance movement. Kansas Mennonites were increasingly aware that their 1879 moderation stand was harmonious with neither popular sentiment nor the Kansas law. The 1883 Kansas Conference response stated that "sobriety and temperance in all things should be an indispensable virtue in all Christendom."[15] Although this addendum to the 1879 statement did not technically change the Kansas Conference stand, it had the effect of reducing any previous ring of defiance in their moderation position.

When the Kansas Conference joined the General Conference Mennonite Church in 1892 and became the Western District Conference, it also became a part of a much larger response to the temperance movement. The Mennonite, an eastern periodical recognized in 1893 as the official English-language newspaper of the General Conference, printed numerous articles on the evils of "demon rum." Editorials included testimonies of converted drunks strongly favoring abstinence. In July 1900 an article entitled "What is Temperance?" offered clear evidence that temperance meant total abstinence from alcohol.[16] This clearly deviated from the traditional Mennonite stand of moderation. Although the Mennonite supported the objectives of the temperance movement, it denounced the methods of Carrie Nation as destructive and excessively violent.[17]

The German-language newspaper of the General Conference Mennonite Church, Christlicher Bundesbote, also supported the cause of prohibition. An 1896 article attacked the moderate drinking position as dangerous. The editor suggested that Mennonite lips should not touch alcohol.[18]

In 1896 the General Conference adopted a statement indicative of a growing pro-temperance sentiment among Mennonites:

> A congregation that tolerates among its members the drink evil, cannot be regarded as Christian, and can therefore not be a congregation in this Conference. Recognizing in the so-called saloons and all kinds of drink houses one of the greatest and most common evils in human society, these should in no wise be countenanced by our congregations and members of our Conference.[19]

The 1896 stand on alcoholic consumption was as close as the General Conference came to an abstinence position prior to twentieth century prohibition. It carefully avoided any mention of drinking in moderation, yet did little to undermine the original position of the 1879 Kansas Conference. At the same time the 1896 statement openly condemned the evil effects of alcohol and in this respect became a part of the American temperance movement. Even as they kept the method-ology of the radical elements of the temperance cause at an arms length, General Conference Mennonites in Kansas adopted the prohibition theme.

Between 1900 and the First World War, Mennonites in central Kansas were generally supportive of the temperance movement. Their conversion to temperance was not simply a matter of conformity. Rejec-tion of the temperance cause may have been perceived improperly by the non-Mennonite Christian community. Christian Krehbiel, the Mennonite patriarch of the WDC, announced his conversion to prohibition to a group of ministers at the Alexanderwohl church: "Brethren, we have made a name unto ourselves that stinks, and we must change our attitude if we want to keep the respect of our English-speaking Christians."[20] Krehbiel realized the necessity of shedding the image of "sipping saints" so that Mennonites might project a proper moral image in their communities, especially in prohibitionist Kansas.

World War I momentarily distracted attention from the alcohol question. However, in 1919 Kansas Mennonites picked up the prohibition cause again. The First World War brought into question the loyalty of the Mennonite Church to the United States; prohibition extended the opportunity to reaffirm its patriotic support. In an April 10,

1919 editorial, Der Herold claimed that although prohibition would
not defeat the devil, it was a move in the right direction.[21] In
March 1920, C. H. Regier, elder of the Zion Mennonite Church (Elbing),
offered a Biblical basis for prohibition.[22] Numerous references supporting prohibition usually included attacks on smoking, dancing,
card playing, and other vices. Apparently some Mennonites felt more
comfortable dealing with the alcohol question within context of a
variety of social evils.

As prohibition continued throughout the 1920s, it gained stronger
support in Kansas Mennonite communities. Temperance was no longer
a matter of conscience or testimony for Mennonites; it was a matter
of civic duty. In 1923 the General Conference expressed its sentiments
toward prohibition with three resolutions including a hearty
endorsement, recognition of prohibition as the greatest progressive
step in the United States since the Emancipation Proclamation, and
a call for public support.[23] On November 7, 1928, an editorial by
Henry P. Krehbiel in the Mennonite Weekly Review proclaimed Hoover's
election as a victory for Kansas dry forces. Krehbiel's zealous support
of prohibition moved him to claim that the issue had been settled
once and for all - never to be debated again.[24]

Mennonite support for prohibition was not unanimous. In his
report to the 1926 General Conference, C. E. Krehbiel noted: "The
sentiment for prohibition is not uniform among us; but we urge, teach,
and practice strict conformity and obedience to law and order."[25]
In 1934 Kansas Mennonites were given the opportunity to display their
support for prohibition. A state vote to repeal prohibition produced

the highest Mennonite turnout in any nonpresidential election year before or since. Prior to the state vote, the Western District Conference ratified the "Temperance Resolution" of the Young People's section of the conference:

> Whereas, we, the young people of the Mennonite Church, believe that our bodies are temples of God, and that the use of intoxicating beverages weakens and defiles them, and in view of the fact that few of us are voting age, we feel constrained to ask our elders who reside in Kansas, that on November 6, they register their votes against the repeal of the Kansas Prohibition Law. We feel certain that through this law we have lost nothing and gained much.[26]

Kansas voters rejected prohibition repeal in 1934 by a vote of 55.7 percent to 44.3 percent. In predominant Mennonite precincts the vote was even stronger against repeal: 75.3 percent to 24.7 percent. Compared with the 1880 vote on prohibition when they voted 57.1 percent in favor and 42.9 percent opposed, Kansas Mennonites had come a long way on the temperance question. The transition of the Mennonite position on alcohol from one of moderation in 1879 to that of active support for the temperance movement in the early twentieth century is a clear indication of Americanization.[27] American revivalism plays no small part in this transition.

Church Schisms

Periodically, Mennonites have been subject to internal squabbles. Some of the greatest struggles in the Anabaptist movement have resulted from internal strife. American revivalism was the cause for certain church schisms in the WDC. The best known was the "Foster Schoolhouse Movement" in the Elbing-Whitewater area around the turn of the century.

One of the earliest reports of revivalism among the Kansas Mennonites came in 1880 near Peabody. In that year Daniel Brenneman and Solomon Eby, two excommunicated elders from the (Old) Mennonite Church in Indiana and Ontario, visited a group of Ontario Mennonites who settled in the area a year before. For several weeks the two men conducted protracted meetings in a tent erected for the occasion. Both non-Mennonites and Mennonites attended these emotionally charged services and sufficient conversions were recorded to establish a congregation. Before Brenneman and Eby left Peabody, they organized a local Mennonite Brethren in Christ congregation.[28]

Other evangelists visited the Peabody congregation and conducted special services during the 1880s. The revival fires spread from Peabody to three Kansas Conference congregations: Zion (Elbing), Grace Hill (Whitewater), and the Swiss Church (Whitewater). As a result, several members of these congregations held "cottage prayer meetings" in a nearby schoolhouse, while retaining regular attendance in each of their respective churches. These Sunday afternoon meetings consisted of informal Bible studies, testimonials, gospel singing, and revivalistic preaching. They soon became known as the "Foster Schoolhouse" group, named after the building in which they met.

Their informal style of worship and lively singing attracted Mennonites weary of formalism and in need of a "frontier religion" to parallel a rugged frontier experience. Dissident Mennonite evangelists from the East periodically visited the "Foster Schoolhouse" group and in August 1901 its leader, G. J. Kliewer, was invited to a convention of the Missionary Church Association (MCA) near Nickerson, Kansas. At this convention Kliewer was ordained by the leaders of the MCA.[29]

The Missionary Church Association was similar to the Mennonite
Brethren in Christ. In fact, after years of negotiations, the two
groups eventually merged in 1969. Both bodies emerged from revivalistic
schisms in Mennonite congregations. Among the revivalistic emphases
of the Missionary Church Association was a Wesleyan belief calling
for the crisis act of sanctification subsequent to a personal salvation
experience, an emphasis on evangelism, the imminent return of Christ,
baptism by immersion, and a clear missions orientation. The leader
of the MCA, Joseph Ramseyer, was a powerful speaker well known for
revival preaching and the founding of Fort Wayne Bible College (1904).[30]

Kliewer's ordination by MCA leaders in 1901 brought action
from his home congregation, Grace Hill. For a number of years the
church carefully avoided conflict over various members' involvement
in the Foster Schoolhouse prayer meetings. In fact, as a minister
at Grace Hill, Kliewer was even elected to the position of church
evangelist, a promotion he refused. However, in 1901, the WDC intervened in an attempt to resolve an impasse between Kliewer and the
Grace Hill congregation. All efforts to reconcile the two parties
failed and in 1902 the Foster School group formed the Elbing Missionary
Church with Kliewer as minister. Of the twenty charter members, thirteen were from Grace Hill, four from Zion, and three from the Swiss
Church.[31]

Meanwhile two enthusiastic young men in the Zion Mennonite
Church were significantly affected by American revivalism. Henry
J. Dyck and Abraham H. Regier felt the "call" to religious ministry
shortly after the turn of the century. Neither was nominated to the

ministry in the Zion Church. Thus, the opportunity to speak in special services was the only means of fulfilling their "call." They both traveled east to engage their ministerial yearnings with a nondenominational agency headed by a controversial Mennonite evangelist, J. A. Sprunger. Sprunger was well known to the Foster Schoolhouse group since he previously conducted protracted meetings in Kansas and took part in the ordination of G. J. Kliewer in 1901.[32]

In 1905 Dyck and Regier returned to Kansas with Sprunger who ordained them to the ministry in the Elbing Missionary Church. This action resulted in their excommunication from the Zion Mennonite Church. Since both Dyck and Regier had relatives in the Zion congregation who objected to the church action (the Zion elder was an uncle to Regier and Dyck's wife), a schism resulted. The division prompted eleven Zion members to join the Missionary Church between 1908 and 1914.[33]

The Elbing Missionary Church transformed an immigrant group into an American revivalistic congregation. In 1910 when its members constructed their first church building, evangelistic zeal abounded. They purchased a tent and held protracted meetings throughout Kansas and Oklahoma. They also built a tabernacle for the workers in nearby oil fields and held regular Sunday school and preaching services for many years. The church produced a number of ministers and missionaries who in turn planted congregations in other communities. A number of young people attended Fort Wayne Bible College, the Missionary Church School in Indiana. Here they assimilated further into the American evangelical community.[34]

Early in the schism several participants summoned assistance from the Western District Conference. The Committee for Congregational Affairs responded to the invitation to serve as a third party. However, the elder of the Zion congregation made it known from the beginning that any outside involvement was perceived as an unwelcome intrusion.[35] In spite of numerous efforts to reconcile the various factions in the conflict, WDC involvement was to no avail. The General Conference structure of locally autonomous congregations was not conducive to mediating a solution. One of the members of the WDC Committee for Congregational Affairs succinctly assessed the situation: "I can hardly see how we can achieve much if the ministers of the church do not want us."[36]

The Foster Schoolhouse affair was indicative of a certain susceptibility on the part of Kansas Mennonites to encroachment by American revivalism. By virtue of a congregational form of church polity, local Mennonite congregations were vulnerable to various influences of American religious trends. The structure of the General Conference Mennonite Church simply did not lend itself to any district involvement beyond that requested by the local church. According to its constitution the WDC was required to become involved if one-fifth of the local membership invited them. However, if the invitation was not also from the elder, a solution was highly unlikely. In any case, WDC involvement was usually in the form of an advisor, rather than that of a disciplinarian.

The Foster Schoolhouse movement dramatically illustrated the impact of American revivalism upon the Mennonites of central Kansas.

As far away as Mountain Lake, Minnesota, it was referred to as the "Great Reformation at Elbing." However, it was not the only schism to result from the infiltration of American Pietism into the Mennonite church.

The Bergthal Mennonite Church at Pawnee Rock experienced two schisms resulting in the creation of two non-Mennonite churches. In 1874 Dutch Volhynians settled near Pawnee Rock, several miles from the hub of Kansas Mennonite settlements. Until 1895 the Bergthal congregation was without an elder and used the services of the elders in the Canton and Pretty Prairie churches.

In 1888 a group of twenty-one members withdrew from the Bergthal congregation and organized the New Jerusalem Church.[37] Based on the teachings of Emanuel Swedenborg (1688-1772), the "Swedenborgian movement" was symbolic of the character of American religious pluralism. In 1893 and again in 1894, the WDC identified the movement as especially dangerous for weak and unestablished members. "Great power and much cunning is his terrible armor."[38] The organization of the New Jerusalem Church further illustrated the vulnerability of isolated Mennonite settlements in central Kansas. The Bergthal schism in the late nineteenth century was indicative of the splintering effect of American denominationalism.

In the 1920s another schism occurred in the Bergthal Church. It resulted from contact with a nearby Pentecostal group. As the holiness movement fragmented near the end of the nineteenth century, a new movement--Pentecostalism--developed within American revivalism. It was characterized by heightened emotionalism and the New Testament practice of glossolalia, or speaking in unknown tongues. In 1914 the Assembly of God Church organized from this movement.[39]

During the 1920s revivalistic Pentecostals established a church in nearby Great Bend. Several Bergthal members were drawn away from the Mennonite Church claiming that it lacked the vibrant spirituality of the Pentecostal group. In 1936 around a dozen disenchanted Mennonites joined the Assembly of God Church in Great Bend.[40]

Aspects of American Revivalism

Most Mennonite congregations in central Kansas survived the impact of American revivalism without a church split. However, every local church showed at least some of the evidence of revivalistic trends.

More than one Mennonite scholar studied at a Bible institute early in the twentieth century (table 6-1). The growth of Bible institutes in America was a powerful expression of American revivalism. The first such school was founded by D. L. Moody in Chicago in 1886. Shortly thereafter, R. A. Torey, former dean at Moody, organized the Bible Institute of Los Angeles (BIOLA). Literally hundreds of American Mennonites attended non-denominational Bible institutes during the first half of the twentieth century.[41]

TABLE 6-1

ATTENDANCE IN NON-MENNONITE BIBLE INSTITUTES
BY WESTERN DISTRICT CONFERENCE MENNONITES, 1925-1936

Church	No. Attending Bible Institutes
Emmaus Mennonite	19
First Mennonite of Newton.	8
Bergthal Mennonite	6
Zion Mennonite	6
First Mennonite of Ransom.	5

SOURCE: Taken from a survey by the Committee on Education, Western District Conference, 1925-1936, Mennonite Library and Archives, Bethel College, North Newton, Kansas.

Although no Bible institutes existed within the Western District Conference, several Mennonite young people attended BIOLA and Moody. A survey in 1937 by the WDC Committee on Education revealed that between 1925 and 1936 a total of forty-four WDC Mennonites enrolled at BIOLA while eight attended Moody. An additional seventeen attended John Brown University and Wheaton College, two fundamentalist liberal arts colleges. The Emmaus Mennonite Church (Whitewater) alone produced nineteen BIOLA students; the First Mennonite Church of Newton had three students at Moody, five at BIOLA, and four at Wheaton.[42]

Many of these students returned to their home congregations, freshly infused with revivalistic fervor. It is impossible to measure the full impact of a Bible institute education on the local church. It appears, however, that American revivalism gained a stronger foothold in Mennonite congregations through Bible institute alumni. A careful look at the five leading congregations producing Bible institute students verifies this assumption (Table 6-1). Bergthal and Zion both suffered revivalistic schisms in the twentieth century. Emmaus and First Mennonite of Newton displayed strong leanings toward American revivalism at various junctures in their histories.[43] There is no evidence concerning the impact of revivalistic schools on the Random congregation. It is clear that the enrollment of Kansas Mennonites in non-Mennonite Bible institutes was a further sign of acculturation. In 1938 Mennonite historian C. Henry Smith lamented the fact that too many Mennonites returned home from Bible institutes with their Anabaptist faith weakened.[44]

Nineteenth century American revivalism also prompted a twentieth century Mennonite emphasis on evangelism and missions. A number of interdenominational missionary agencies developed in conjunction with the 1870-1890 revivals in America. At about the same time, the General Conference Mennonites established their first mission work in the Indian Territory of Oklahoma. By 1900 over one hundred Mennonite missionaries, many of them from central Kansas, had served the Cheyenne-Arapaho Indian mission field. Several WDC churches supported the Indian work with finances and materials.[45]

The impetus to evangelize American Indians was not simply a result of Mennonite acculturation. The first Mennonite missions effort in America had European roots. South Germans participating at the 1860 organization of the General Conference established a missions theme for the GCM church. Russian and East European Mennonites who migrated to Kansas in the 1870s included a number of zealous missions advocates. Their association with the General Conference Mennonites strengthened the missions emphasis of both immigrants and American Mennonites.[46]

209

A conducive American religious environment served to activate
the existing missions zeal. American revivalism, in part, produced
such an environment with its emphasis on evangelism. Initially, a
lack of missions strategy hindered the Mennonite effort. Meanwhile,
other interdenominational mission agencies enlisted the assistance
of early Kansas Mennonites. One was the Gospel Missionary Union founded
by R. A. Torey. Although the organization did not support any doctrinal
positions contrary to those of the General Conference, it emphasized
experiential salvation, holiness of life, and an immersion form of
baptism.[47]

In a number of Kansas Mennonite churches, the roll call of
locally supported missionaries in the early twentieth century included
a significant number affiliated with interdenominational mission agencies. One study estimated that General Conference Mennonite Churches
supplied as many missionaries to non-Mennonite mission programs as
they did to their own denomination.[48] The Emmaus Mennonite Church
(Whitewater) illustrates this. Its centennial publication (1978)
listed thirty-one missionaries from the Whitewater congregation.
Only six served with the General Conference while the remainder served
under interdenominational mission agencies such as the Gospel Missionary
Union, Wycliffe Translators, and Go Ye Missions.[49]

Mennonite historian James C. Juhnke recognized the impact of
American religion on early General Conference mission efforts:

> At the same time North American Mennonites cannot deny that
> they have taken on the institutional shape, and much of the
> theology, of Protestant denominationalism. That Mennonites
> went into all the world to spread the gospel was due to a
> movement of Protestant renewal, not of Anabaptist renewal.[50]

A desire to emphasize the Anabaptist-Mennonite witness in missions
has been a relatively recent trend for Kansas Mennonites.[51]

The full impact of American revivalism on Kansas Mennonites
is, at best, difficult to assess. A varied response existed in each
local congregation and differed with every elder. In some respects,
American revivalism was an impetus to the growth of Sunday schools,
the language transition, the spread of gospel singing, and informal
services in local churches; it also led to church schisms and ingroup
bickering.

In a 1955 survey, 51 percent of the WDC held regular evangelistic
services for the sake of conversions while an additional 18 percent
used special meetings on an occasional basis.[52] However, these services
seldom involved the emotional appeal of nineteenth century revivalism.
They were modified to incorporate a distinctive Mennonite catechism
and believer's baptism as integral parts of salvation. This was typical
of the Mennonite response to American religion. Mennonites usually
accepted American innovations with certain modifications. The American
religious environment produced a fascinating paradox in the Mennonite
Church: as it acculturated an emerging consciousness developed.
No doubt the jolting experience of a world war reminded Mennonites
of their ethnoreligious distinctiveness. However, by 1939 their distinctiveness was less ethnocentric and increasingly religiocentric.

Modernist-Fundamentalist Controversy

Revivalism was not the only religious influence upon Kansas
Mennonites; modernism also made inroads into the WDC in the twentieth
century. There is a great deal of ambiguity in the entire matter

of the fundamentalist-modernist debate in American religious history.
The involvement of Kansas Mennonites is even more complex.

Generally speaking, fundamentalism was a response to growing
modernism in a number of denominations and church colleges across
America during the first half of the twentieth century. In 1909 a
series of twelve volumes of defense of conservative theology was published and over 3,000,000 copies distributed. Fundamentalism attacked
the higher criticism of modernist theologians. In 1922 Harry Emerson
Fosdick delivered a sermon entitled, "Shall the Fundamentalists Win?"
In this, he clearly joined the ranks of the modernists and sparked
a direct confrontation between modernists and fundamentalists.[53]

American fundamentalism was rooted in nineteenth century American
revivalism. Unlike the 1870-1890 period of revivalism, fundamentalism
was primarily a reactionary movement. When the revival fires of the
nineteenth century began to die down, there emerged a group of "modernists" who assimilated modern assumptions and values into the Christian
tradition. As theological liberals, they emphasized (in varying
degrees) God's divine work through evolutionary, natural, and historical
forces, the development of scripture out of natural processes, and
the continuing revelation of God, especially in the growing application
of Christian principles to society.[54]

It is difficult to imagine a Mennonite farmer engaging his
Presbyterian neighbor in a debate over the issues of modernism around
the turn of the century. The truth is the modernist-fundamentalist
controversy was a nonissue among most Kansas Mennonite laity. It
rarely made its way into Sunday school classes and seldom merited

reference from the pulpit. Most elders, with their limited theological training, would have been hard pressed to identify the issues of the modernist-fundamentalist debate, let alone take sides. The real battleground for the controversy was Bethel College, the educational extension of the Kansas Mennonites.

Mennonite colleges sailed turbulent waters in the 1920s. Bethel, Goshen, Bluffton, and Witmarsum Theological Seminary all experienced, in varying degrees, the impact of the modernist-fundamentalist controversy. John Horsch, an historian of the (Old) Mennonite Church, wrote several books and articles attacking modernist professors at Bluffton and Witmarsum Theological Seminary. In 1923 the controversy resulted in the closing of Goshen College for one year in an attempt to purge the school of elements of the modernist-fundamentalist debate.[55]

The very fact that Bethel was a liberal arts college engendered suspicions among Kansas Mennonites. In 1916 these suspicions reached a boiling point when two professors publicly disagreed over the dating of the book of Daniel. The ultimate issue was the teaching of higher criticism at Bethel, a modernist characteristic. The board of directors finally dismissed one of the participants in the debate, Gustav Enss. Enss had severely criticized other Bethel professors for teaching what he perceived to be modernism. However, the departure of Enss did not terminate the controversy.[56]

In 1918 the college board investigated two Bible professors for reportedly teaching modernism. Both subsequently resigned their positions. A year later President J. W. Kliewer also tendered his resignation, at least in part as a response to this incident. The board then drafted a set of twelve basic doctrines that faculty members had to sign as a condition of continued employment. At the same time the Western District Conference brought Bethel under conference control by means of a $100,000 WDC contribution. After 1921 Bethel was no longer controlled by a private corporation.[57]

Although suspicions continued to exist, both sides avoided a major confrontation until 1932 when a financial crisis precipitated an eruption. Indebtedness increased from $16,276.59 in 1923 to $100,834.91 in 1930, mostly as a result of a depressed agricultural market in the 1920s. Kansas Mennonites were forced to reevaluate their commitment to higher education and Bethel College.[58]

At this point in the school's history an old debate emerged, this time staged within the context of the modernist-fundamentalist controversy. A major faction of the WDC had always felt uncomfortable with the idea of a liberal arts Mennonite college. Instead, they preferred an institute exclusively designed for the training of ministers, missionaries, and parochial school teachers. By 1930 Bethel had strayed a long way from the 1883 Halstead Seminary concept. To many observers, the clamor for a ministerial training school in 1930 sounded very much like a demand for a fundamental Bible institute.

The leader of the Bible school concept was Mennonite elder and publisher H. P. Krehbiel. Krehbiel requested that the WDC take back its $100,000 from the Bethel College endowment fund and use the money to found a Bible school. Krehbiel was no rapid assimilator seeking to establish a Bible institute along fundamentalist lines. His desire to establish a "Christian Workers School" was, in part, a reaction to the secularized, worldly development of Bethel College in its first three decades. Personal conflicts also figured into the crisis.[59]

The entire issue came to a head at a special session of the WDC on April 6, 1932. A vigorous debate resulted over the purpose of the college and the ownership of the WDC contribution of $100,000. In a close vote (149 to 131) the WDC decided that the $100,000 could not be withdrawn from Bethel's endowment. In doing so, the WDC reaffirmed its confidence in Bethel College and opted not to establish a Bible institute.[60]

Bethel survived the modernist-fundamentalist debate by the narrowest of margin. Interestingly enough, no actual modernists or fundamentalists were directly involved in the debate. Kansas Mennonites certainly supported the preservation of doctrinal absolutes but hesitated to affiliate completely with the fundamentalist movement because of its non-Mennonite origins. On the other hand, even the most progressive Mennonite educators stopped short of a full modernist stance. The controversy was further complicated by an unusual alliance between liberals and conservatives, progressives and traditionalists, and Americanizers and anti-Americanizers. Both liberals and conservatives supported Bethel. Both progressives and traditionalists supported Krehbiel's Bible school concept. The sides were too thoroughly mixed to present a simple struggle between modernists and fundamentalists.

At the same time the Bethel College controversy of 1916-1932 revealed the impact of the national modernist-fundamentalist debate on Kansas Mennonites. The controversy was preceded by a nine year General Conference membership (1908-1917) in the Federal Council of Churches. Little mention of the Federal Council existed in the WDC minutes. One exception was the WDC resolution in 1913 to support Federal Council opposition to "licensed vice" during the Panama Exposition in San Francisco in 1915.

When the Tabor Mennonite Church (Goessel) joined the Federal Council in 1911, it reported its affiliation to Senators Joseph Bristow and Charles Curtis in Topeka as if to affirm patriotic credibility. Although membership in the Federal Council of Churches was an attempt to identify with a larger American religious body, Mennonites were not prepared to accept a complete deviation from their historical distinctives. The Federal Council decision to endorse American involvement in the First World War resulted in the withdrawal of the General Conference.[61]

The post-war modernist-fundamentalist controversy further alienated many Mennonites from the Federal Council of Churches. Meanwhile, the Bethel College controversy (1916-1932) served to alienate progressive Mennonites from traditional Mennonites. In subsequent years, the support of Bethel by local congregations was closely related to the 1916-1932 controversy. David Haury noted in his history of the WDC that conservative congregations posed the greatest opposition for Bethel. Many of these same churches reflect various levels of fundamentalist practices.[62]

One obvious evidence of the modernist-fundamentalist debate at Bethel College was the establishment in 1943 of Grace Bible Institute

in Omaha, Nebraska. Several General Conference Mennonites were extensively involved in the planning and operation of the Omaha school.
In some respects, Grace was the fruition of H. P. Krehbiel's desire
to establish a Bible school in Kansas in 1931. Although the WDC refused
to endorse Grace, a number of Kansas Mennonites continued their studies
at the Omaha school.[63]

The fact that Kansas Mennonites were drawn into the national
modernist-fundamentalist debate in spite of an historical position
of noninvolvement in ecumenical issues is further evidence of their
assimilation from 1874 to 1939. Although most WDC leaders tried to
avoid conflict over the modernist-fundamentalist controversy, Kansas
Mennonites in the early twentieth century no longer maintained a safe
distance from American Protestantism. Their nineteenth century involvement in American revivalism and the temperance movement and the decision
of the General Conference to join the Federal Council of Churches
in 1908 precluded any desire to remain aloof of the modernist-fundamentalist debate. As in other American denominations, the debate was
divisive, both within the WDC and in local churches. Although most
WDC churches by 1939 chose to side with neither modernism nor fundamentalism, hardly a congregation escaped the impact of the debate.

Secularism

Secularism is difficult to define in relation to assimilation.
Simply defined secularism is "not religious in character nor devoted
to religious ends."[64] Various aspects of secularism confronted Russian
and East European Mennonites upon their arrival in central Kansas.
Growing materialism, Sunday baseball and other Sabbath activities,

patriotic expression exceeding the boundaries of traditional Mennonite nonconformity, and the attraction of secret societies were a few of the secularizing influences in late nineteenth century America. These influences had their origins in neither fundamentalism nor modernism; they were distinctly secular, "not religious in character nor devoted to religious ends."

As model subjects for Max Weber's concept of the Protestant work ethic, most Kansas Mennonites made significant material gain from 1874 to 1939. Economic success naturally enhanced secularization. The growth of a secularist spirit among Kansas Mennonites may be observed in their Sabbath activities. Although congregational records do not reveal formal changes, the fact remains that typical church members gradually moved away from strict sabbatarianism and the traditional custom of Sunday visiting to working in the fields when necessary and enjoying recreational activities on Sunday.

Historically, a number of Mennonite communities managed to keep businesses closed on Sundays and on at least one occasion, protested the opening of the Kansas State Fair on the "Lord's day."[65] At least three congregations expressed concern over the issue of Sunday baseball; Mennonite legislator H. P. Krehbiel sponsored a bill to outlaw Sunday baseball in Kansas.[66] During the Great Depression, however, some Mennonites agreed to work in the oil fields in an attempt to maintain hard-to-find jobs.[67]

The most thorough treatment of the Mennonite response to a secular government is James C. Juhnke's A People of Two Kingdoms (1975). Juhnke traced the reaction of Kansas Mennonites to American politics and patriotism from 1874 to 1940. He determined that Kansas Mennonites were reluctant participants in American politics due to their historical suspicion of worldly governments. The First World War forced Mennonites into a painful conflict between the display of American patriotism and the maintenance of the doctrine of nonresistance and a sense of Deutschtum.[68]

Juhnke concluded that out of the tension of a Mennonite encounter with secular patriotism during World War I, there arose a creative, positive Mennonite response: Mennonite relief programs, alternative service, and a heightened sensitivity to the evils of American national-ism. By 1940 a reverse acculturation began among Mennonites who perceived the critical necessity of preserving group identity in the face of American patriotism.[69]

An issue that clearly reflected the threat of American secularism as an assimilating agent was the secret society, or lodge question. Milton M. Gordon viewed entrance by immigrants into clubs, cliques, and institutions of the host society as structural assimilation. According to Gordon, the key to the assimilation process is structural assimilation. Once this level occurs, all other forms of assimilation naturally follow.[70] Practically speaking for Mennonites, lodge member-ship meant complete assimilation and eventual dissociation with a Mennonite identity.

American Mennonites historically maintained opposition to secret societies. The lodge question was germane to the Mennonite concept of nonconformity. It stemmed from the apostolic admonition:

Be ye not unequally yoked together with unbelievers; for what fellowship hath righteousness with unrighteousness? Or what communion hath light with darkness? And what concord hath

Christ with Belial? Or what part hath he that believeth with
an infidel? (II Cor. 6:14-15)

Mennonites objected to secret societies because of their
oathbound, secretive nature. The lodge title of "Worshipful Grand
Master" smacked of blasphemy. Mennonites especially took issue with
the Masonic promise of "salvation" to those who kept lodge rules and
maintained the concept of "work righteousness."

The General Conference established one of its strongest stands
on the lodge question. In 1861 the conference stated that a member
of a Mennonite congregation could not be a member of a secret society.
In 1896 the conference issued a terse statement on secret societies:
"It is the conviction of the General Conference that all secret
societies without exception are in direct opposition to the letter
and spirit of the Word of God."[71] The conference refused to admit
new churches that allowed lodge members to hold church membership
and requested existing member congregations to purge themselves from
"the lodge evil."[72]

Since nineteenth century European Mennonites knew little of
secret societies, the General Conference stand was important to Kansas
Mennonites. The conference provided an infexible position on the
lodge question and aided in the battle against the invasion of secret
societies in local congregations. In 1899 "the sinister encroachment"
of secret societies again surfaced in General Conference sessions.
The conference introduced a letter from the president of Wheaton College
condemning secret societies as "enemies of Jesus Christ." The 1899
conference adopted two resolutions: one called for all delegates
to make open statements on the subject; the other sought to expel

all conference churches that did not remove lodge-attending members.[73]

The 1902 General Conference session added to its previous stand by providing a definitive examination of secret societies. In 1914 a lodge committee was formed to draft a plan by which General Conference Churches could be freed of lodge members. In 1917 the committee brought a detailed report to the General Conference session describing proper steps for the elimination of body lodge members and churches that refused to discipline lodge members. In 1926 the conference requested that pastors use the pulpit to do battle with secret societies. The lodge committee was summoned to conduct periodic surveys to maintain a watchful eye on conference churches for the infiltration of lodge members.[74]

In some respects, the General Conference response to the secret society issue was directly associated with the lodge activities of Kansas Mennonites. Many of the original church constitutions of Russian and East European congregations failed to address the issue of secret societies. The 1876 constitution of the First Mennonite of Halstead merely stated that members were "expected to avoid secret societies." However, when the question became a hotly contested issue in the Kansas Conference during the 1880s, the Halstead Church strengthened its stand with the statement that "no one can be a member of a secret society and of this church at the same time."[75]

The conflict that drew Kansas Conference attention to the lodge question took place in the First Mennonite Church of Newton in 1885-1886. During a congregational meeting (Bruderschaft) on September 27, 1885, elder Leonhard Sudermann addressed the group on the evils

their reference as "liberals." They stated that they preferred not
to associate with the Kansas Conference if it meant changing their
constitution to exclude secret society members. This action had the
effect of withdrawing their application.[78]

The Newton affair had repercussions for the entire Kansas Conference. Prior to 1886 the lodge question was practically a nonissue
for Kansas Mennonites. Their European experience gave no indication
that secret societies posed a threat to Mennonite identity. The 1882
position of the Kansas Conference on secret societies was worded in
a mild, nonoffensive manner: ". . . it is not necessary for any Mennonites to join a secret society."[79] However, the Newton conflict provided
a strongly worded Kansas Conference stand forbidding admittance of
secret society members into the church as well as churches with secret
society members into the conference. Local congregations followed
the lead of the Kansas Conference after 1887 and included constitutional
statements prohibiting membership in secret societies.[80]

What attracted Mennonites to secret societies? Why would an
immigrant willingly terminate his church affiliation simply to gain
membership in a Masonic Lodge? No doubt the actual reasons varied
for different individuals. Some united with secret societies for
the fellowship they provided. Certainly it was a much broader fellowship than what an immigrant church allowed. However, it is hard to
imagine that Mennonites were willing to sacrifice the fellowship of
the church for that of a lodge after a mere decade in America. Some
may have joined secret societies for their patriotic appeal. The
1899 General Conference was careful to point out that its opposition

to secret societies was not an "unAmerican" stand.[81]

Some Mennonites may have joined secret societies for financial benefits, or for the benevolence that characterized lodges. Whatever the cause, secret societies continued to attract Kansas Mennonites and the church maintained its opposition into the twentieth century. At times church leaders were uncertain as to what constituted a secret society. In 1889 the First Mennonite Church of Newton decided that the Farmers Alliance was a secret society and in 1891 refused membership to a young man because he belonged to the Newton Athletic Club. The Tabor Mennonite Church (Goessel) concluded in 1917 that the Grange in the South was similar to the Free Masonry and "membership should be avoided for all Mennonites."[82]

The issue of secret societies once again surfaced at the 1927 Western District Conference session. The WDC restated its previous stand and pledged to assist local congregations in the fight against the "lodge business." Furthermore, it resolved that congregations with lodge members could continue to send delegates to WDC sessions as long as the local church maintained a battle against secret societies.[83] Although the WDC retained a strong anti-secret society position from 1886 to World War II, it became increasingly difficult to enforce its position at the local level. New churches seeking admission to the WDC, however, were carefully scrutinized for lodge membership. A new group in McPherson was denied admission for three years in the 1940s until the congregation ridded itself of two Elks Club members. It was not until 1976 that a revised constitution dropped the traditional WDC opposition to secret societies.[84]

The secret society issue was indicative of pervasive secularism amongst Kansas Mennonites. Unlike revivalism, modernism, and fundamentalism, secularism had few outspoken supporters in the church. Its threat was less obvious; the exception was the lodge issue with its direct confrontation to nonconformity. This prompted the Kansas Conference and WDC leaders to respond with their strongest, most unified voice, condemning secret society membership for Mennonites. The very fact that the lodge question was such a hotly contested issue among Kansas Mennonites is evidence of structural assimilation and its growing attraction to immigrants and their children from 1874 to 1939.

Nonresistance

The matter of nonresistance figured largely in Mennonites immigration to North America in the 1870s. Russian and East European Mennonites arrived in a period marking the longest interval of peace in American history. However, beginning in 1898, America was at war three times in less than a half century. American religion made important inroads into the Mennonite doctrine of nonresistance. Certain nonreligious factors also figured along with the influences of revivalism, modernism, and fundamentalism.

The initial Mennonite response to the War of 1898 was one of embarrassment. A special meeting by the WDC on May 7, 1898 revealed the nature of their dilemma. Mennonites wished to remain true to their historical confession of nonresistance, but also desired to prove their loyalty to the United States. In an apologetic manner, a carefully worded WDC statement reflected the inability of Mennonites to join in the actual fighting. At the same time they commended

President McKinley for avoiding war with Spain for as long as possible. Although few Mennonites actually volunteered for military service, most proclaimed their willingness to be involved in the war in a noncombatant role (Red Cross). These were the same people who just twenty-five years earlier refused to render alternative service to the Czar of Russia in the form of forestry service (Forsteidienst).[85] A slight but noticeable crack was evident in the historical Mennonite position of nonresistance.

America's entry into World War I again challenged the Mennonite stand on nonresistance. When war broke out in Europe in 1914, Mennonites asserted their Germanic national identity. When America declared war on Germany in 1917, Kansas Mennonites sought to emphasize their religious identity. The Mennonite image suffered greatly from their initial Germanic identity and a subsequent refusal to fight. Admittedly, the war caught Mennonites by surprise. As a result of four decades in America without a draft, nonresistant Mennonites were not prepared for the challenge of World War I. As a result, less than half of those drafted, 45 percent, refused service of any kind, while 48 percent accepted noncombatant service, and 7 percent accepted regular army service.[86]

Kansas Mennonites learned several painful lessons from World War I. The war revealed the stark reality of an unchallenged stand on nonresistance weakened by four decades of acculturation. American revivalism and fundamentalism provided a capable ally for Mennonites on such issues as temperance, secret societies, Sunday schools, and evangelism. Their brief association with the Federal Council of

Churches provided further allies with regard to temperance, Sunday observance, higher education, and various issues of morality. However, when America entered the war, Kansas Mennonites found themselves standing alone on the issue of nonconformity. Both fundamentalists and modernists enthusiastically supported America's entry into World War I. Kansas Mennonites did not actively seek out an alliance with historic peace churches until after the war.

The abandonment of Mennonites by American Protestantism in 1917 had a greater impact than simply standing alone on the nonconformity issue. As a "church of the disinherited," the Anabaptist-Mennonite tradition was steeped in lonely stands. What made nonconformity so difficult for Kansas Mennonites in 1917 was the fact that during the previous four decades they had courted and periodically joined hands with American Protestantism on various issues. In World War I there were no allies with whom Mennonites could join forces.

Nineteenth century American revivalism and its twentieth century step-child, fundamentalism, had an eroding impact on Mennonite nonresistance. Mennonites attending fundamentalist Bible institutes encountered superpatriotism during World War I. Mennonite historian Robert Kreider traced a lack of conscientious objectors in World War II to the influence of fundamentalist Bible institutes. Mennonite enrollment at Moody and BIOLA did little to bolster the Anabaptist position on nonresistance. Rodney J. Sawatsky, in a 1973 University of Minnesota thesis, blamed fundamentalism for undermining the stand of nonresistance in the (Old) Mennonite Church. If this was true for the (Old) Mennonites, Sawatsky concluded it was even more applicable

to the General Conference Mennonite Church. James C. Juhnke agreed
that fundamentalism shook a few Kansas Mennonites and congregations
loose from their traditional doctrine of nonresistance.[87]

Fundamentalism alone was not responsible for the majority of
Kansas Mennonite draftees who accepted some form of military service
barely four decades after refusing the same in Russia. Mennonite
identification with progressive American Protestantism also contributed
to a weakened position of nonconformity in 1917. For nine years (1908-
1917) the General Conference was a charter member of the Federal Council
of the Churches of Christ in America (FCCCA). The FCCCA organized
in 1908 as a reaction to "sensational commercialism presently demonstrated by evangelists." Although there were certain elements of
the FCCCA which supported principles contrary to those of traditional
Mennonites (secret societies, higher Biblical criticism, etc.),
Mennonite delegates usually reported only the most positive aspects
of FCCCA conventions.[88]

In April, 1917, the FCCCA called a special meeting in response
to America's entry to the war. It subsequently registered complete,
unrestricted support for the United States war effort. General Conference Mennonite leaders selected a committee to investigate the FCCCA
decision. The committee returned to the General Conference with two
reports: a majority and a minority report. The majority report favored
the retention of FCCCA membership while the minority report dissented.
After a lengthy debate, the General Conference voted to accept the
minority report and severed ties with the FCCCA.[89]

The report of the vote in the September 27, 1917, _Mennonite_
indicated that the conference relinquished FCCCA membership with serious

227

reservations. Even though the FCCCA thoroughly supported America's war effort, a majority of the investigating committee still preferred membership. The fact that the decision to sever ties was difficult and based upon the minority report was evidence of a General Conference affinity for progressive American Protestantism. It is conceivable that modernism also contributed to the weakening of Mennonite nonresistance by 1917.[90]

It is difficult to evalute the impact of secularism on nonresistance. As Kansas Mennonites gained materially during the first four decades in America, they became vulnerable to pervasive secularism. Kansas Mennonites demonstrated little systematic effort to perpetuate the principle of nonresistance in either churches or parochial schools from 1874 to 1898. Since the War of 1898 was so brief and did not include a draft, a brief Mennonite interest in nonresistance quickly disappeared.

World War I did more than reveal a weakening in the Mennonite doctrine of nonresistance. It forced Kansas Mennonites to develop an organized response to future American militarism. In 1921 the WDC petitioned the president of the United States to pursue disarmament. In 1922 Kansas Mennonites sent a delegate to Bluffton, Ohio, to affiliate with other historic peace churches. In 1925 the WDC joined forces with Friends University in Wichita for the promotion of the peace cause. In the fall of 1935 as the clouds of war again gathered on the European horizon, Kansas Mennontes joined forces with Brethren and Friends in Newton to establish a "Statement of Position" on war and a proper concept of patriotism. They had learned the lessons of war well.[91]

Mennonites across North America learned other lessons through the disastrous experience of World War I. The war hindered any Mennonite display of loyalty and patriotism. Without the ability to fight, Mennonites floundered in an attempt to show support for the United States. Following the war, nonresistant Mennonites engaged in visible programs of service and relief. Refugees from Russia prompted a benevolent response from Mennonites across North America. Kansas Mennonites participated in a number of relief programs beginning in the 1920s and expanding to the present time.

The Mennonite search for sacrifical, benevolent enterprises was compensation for their inability to fight. The rapid development and growth of the Mennonite Central Committee (MCC) and its affiliated relief programs reflected the need of Mennonites to sacrifice so that they might be perceived as acceptable citizens. The dilemma of the War of 1898 continued in World War I -- how to maintain nonresistance while demonstrating loyalty to the United States. Visible programs in the 1920s such as disaster relief, refugee relocation, and food distribution provided a solution to the dilemma. Thus, concluded James C. Juhnke, Mennonite benevolence is a product of Americanization.[92]

The First World War caused Kansas Mennonite churches to reconsider alliances with both modernism and fundamentalism, not just on the issue of nonresistance. Although local congregations occasionally joined hands with one or the other force during the 1920s and 1930s, WDC leaders maintained a position of cautious distance from both extremes of modernism and fundamentalism due to the lessons of the First World War.

Conclusion

Kansas Mennonites encountered a religious paradox in nineteenth century America. On one hand a pluralistic environment tolerated the pursuit of group distinctiveness by European immigrants. At the same time, the trends of American Protestantism were emphatic, diverse, individualistic, and nearly impossible to escape. America was a polychotomy of religious influence. What immigrants initially perceived as an environment conducive to ethnoreligious preservation turned out to be far more divisive and influential than that of eastern Europe and southern Russia.

American revivalism made inroads into Kansas congregations by means of protracted meetings, evangelism, the temperance movement, and Bible institutes. Although revivalism took on a modified form in Mennonite churches, special meetings and certain ingroup quarrels were evidence of its presence. Each church varied in its response to American revivalism; congregations outside the center of Mennonite settlements usually revealed the greatest impact. Schisms producing splinter groups at Elbing and Pawnee Rock reflected the extreme influence of revivalism.

Even though most Mennonite leaders tried to steer clear of the national modernist-fundamentalist debate, Bethel College experienced a small scale version of the controversy between 1916 and 1932. The fact that no actual fundamentalists or modernists were involved in the college debate did little to reduce accusations and suspicions. Kansas Mennonites were attracted to fundamentalism by its emphasis on personal piety, Bible teaching, and evangelistic fervor. Tension of secret societies. During the brief discussion that followed, a member questioned the elder on certain accusations regarding Masons. In a spirited exchange the elder found himself challenged by a Mason who was also a member of his own flock. Noting that Mennonites could not be members of secret societies, Sudermann ruled the protestor out of order and abruptly adjourned the congregational meeting. However, this did not end the conflict.[76]

A group of families supportive of the Masonic Lodge withdrew from the First Mennonite Church of Newton and organized another congregation in 1886. Had their relationship with other Kansas Mennonites terminated at that point, the lodge question might never have become an issue in the Kansas Conference. However, members of the new congregation wished to retain their identity as Mennonites and at the next Kansas Conference (October 11-13, 1886), they petitioned for admittance.

When the 1886 Kansas Conference realized that the petitioning group was the result of a schism over the lodge issue, admission was denied. The Kansas Conference indicated that its stand on secret societies was the same as that of the First Mennonite Church of Newton. Conference leaders encouraged the petitioning group to purge itself of secret society members before further seeking Kansas Conference membership.[77]

At the October 1887 session, a committee on the lodge question reported to the Kansas Conference. Leaders of the First Mennonite Church of Newton, the Kansas Conference, and the petitioning group had gathered the previous March to iron out differences. At one point in the meeting the leaders of the petitioning group took offense to between fundamentalism and traditional Anabaptism grew out of the former's militaristic nationalism during World War I. By 1939 most Kansas Mennonites pursued a precarious path between American fundamentalism and modernism.

Kansas Mennonites did not escape the impact of pervasive secularism. In spite of an adament stand against secret societies, the Western District Conference found it increasingly more difficult to combat the "lodge evil."

The First World War revealed the impact of revivalism-fundamentalism, modernism, and secularism on the basic Anabaptist doctrine of nonresistance. Kansas Mennonites were jarred into the realization that worldly materialism and a whirlwind courtship with American Protestantism had weakened their historic stand on nonresistance.

From 1920 to 1939 Kansas Mennonite church leaders reflected upon the experiences of World War I. Rather than seeking alliances with the modernist Federal Council of Churches or various fundamentalist organizations, they sought out historic peace churches and established a coalition stand on nonresistance. At the same time, Kansas Mennonites asserted their own sense of loyalty and patriotism through the development of numerous relief programs. This required cooperation with other Mennonite groups and resulted in an emerging consciousness of a larger Mennonite body. However, by 1939 this emerging identity was less ethnocentric and religiocentric.

CHAPTER VI - ENDNOTES

1. Andrew M. Greeley, The Denominational Society (London: Scott, Foresman, and Company, 1972), pp. 102-07.

2. Mennonite Encyclopedia, s.v. "Pietism," by Cornelius Krahn.

3. George M. Thomas, "Rational Exchange and Individualism: Revivalism Religion in the United States, 1870-1890," in The Religious Dimension: New Directions in Quantitative Research, ed. Robert Wulknow (New York: Academic Press, 1979), pp. 351-72; Timothy L. Smith, Revivalism and Social Reform in Mid-Nineteenth Century America (New York: Abingdon Press, 1957). For a detailed account of the holiness movement see Melvin Easterday Dieter, The Holiness Revival in the Nineteenth Century (Metuchen, New Jersey: Scarecrow Press, Inc., 1980); Charles E. Jones, Perfectionist Persuasion: The Holiness Movement and American Methodism (Metuchen, New Jersey: Scarecrow Press, Inc., 1974); Timothy L. Smith, Called Unto Holiness (Kansas City, Missouri: Nazarene Publishing House, 1962).

4. George M. Marsden, Fundamentalism and American Culture: The Shaping of Twentieth Century Evangelicalism: 1870-1925 (New York: Oxford University Press, 1980).

5. Mennonite Encyclopedia, s.v. "Revival," by Harold S. Bender; Samuel F. Pannabecker, Open Doors (Newton, Kansas; Faith and Life Press, 1975), pp. 12, 112; C. Henry Smith, The Story of the Mennonites (Newton, Kansas: Faith and Life Press, 1964, fifth edition), pp. 399-409; Cornelius J. Dyck, An Introduction to Mennonite History (Scottdale, Pennsylvania: Herald Press, 1981), pp. 307-09; John C. Wenger, Glimpses of Mennonite History and Doctrine (Scottdale, Pennsylvania: Herald Press, 1981), pp. 307-09; John C. Wenger, Glimpses of Mennonite History and Doctrine (Scottdale, Pennsylvania: Herald Press, 1947), pp. 107-09, and The Mennonite Church in America (Scottdale, Pennsylvania: Herald Press, 1966), pp. 91-92, 238-39; John A. Toews, A History of the Mennonite Brethren Church (Fresno, California: Board of Christian Literature, General Conference of Mennonite Brethren Churches, 1975), pp. 195-96, 364-67; Jasper Abraham Huffman, History of the Mennonite Brethren in Christ (New Carlisle, Ohio: The Bethel Publishing Co., 1920); Jared F. Gerig and Walter H. Lugibihl, The Missionary Church Association (Berne, Indiana: Economy Printing Concern, 1950); Eileen Lageer, Merging Streams: The Story of the Missionary Church (Elkhart, Indiana: Bethel Publishing Co., 1979); Kevin Rempel, "The Evangelical Mennonite Brethren" (Unpublished paper, Mennonite Library and Archives, Bethel College, North Newton, Kansas, 1982).

6. Minutes of the Western District Conference, 7-9 November 1894, Mennonite Library and Archives, Bethel College, North Newton, Lageer, p. 109-11; Emma King Risser, History of the Pennsylvania Mennonite Church in Kansas (Scottdale, Pennsylvania: Mennonite Publishing House, 1958), pp. 72-82.

7. Minutes, 8-9 November 1897; 19-21 October 1910; 28-30 October 1914

8. Jonas A. Stucky, Epochs of History of First Mennonite Church of Pretty Prairie, Kansas (n.p., 1954), p. 55; Minutes, 19-21 October 1921.

9. Henry Peter Krehbiel, The History of the General Conference of the Mennonite Church of North America, vol. 2 (Newton, Kansas: Herald Publishing Co., 1938), p. 255.

10. Minutes, 5-7 November 1919.

11. Timothy L. Smith, Revivalism and Social Reform, pp. 167-68.

12. Cornelius C. Janzen, "Americanization of Russian Mennonites in Central Kansas" (M.A. thesis, Kansas University, 1914), p. 68; Ronald J. Andres, Centennial Reflections: Zion 100 (n.p., 1983), p. 15; David Haury, Prairie People (Newton, Kansas: Faith and Life Press, 1981), p. 70; David C. Wedel, The Story of Alexanderwohl (North Newton, Kansas: Mennonite Press, 1974), p. 160.

13. Don W. Wilson, Governor Charles Robinson of Kansas (Lawrence, Kansas: The University Press of Kansas, 1975), pp. 116-18; Kenneth S. Davis, Kansas: A Bicentennial History (New York: W. W. North and Co., Inc., 1976), pp. 143-47.

14. Minutes, 27-29 October 1879.

15. Minutes, 16-17 October 1883.

16. D. L. Funk, "What is Temperance?" Mennonite 15 (July 1900): 75.

17. H. G. Allebach, "Mrs. Carrie Nation," Mennonite 16 (April 1901): 51.

18. "Maessiges Trinken," Christlicher Bundesbote, 1 January 1896, p. 3.

19. Henry Peter Krehbiel, History of the Mennonite General Conference, vol. 1 (St. Louis: A. Wieblisch and Son Printing Co., 1898), pp. 479-80.

20. Quoted in James C. Juhnke, A People of Two Kingdoms (Newton, Kansas: Faith and Life Press, 1975), p. 44.

21. "Prohibition," Der Herold 4 April 1919, p. 4.

22. "Die Prohibition," Der Herold 11 March 1920, p. 2.

23. Henry Peter Krehbiel, vol. 2, p. 292.

24. "The Dry Issue Has Won," Mennonite Weekly Review 7 November 1928, p. 4.

25. Henry Peter Krehbiel, vol. 2, p. 254.

26. Minutes, 24-25 October 1934.

27. James C. Juhnke, A People of Two Kingdoms, pp. 43, 123.

28. Records of the Mennonite Brethren in Christ Church, Peabody, Kansas (Midwest District Headquarters of the Missionary Church, Lincoln, Nebraska); Lageer, pp. 93-95.

29. Gerig and Lugibihl, p. 80; Lageer, pp. 109-11; Louis A. Janzen, "Forbid Him Not" (Unpublished paper, Mennonite Library and Archives, Bethel College, North Newton, Kansas, 1978), pp. 62-73.

30. Lageer, pp. 1-39.

31. Records of the Missionary Church, Newton, Kansas.

32. Louis A. Janzen, pp. 62-79; John M. Janzen, "Schism and Renewal in Three Central Kansas Mennonite Congregations" in The Quest for Community: Mennonite Separation and Integration, eds. Leo Driedger and Calvin Redekop (forthcoming); Mennonite Encyclopedia, s.v. "John A. Sprunger," "Light and Hope Orphanage," and "Light and Hope Publishing Company," by Harold S. Bender; Lageer, pp. 109-10.

33. John M. Janzen, "Schism and Renewal in Three Kansas Mennonite Parishes" (Unpublished paper, Mennonite Library and Archives, Bethel College, North Newton, Kansas, 19750, pp. 9-11.

34. Records of the Missionary Church, Newton, Kansas; Lageer, pp. 109-10.

35. C. H. Regier to Wilhelm J. Ewert, 12 April 1910, "Private Correspondence of Rev. Wm. J. Ewert," Mennonite Library and Archives, Bethel College, North Newton, Kansas.

36. J. J. Flickinger to Wilhelm J. Ewert, 23 May 1910, "Private Correspondence of Rev. Wm. J. Ewert, "Mennonite Library and Archives, Bethel College, North Newton, Kansas.

37. Haury, pp. 50-51, 182-83; Grant Siebert, History of the Bergthal Mennonite Church, Pawnee Rock, Kansas (Great Bend, Kansas: Grant Siebert, 1976), p. 45.

38. Minutes, 7-9 November 1894.

39. Vinson Synan, The Holiness-Pentecostal Movement in the United States (Grand Rapids, Michigan: William B. Eerdman's Publishing Company, 1971), pp. 95-116, 137.

40. Maxlyn Smith, "A Brief History of the Mennonites of Barton County, Kansas" (Unpublished paper, Mennonite Library and Archives, Bethel College, North Newton, Kansas, 1940), pp. 33-34.

41. Mennonite Encyclopedia, s.v., "Bible Institutes," by Harold S. Bender.

42. Survey by the Committee on Education, Western District Conference, 1925-1936, MLA.

43. Haury, pp. 251, 349-50; John D. Thiesen, "The More Things Change, the More They Stay the Same: A History of the First Mennonite Church, Newton, Kansas, 1878-1982" (Unpublished paper, Mennonite Library and Archives, Bethel College, North Newton, Kansas, 1982), p. 83.

44. C. Henry Smith, "Mennonite and Culture," Mennonite Quarterly Review 12 (April 1938): 80.

45. James C. Juhnke, "General Conference Mennonite Missions to the American Indians in the Late Nineteenth Century," Mennonite Quarterly Review 54 (April 1980): 117-34.

46. James C. Juhnke, A People of Mission (Newton, Kansas: Faith and Life Press, 1970), pp. 5-9.

47. Richard Harder, "A Comparison of the Gospel Missionary Union and the General Conference Commission of Overseas Missions" (Unpublished paper, Mennonite Library and Archives, Bethel College, North Newton, Kansas, 1969), p. 3.

48. James C. Juhnke, A People of Mission, pp. 97, 102.

49. Frank Busenitz, Ernest Claassen, Mrs. Henry Claassen, Mrs. B. G. Harder, and Walter Penner, History of the Emmaus Mennonite Church (Hillsboro, Kansas: Mennonite Brethren Publishing House, 1978), pp. 134-36.

50. James C. Juhnke, A People of Mission, p. 215.

51. Ibid., p. 107.

52. Maynard Shelly, "Practices and Trends in Mennonite Congregations," in Proceedings of the Study Conference on the Believer's Church (North Newton, Kansas: Mennonite Press, 1955), p. 30.

53. George M. Marsden, Fundamentalism and American Culture; Sameul Floyd Pannabecker, Faith in Ferment (Newton, Kansas, Faith and Life Press, 1968), pp. 221-27.

54. George M. Marsden, "From Fundamentalism to Evangelicalism: A Historical Analysis," in The Evangelicals, eds. David F. Wells and John D. Woodbridge (Grand Rapids, Michigan: Baker Book House Company, 1977), p. 144.

55. Pannabecker, Faith in Ferment, pp. 221-27; also see Rodney James Sawatsky, "The Influence of Fundamentalism on Mennonite Nonresist-ance 1908-1944" (M.A. thesis, University of Minnesota, 1973). Sawatsky examined only the (Old) Mennonite Church but made application to General Conference Mennonites as well. He concluded that fundamentalism was a greater threat to Mennonite nonresistance than either modernism or liberalism.

56. Haury, pp. 233-34.

57. Ibid., pp. 234-35; James C. Juhnke, A People of Mission, pp. 91-93; Peter J. Wedel, The Story of Bethel College (North Newton, Kansas: Bethel College, 1954), pp. 243-52.

58. Haury, pp. 235-36; Peter J. Wedel, The Story of Bethel College, pp. 339-343.

59. Haury, pp. 237-39.

60. Ibid., pp. 239-40.

61. Elias B. Sanford, Federal Council of Churches of Christ in America (Hartford: S. S. Scranton Company, 1916), p. 513; Henry Peter Krehbiel, vol. 2, pp. 279-84; Minutes, 9-11 October 1913; "Secretary's Report of the Congregational Meetings of the Tabor Mennonite Church, 1907-1926" (Mennonite Library and Archives, Bethel College, North Newton, Kansas), p. 13.

62. Haury, p. 252.

63. Ibid., pp. 240-44.

64. Webster's New International Dictionary of the English Language, 2nd ed. (1953), s.v. "secular."

65. Andres, p. 9; Minutes, 21-23 October 1925.

66. David C. Wedel, p. 68; James C. Juhnke, A People of Two Kingdoms, p. 77.

67. Otto D. Unruh, "Schisms of the Russian Mennonites of Harvey, McPherson, and Reno Counties, Kansas" (M.A. thesis, Kansas University, 1939), p. 157.

68. James C. Juhnke, A People of Two Kingdoms, pp. 153-57.

69. Ibid.

70. Milton M. Gordon, Assimilation in American Life (New York: Oxford University Press, 1964), pp. 67-71.

71. Henry Peter Krehbiel, vol. 1, p. 479.

72. Ibid.

73. Henry Peter Krehbiel, vol. 2, p. 73.

74. Ibid., pp. 74, 272-79, 413-15.

75. Loris Habegger, ed., The Flock and the Kingdom (n.p., 1975), p. 24.

76. Congregational minutes, 27 September 1887, First Mennonite Church of Newton, Newton, Kansas; Thieson, pp. 54-55; Menno Schrag, First Mennonite Church (n.p., 1978).

77. Minutes, 11-13 October 1886.

78. Minutes, 3-5 October 1887.

79. Minutes, 24 October 1882.

80. The Tabor Mennonite Church (Goessel) included a constitutional reference to secret societies typical of the churches in the WDC: "A member who joins some secret society, cannot at the same time be a member of the church." Tabor Mennonite Church Constitution, 1908, XIV-2 (Mennonite Library and Archives, Bethel College, North Newton, Kansas).

81. Encyclopedia Americana, 1978 ed., s.v. "Masonic Fraternity," by Henry Wilson Coil; Henry Peter Krehbiel, vol. 2, p. 73.

82. Thiesen, p. 54; "Secretary's Report," p. 24, 27.

83. Minutes, 19-20 October 1927.

84. Haury, pp. 309-10.

85. Minutes, 7 May 1898; James C. Juhnke, "Kansas Mennonites During the Spanish-American War," Mennonite Life 26 (April 1971): 70-72. At the First Mennonite Church of Newton, one individual actually volunteered for military service and saw combat in the Philippines. He was excommunicated but in 1905 was readmitted without question. See John D. Thiesen, p. 58; Congregational Minutes, 18 June 1905, 4 September 1905, First Mennonite Church of Newton, Newton, Kansas.

86. For a thorough treatment of the Kansas Mennonite response to World War I, see James C. Juhnke, A People of Two Kingdoms, pp. 95-110.

87. Robert Kreider, "Environmental Influences Affecting the
Decision of Mennonite Boys of Draft Age," Mennonite Quarterly Review
16 (October 1942): 250; Rodney J. Sawatsky, "The Influences of Fundamentalism on Mennonite Nonresistance" (M.A. thesis, University of Minnesota,
1973); James C. Juhnke, A People of Two Kingdoms, p. 134.

88. Henry Peter Krehbiel, vol. 2, pp. 279-84. Reports of
FCCCA conventions were common in the Mennonite. See "The Coming Inter-
Church Conference," Mennonite, 19 October 1905, p. 4; "Editorial,"
Mennonite, 17 December 1908, p. 4; "The Federation of Churches," Mennonite
13, February 1913, p. 4; "The Federal Council - What is it? What
does it do?", Mennonite, 29 March 1917, p. 2; "The Special Meeting
of the Federal Council," Mennonite, 17 May 1917, pp. 3-5; "Our Conference,"
Mennonite, 27 September 1917, p. 4.

89. Henry Peter Krehbiel, vol. 2, pp. 279-84.

90. "Our Conference," Mennonite, 27 September 1917, p. 4.

91. Minutes, 19-21 October 1921; 18-20 October 1922; 21-23
October 1925; 23-25 October 1935.

92. James C. Juhnke, "Mennonite Benevolence and Civic Identity:
The Post-War Compromise," Mennonite Life 25 (January 1970): 34-37.

CHAPTER VII

THE AMERICANIZATION OF CHURCH CUSTOMS

How shall we maintain and cultivate that reverence for spiritual values, for the Christian home, the school, and the Church which stamp us indelibly as a "peculiar people"?[1]

Henry Peter Krehbiel
1926

One of the basic tenets of Anabaptist-Mennonite doctrine over the past four and one-half centuries has been the concept of nonconformity. It is imbedded in Paul's admonition to the Roman Christians:

I beseech you therefore, brethren, by the mercies of God, that ye present your bodies a living sacrifice, holy, acceptable unto God, which is your reasonable service. And be not conformed to world: but be ye transformed by the renewing of your mind, that ye may prove what is that good, and acceptable, and perfect, will of God. (Romans 12:1,2)

Early Anabaptists clung to the notion that believers were to be separate from the world with its "fleshy lusts." They took seriously the warning of John:

Love not the world, neither the things that are in the world. If any man love the world, the love of the Father is not in him. For all that is in the world, the lust of the flesh, and the lust of the eyes, and the pride of life, is not of the Father, but is of the world. (I John 1:15, 16)

One of the earliest confessions of the Anabaptists, the Schleitheim confession of 1527, addressed the matter of nonconformity. Separation from the world was one of seven topics treated by the Confession, but each was embellished in the idea of nonconformity. Baptism was understood as a public acknowledgment of the believer's separation from the world. Nonresistance rejected the use of the "worldly sword." Anabaptist refusal to take the oath was consistent with nonconformity. Communion included only true believers. Excommunication was an instrument of purification, purging the church from worldliness (Weltlichkeit). The Elder served as a watchdog against conformity. The Schleitheim Confession did not offer a complete summary of the Christian faith, but treated extensively the matter of nonconformity. It called on the children of God to withdraw from every institution and person that was not truly Christian.[2] The strength of a local congregation's nonconformist stance was contingent upon the unquestionable authority of its elder.

Nonconformity produced a cornucopia of practices that distinguished Mennonites from other Protestant groups. Some practices were more directly related to nonconformity than others. Plain garb, hair covering for women, beards, German-language services, and restrictions on wearing jewelry, playing musical instruments, enjoying worldly recreation, desecrating the sabbath, joining secret societies, and indulging in materialist pursuits all were responses of Mennonite nonconformity to worldliness. Mennonite groups most successful in maintaining the outward signs of nonconformity are those who have "retreated to an island," as Mennonite historian Robert Friedmann observed.[3] This "anti-world" posture led theologian H. Richard Niebuhr to characterize Anabaptism as a "Christ against culture" prototype. Mennonite sociologist John C. Bennett perceived the Mennonite ethic as a "strategy of withdrawal."[4]

There is probably no other issue among Mennonites that has produced a more diversified response than that of nonconformity. Generally speaking, Mennonites who migrated "for sake of conscience" were more successful at maintaining the outward appearances of worldly separation. They usually abandoned an urban setting for a closed, rural environment, a "retreat to an island." The Amish, Hutterites, and Old Order Colony Mennonites best exemplify Niebuhr's radical type of "Christ against culture." Mennonites who refused to retreat from European urban centers were the least successful in maintaining the outward signs of nonconformity. In Holland, for instance, Mennonites choosing to remain in integrated communities rather than in closed groups displayed little external evidence of nonconformity by the late nineteenth century.[5]

An understanding of nonconformity is germane to any treatment of distinctive Mennonite church customs. Mennonites in central Kansas brought with them an Old World belief system that included various levels of response to the issue of nonconformity. Few practices were commonly shared by all Kansas Mennonites upon their arrival in the 1870s. This was due to their diverse European origins. The dominant group of Black Sea Mennonites experienced nearly a century of closed settlement in Russia. A high level of Mennonite ethical and cultural life discouraged any attraction to the surrounding Russian culture. Far removed from the influences of urban culture and fashion, Mennonite church customs in the nineteenth century were never exposed to any real danger of acculturation in Russia.[6]

Kansas Mennonites from other areas of Europe did not share the same European experience as Black Sea Mennonites. Rural West

242

Prussians, South Germans, and Swiss Mennonites maintained a conservative rural perspective on nonconformity until the nineteenth century when modern culture began to penetrate even isolated agrarian Mennonite groups. Swiss Volhynian Mennonites were of Amish background and retained some distinctive Amish traits in church worship during their stay in Russia. Even in Kansas their traditional religious practices reflected their Amish beginnings. By contrast, Dutch-Prussian Volhynians, or "Polish" Mennonites, experienced frequent contact with Polish and Russian environmental influences which in turn transformed their position of nonconformity. A loss of ethnoreligious cohesiveness was evident in their early years in Kansas. Swiss Galicians managed to maintain separation from the world during a century of relative isolation from other Mennonites in Europe. Dutch-Prussians via Polish Russia were similar to the South Russians in culture and church customs. They too managed to maintain separate settlements in a rural, Old World environment.[7]

The adjustment of long-held church customs to the new environment of America was a complex process. It was not simply a matter of encountering the influences of American Protestant church customs. Nineteenth century Mennonites in central Kansas represented a wide range of church practices indicative of the heterogeneous nature of the Kansas Conference. From 1874 to 1939 a dual acculturation process emerged -- Americanization and denominationalization. Denominationalization was the process by which Mennonite churches adapted customs and practices that were neither American nor common to their own group experience. They were common, however, to the experience of other Mennonite groups and prescribed to the concensus of the Kansas Conference. For instance, upon their arrival in America, some congregations practiced footwashing while others did not. Although autonomous decisions were permitted by local churches in the Kansas Conference in regard to such church customs, after several decades a more uniform "denominational" posture was adopted by most congregations which led to the disappearance of footwashing.

Sociologist Andrew Greeley identifies denominationalism as an Americanization phenomenon that results from a "belonging vacuum" created by the social disorganization of immigration. Denominationalism was only one level of assimilation for Kansas Mennonites. Philosopher Will Herberg's concept of "multiple melting pots" is also applicable to Mennonites. While the Kansas and Western District Conferences provided one melting pot for church customs, the Protestant American church environment provided another.[8]

As a consequence of Americanization, the Mennonite churches of central Kansas experienced significant changes in church customs, as did the clergy who carefully preserved these traditions. By the time of World War II, they had less an appearance of immigrant churches and more closely took on the characteristics of American congregations. This transformation may be observed in various church ordinances as well as in a clerical transition.

Ordinances

The early Anabaptists generally acknowledged three basic ordinances of faith: baptism, communion, and footwashing.[9] Each of these were affected by the Americanization of the church.

The most crucial issue in the formation of the sixteenth century
Anabaptist Movement centered on the practice of baptism. Early Anabaptists differed from both the Roman Catholic and Lutheran churches
in meaning and method of baptism. The latter reflected the notion
that baptism symbolically washed away sin and, as a sacrament, automati-
cally conveyed divine grace. To Anabaptists it merely symbolized
regeneration and a pledge to holy living. Anabaptists did not subscribe
to the practice of infant baptism as maintained by most sixteenth
century Christians. Instead, Anabaptists opted for a "believers'
baptism," entered into voluntarily by adults. Believers' baptism
was essential to the Anabaptist claim of separation from the world
and purity from sin. Only baptized believers were members of the
Church.[10]

Baptism usually took place in early adulthood and was preceded
by catechism classes. This marked the most important event in the
life of a Mennonite. The ceremony could be performed only by an elder
and usually took the form of pouring as opposed to immersion. Itinerant
ministers provided baptismal services for Kansas Conference churches
without an elder.

Two notable changes occurred in the baptismal practices of
East European and Russian Mennonites in central Kansas from 1874 to
1939: the tendency to receive infant-baptized members from
non-Mennonite churches without rebaptism and the lowering of the age
of baptismal candidates.

Initially, the Kansas Conference required individuals transfer-
ring memberships from denominations that practiced infant baptism

to submit to adult baptism before receiving membership status in a Mennonite church. In 1886 the Kansas Conference denied a Newton congregation conference membership because the new church's constitution accepted infant-baptized membership transfers without rebaptism. In 1888 the Garden Township Church applied for admission to the Kansas Conference under similar circumstances. The conference delayed a church's entry until it made a constitutional revision requiring rebaptism of child-baptized transfers. Garden Township refused to do so, stating that mandatory rebaptism restricted opportunities for church growth. The issue reached a standstill until the conference changed its own policy and allowed the admission of infant-baptized transfers into church membership. In 1892 Garden Township and another new congregation with a similar stance, West Zion (Moundridge), joined the conference.[11]

By 1939 most of the Western District Conference congregations had dropped the requirements for adult rebaptism of infant-baptized transfers. Membership was conferred on such persons "so long as they were satisfied with their infant form of baptism."[12] Eventually, this became the stand of the General Conference Mennonite Church. In light of an historical emphasis on a believer's baptism, the acceptance of infant-baptism members without required rebaptism was a significant sign of acculturation.

The other change in baptismal practices had to do with the ages of baptismal candidates. Russian and East European Mennonites traditionally practiced "adult" baptism in the nineteenth century. By 1939 the practice changed to include "adolescent" and even "child" baptism. Although baptismal records of WDC churches are not generally available, a close look at five congregations reveals the trend of lowering baptismal ages (table 7-1).

In each case the average baptismal age had dropped by 1939. Alexanderwohl (Goessel) and Hoffnungsau (Inman) were both South Russian congregations from the same Old World mother church. During the first four decades of their existence in America, the average baptismal age consistently remained in the nineteen to twenty-year-old range. However, after World War I baptismal ages were lowered. In the 1920s the average baptismal candidate was less than nineteen in both congregations (Alexanderwohl - 18.6; Hoffnungsau - 18.7). In the 1930s the average baptismal age of Alexanderwohl dropped to 18.1, while at Hoffnungsau the average age fell dramatically to 16.0. A further indication of the adult to adolescent baptism trend was the average age in the 1940s: 16.3 for Alexanderwohl and 16.3 for Hoffnungsau. By 1950 the average baptismal candidate at Alexanderwohl was fourteen years old, a convergence with confirmation practice in other churches.

A similar trend took place in the other three churches. Emmaus Mennonite Church (Whitewater) was a Prussian congregation with a few South Russian additions. In the nineteenth century, the average age of baptism (17.7) was nearly two years younger than that of the Alexanderwohl and Hoffnungsau churches (19.1 and 19.6). From 1900 to 1939 the average age gradually dropped from 17.7 to 16.7.

Burrton and Arlington were both twentieth century additions to the Western District Conference. As smaller congregations they allow interesting comparisons with the larger Alexanderwohl, Hoffnungsau, and Emmaus churches. Burrton was organized in 1907 from a mixed,

247

TABLE 7-1

AVERAGE AGE OF BAPTISM IN FIVE MENNONITE CONGREGATIONS

years	Emmaus ave. age (no. bap.)		Burrton ave. age (no. bap.)		Arlington ave. age (no. bap.)		Alexanderwohl ave. age (no. bap.)		Hoffnungsau ave. age (no. bap.)	
Before 1900	17.7	(71)	-	-	-	-	19.1	(693)	19.6	(250)
1900-1909	17.2	(47)	26.9	(12)	16.3	(17)	19.5	(299)	19.7	(169)
1910-1919	17.0	(68)	18.2	(43)	16.3	(13)	19.7	(343)	20.0	(163)
1920-1929	16.9	(98)	18.4	(30)	16.1	(25)	18.6	(229)	18.7	(96)
1930-1939	16.7	(92)	16.3	(42)	14.9	(13)	18.1	(199)	16.0	(86)

SOURCE: Compiled from the family records books of the Alexanderwohl Mennonite Church, Huffnungsau Mennonite Church, Emmaus Mennonite Church, Burrton Mennonite Church, and the Arlington Mennonite Church. All of these records are located in the Mennonite Library and Archives, Bethel College, North Newton, Kansas. Also see Carol D. Gaeddert, "A Study in the Change of Baptismal Age in the Alexanderwohl and Huffnungsau Churches" (Unpublished paper, MLA, Bethel College, North Newton, Kansas, 1953).

South Russian dominant constituency. Baptisms during the first three years were few (12) and included six persons over thirty years of age. This accounts for the unusually high average age of 26.9. By the end of the first World War, the average age of baptism was 18.2. Twenty years later it had fallen to 16.3, similar to that of Emmaus and Hoffnungsau in the 1930s and Alexanderwohl in the 1940s.

Arlington was a Galician congregation organized in 1905. Swiss and South Germans later joined the church. The average baptism age was comparatively young during the church's first five years (16.3). However, it was even younger by 1939 (14.9), the lowest average baptismal age of the five churches in table 7-1.

Not only did the average baptismal age drop in each of the five congregations in the twentieth century; a number of eleven, twelve, and thirteen year-olds made their way into the baptismal record books for the first time in many congregations during the 1920s and 1930s. Adolescent baptisms led to child baptisms by the middle of the twentieth century. Professor J. Winfield Fretz of Bethel College noted in 1949 "the shift from adult baptism, a doctrine which cost our forefathers so much, to adolescent or child baptism."[13]

There was no single cause for the changing age of baptism. Several factors combined to contribute to the transition. As with so many other adaptations of the Mennonite Church, the lowering of the baptism age was an attempt to keep Mennonite youth in the fold. Church membership was limited to only those who had experienced believers' baptism. Since fewer twentieth century Mennonites remained on the farm upon the completion of a formal education, there was a greater likelihood of leaving the home church. Leaders may have reasoned that admitting adolescents into membership through baptism at a younger age might succeed in retaining their church involvement.

The pull of American denominations was complicated by the evangelizing efforts of nearby Mennonite Brethren. The product of a pietistic revival in Russia during the middle of the nineteenth century, the Mennonite Brethren settled close to Kirchliche congregations in America. With a strong emphasis on evangelism and missions, they frequently perceived General Conference congregations as mission fields and at times aggressively proselyted. WDC churches baptized at an earlier age to keep young people from falling prey to the Mennonite Brethren belief that a valid baptism experience required immersion.[14]

Certain Mennonite historians and sociologists perceive the lowering of the baptism age as evidence of "infiltration and secularization" by American civil religion. J. Winfield Fretz contends that the shift "seems not to be on the grounds of principle but on the grounds of imitation of other religious groups." David A. Haury suggests that the baptism of adolescents "may indicate a weakening of the concept of believer's baptism through contact with fundamentalist practices."[15]

Another explanation of the baptism age shift stems from the Mennonite experience in World War I. With America's entry into the war in April, 1917, the United States enacted a draft. Although a draft exemption law was not passed until the later stages of the war, rumors of exemption and alternative service circulated wildly in Mennonite communities during 1917. However, any projected exemptions were based on current membership in a historic peace church. For Mennonite youth of draft age membership meant baptism.

Since the average age of baptism in 1917 was twenty or above in several churches (Hoffnungsau - 21; Alexanderwohl - 20), a number of Mennonite youth faced military conscription without the required _enet of exemption - church membership. Thus, the war years produced the largest bumper crop of baptisms in the history of the church. Mennonite youth who normally would have procrastinated in regards to baptism were forced into earlier decisions by the prospects of military service. In 1917 the Alexanderwohl congregation recorded eighty-one baptisms, nearly double that of any previous year. Hoffnung-sau recorded twenty-six baptisms in 1917, twenty-one in 1918, and seventeen in 1919, all well above the 12.3 yearly average from 1875 to 1917. Emmaus had the largest group of baptisms in 1918 since the turn of the century. The total baptisms in the Burrton church in both 1917 and 1918 surpassed any previous year. The Arlington congregation conducted its only baptisms between 1913 and 1,920 in 1917.[16]

The First World War forced Mennonite youth to decide on baptism at an earlier age. It reduced the likelihood of procrastination. It may have even drawn in some who might have allowed the membership issue to go unanswered indefinitely and thus be absorbed into American churches.

The acceptance of infant-baptized transfer membership and the increased practice of adolescent and child baptism are both signs of Americanization in the East European and Russian Mennonite churches in central Kansas.

The Mennonite ordinance of communion seems to have changed as a consequence of interaction with American society. For early Anabaptists, communion was an important means of fellowship. They rejected the concept of transubstantiation, which is the Roman Catholic belief that bread and wine become the actual flesh and blood of Christ. Sixteenth century Anabaptists shared the view of Zwingli who contended that the elements of communion "signified" the body of Christ rather than actually serving as his flesh and blood. The Schleitheim Articles referred to the Lord's Supper as "a remembrance of the broken body and the shed blood of Christ."[17]

Not only did the theological implications of Anabaptist communion differ significantly from both those of the Roman Catholic and Lutheran Churches, the outward form also deviated from the standard practice of the day. In an attempt to do away with "idolatrous implications" of Roman Catholic communion, there was little ceremony, no blessing, and often no words during an Anabaptist communion. Because of severe persecutions, no uniform practice developed among sixteenth century Anabaptists. However, in the following three centuries certain common forms evolved in European and Russian Mennonite churches.

Mennonites who settled in central Kansas during the late nineteenth century often brought their communion ware with them from the Old Country. This included a cruet, or pitcher, and up to six chalices, or common cups. After the bread had been broken and distributed, the common cup was filled with wine and passed from member to member. The elder, assisted by deacons, distributed the elements of communion to members in good standing. Local congregations of the Kansas Conference used various forms of distribution, but few in the nineteenth century deviated from the practice of drinking wine from the common cup.[18]

The primary changes in the Mennonite form of communion during the twentieth century were threefold: grape juice replaced wine, individual cups replaced the common cup, and bread was passed around the congregations rather than distributed by the pastor individually at the front of the church. Available records do not account for the transition of the means of bread distribution; however, the purchase of individual cups and adoption of unfermented grape juice were recorded in several church treasury records and various minutes of congregational meetings (Bruderschaft).

Mennonites arrived in Kansas with diverse opinions on the alcohol question. They had encountered a temperance movement in Russia where both the Krimmer Mennonite Brethren and the Mennonite Brethren developed a stance forbidding alcoholic consumption. However, most of the Kirch-liche congregations had no established provisions in church constitutions addressing the issue. Mennonite communities in Russia and Prussia knew the pleasure and the profits of brewing and inbibing alcoholic beverages.

In 1880, when Kansas became the first state in the union to adopt a prohibition amendment to the state constitution, the Mennonite vote was split: 57.1 percent in favor and 42.9 percent opposed. Although the temperature movement was gaining momentum in the late nineteenth century, prohibition was not enforced in Kansas until swayed by the protests of Carrie A. Nation in the early twentieth century. Kansas Mennonites continued to use wine for communion purposes in the nineteenth century in spite of public sentiment supportive of prohibition.[19]

The shift to grape juice in communion occurred in most Western District Conference churches in the 1920s and 1930s after a national prohibition law was adopted in 1919. The Tabor Mennonite Church (Goessel) expressed concern in 1919 with regard to the continued use of wine. The deacons were instructed to take note of the concern and use their own judgment. In 1920 the Hoffnungsau Mennonite Church switched from wine to grape juice. The Zion Mennonite Church (Elbing) replaced wine in communion in 1922. Although some churches continued to file for a permit to serve wine during the prohibition era, most congregations followed the lead of Tabor, Zion, and Hoffnungsau and switched to grape juice for communion. By 1949 the transition was generally complete.[20]

The use of grape juice in twentieth century Mennonite communion services was a clear sign of acculturation. The use of wine for communion was common to all Kansas Conference churches in the nineteenth century. Its voluntary replacement with grape juice as a result of the temperance movement was clearly an accommodation to American norms.

The common cup was also a regular feature of nineteenth century Mennonite communion services. Larger churches had up to six common cups to serve an entire congregation in a single setting. Smaller congregations usually had two common cups: one for men and one for women. The cup was filled from a cruet or pitcher by the elder and handed to the communicant seated at the end of the pew. After supping from the cup, each person wiped the rim with a folded handkerchief before passing it on. In this way, communion not only had important theological implications; it also strengthened the bond of cohesiveness through the familial practice of sharing the common cup.

The common chalice actually outlived the use of wine in most churches. The Bethel College Church was among the first to adopt individual communion cups in 1912, "because of fear of a tuberculin epidemic."[21] The fact that the Bethel College congregation was far more heterogeneous than any other WDC church may have contributed to a less communal spirit. The existing records of seven churches reveal a pattern characteristic of most Mennonite congregations in the shift from the common chalice to individual cups.

Table 7-2 indicates a diverse range in the rate of shift from the common cup to individual cups. Bethel College (1912) and Emmaus (1951) represented the extremes in the transition. In all likelihood, most congregations first used individual cups in the 1920s and 1930s. The adoption of individual cups may be indicative of a reduced familiarity within a congregation. As local Mennonite churches became more heterogeneous in the twentieth century, American individualism encroached on even the most sacred practices. By 1939 Mennonite communion practices had lost at least two distinctive features: the use of wine and the common cup.

Footwashing was a third Mennonite ordinance affected by acculturation. Actually it was never universally accepted by Anabaptists from the beginning. Groups who had at one time practiced footwashing in Europe discontinued it before arriving in central Kansas. The General Conference dropped compulsory footwashing in North America

TABLE 7-2

SHIFT FROM COMMON CUP TO INDIVIDUAL CUPS IN COMMUNION

Church	Date
Bethel College Mennonite	1912
Tabor Mennonite	1919
Eden Mennonite	1925
Zion Mennonite	1930
First Mennonite of Pretty Prairie	1936
Bergthal Mennonite	1943
Emmaus Mennonite	1951

SOURCE: Compiled from Peter S. Goertz and Harley J. Stucky, Our Church Past and Present (North Newton, Kansas: Mennonite Press, 1954), p. 13; "Secretary's Report," p. 30; John Janzen, pp. 15-16; William Juhnke, ed., p. 41; J. A. Stucky, Epochs of History of First Mennonite Church of Pretty Prairie (n.p., 1954), p. 47; Elma Ruth Smith, "A Brief History of the Berthal Mennonite Church, Pawnee Rock, Kansas" (Unpublished paper, Mennonite Library and Archives, Bethel College, North Newton, Kansas, 1943), p. 4; Ernest Claassen, Mrs. B. G. Harder, Frank Busenitz, Mrs. Henry Claassen, and Walter Penner, comp., History of the Emmaus Mennonite Church (Hillsboro, Kansas: Mennonite Brethren Publishing House, 1978), p. 105.

two decades before East European and Russian Mennonites arrived in Kansas.[22]

For the most part South Russian Mennonites and Swiss Volhynians continued the practice of footwashing in America. Prussian Mennonites dropped footwashing in the old country while South Germans and other Swiss groups never adopted the practice in Europe. The Swiss Volhynians were an exception due to their Amish background.[23]

Although there were some WDC churches that originally abstained from footwashing, a majority maintained the practice in nineteenth century America. At the Brudertal Mennonite Church (Hillsboro), South Russians worshipped together with West Prussians. The South Russians

were familiar with footwashing while the West Prussians had dropped
the practice several decades before immigration. After a brief instruction, Prussian Mennonites at Brudertal again participated.[24]

By 1931 less than half (twenty-three) of the WDC churches still
practiced footwashing. A survey in 1944 revealed that only ten WDC
churches encouraged footwashing ceremonies. It was optional in most
of the ten congregations. When daughter churches were established
in the twentieth century, some failed to include provisions for footwashing in their new constitutions. Such was the case of the Tabor
Mennonite Church (Goessel) in 1908.[25]

In 1914 a group within the Alexanderwohl congregation moved
to have footwashing removed as a part of the communion ceremony.
There was strong resistance, but a short time later it was agreed
that communion would be observed twice a year; once with footwashing
and once without. However, by 1927 when it became obvious that fewer
people attended the communion observances that included footwashing
ceremonies, the practice was made optional. Finally in 1943 with
the retirement of the church elder of twenty-eight years, footwashing
was discontinued. In 1950 it was officially abolished. The discontinuance of footwashing in other congregations followed the Alexanderwohl
pattern.[26]

Clarence Hiebert, tracing the decline of footwashing amongst
Mennonites in his 1954 thesis, concluded that the demise of this practice was due largely to "secularization and the compromising influences
in the church." In addition, Hiebert claimed that the "influence
of the larger denominations upon the Mennonites played no little part

in bringing about compromises in their traditional beliefs."[27] Numerous
young Mennonites of the twentieth century found footwashing to be
an archaic tradition symbolic of an Old World identity no longer germane
to their American experience.[28] A decline of the distinctive practice
of footwashing within the European and Russian Mennonite churches
in central Kansas is further evidence of acculturation from 1874 to
1939.

The Clerical Transition

Mennonite clergy have traditionally wielded an important level
of authority in Mennonite communities. The persecution of early Anabaptists produced emergency conditions that necessitated strong leadership
for the sake of survival. This precedent was important to the development of the elder's position as one of great prestige and considerable
authority. In Russia under the village system of government, the
role of elder expanded into a type of "hierarchial theocracy" in which
elders periodically controlled both the civil and ecclesiastical life
of the community.[29]

As previously explained, Prussian and Russian Mennonites maintained a three tier ministerial structure: elders (Aelteste), ministers
(Vermaaner or Prediger), and deacons (Armendiener or Diakon). The
highest office was that of elder. Among early Anabaptists the term
was used along with bishop (Bischof) until the latter disappeared
in Europe during the eighteenth century. "Bishop" remained the common
term for the highest office among the (Old) Mennonite Church and certain
Amish groups in America. The elder alone administered baptism, communion, and presided at church meetings.[30]

Usually each congregation had several ministers to assist the elder. Ministers (<u>Prediger</u>) preached, taught catechism classes, married, buried, and called on the sick in addition to assisting with communion, baptism, and church meetings.

Deacons (<u>Diakon</u>) made up the third level of the local church leadership. Actually they were not ministers in the same sense as the <u>Prediger</u> or the <u>Aelteste</u>. Deacons were charged with the responsibilities of serving poor and needy members, assisting the elder with communion and baptism when needed, visiting the sick, and often reading scripture or praying in worship services.

All three levels of the ministry were elected to their respective positions for life and usually remained in the same congregation. Elders were chosen from amongst the ministers by lot. Ministers and deacons were nominated by the local church from among their male membership. Campaigning for a clerical office was strictly forbidden, and few dared to refuse the nomination of the congregation. Neighboring elders ordained elder-candidates; ministers and deacons were ordained by the local elder. Eventually the church dropped ordination for deacons.

Certain generalities characterized Kansas Mennonite church leaders in the nineteenth century. They seldom had formal preparation for their position. They received little or no financial compensation. For this reason, elders usually were selected from the wealthy class. A common saying in Russia was that they chose the man with the biggest shed to become an elder. Most were farmers. They grew up in the same congregation they served, accepted their call as a lifetime commitment, and generated a great deal of respect from church members.

The holder of this "farmer-patriarch" position who accompanied nineteenth century Mennonites to Kansas was something of an "enlightened dictator." Empowered with the highest office of the Mennonite community, he had unquestioned authority and prestige. In church matters he answered to no one but God. The conference, the congregation, and his colleagues might make suggestions, but ultimately local church decisions required the support of the elder. He need not worry about offending someone lest he jeopardize his status. A sense of divine-sanctioned permanence fortified his stability.

In some respects the role of the Mennonite elder was similar to that of the Catholic priest. Andrew Greeley traced a struggle in the history of American Catholicism between "Americanizer" and "anti-Americanizer" clergy. The acculturation of the Catholic immigrant depended largely upon the role of the priest and his position on Americanization.[31] Likewise, the local elder largely determined the rate of Mennonite assimilation. Meanwhile, the position of church leadership also underwent a significant transition from 1874 to 1939. The development of Mennonite clergy in central Kansas from the ingroup, uneducated, unsalaried elder to the outgroups, educated, professional pastor over a span of six and one-half decades reflected the impact of American Protestant religious influence.

The American religious experience affected a basic tenet of the Mennonite elder -- the means by which he was called to serve the local congregation. Elders originally were chosen from within the local congregation by vote, lot, or both. An elder-candidate first had to be a minister, and in most cases, a successful farmer.[32] Occasionally he taught in Mennonite parochial schools.

The Prussian and South Russian congregations chose elders by a "double vote" process. The first vote served to nominate candidates from amongst the congregation's ministers. The nominees were placed before the members of the congregation, who cast secret ballots after prayerful consideration.[33] The Swiss and South Germans had a "vote and lot" process of selection. The vote served to nominate candidates while the lot actually determined an elder. J. J. Flickinger, the first elder of the First Mennonite Church of Pretty Prairie, described his own selection:

> Everyone receiving votes should be chosen by lot. In this drawing each candidate would draw a blank except one. So a prayer meeting was held to ask that the Lord might lead and direct in this drawing that everything might terminate according to His holy will and to the welfare of this church. After the prayer meeting the drawing by lot was held in the home of Andrew Schwartz, and the result was that all 21 who had received votes drew blanks except myself.[34]

Selection by lot gave the chosen one a strong sense of divine call which sanctioned his unquestioned authority.

One of the earliest evidences of Americanization was the extension of a call to elders outside the local congregation for a shorter term. Only two of the thirty-four Kansas congregations before 1920 originally chose an outsider as their first elder (table 7-3). Both of these churches had mixed European origins making an ingroup selection undesirable. With the outside call local congregations dropped the lifetime selection by lot.

The transition in the Western District Conference from selecting "home-grown elders" to calling outgroup church leaders was a long process. In 1911 the First Mennonite Church of Halstead dropped the

TABLE 7-3

FIRST MINISTER CALLED FROM OUTSIDE LOCAL CONGREGATION

Church	Year
First Mennonite of Hillsboro*	1884
First Mennonite of Halstead	1911
Garden Township Mennonite	1912
First Mennonite of Hutchinson*	1914
Einsiesedel Mennonite	1915
Hopefield Mennonite	1918
Emmanuel Mennonite	1919
First Mennonite of Pretty Prairie	1919
West Zion Mennonite	1922
Brudetal Mennonite	1924
First Mennonite of Newton	1924
Hebron Mennonite	1925
Bethel College Mennonite	1925
First Mennonite of Ransom	1925
Bethany Mennonite	1932
Buhler Mennonite	1933
Inman Mennonite	1936
Burrton Mennonite	1936
Arlington Mennonite	1937
Johannestal Mennonite	1937
Eden Mennonite	1937
Grace Hill Mennonite	1937
Emmaus Mennonite	1939
Friedenstal Mennonite	1943
Alexanderwohl Mennonite	1944
Bergthal Mennonite	1948
Lehigh Mennonite	1949
Goessel Mennonite	1950
First Mennonite of Christian	1951
Zion Mennonite	1952
Swiss Mennonite	1954
Tabor Mennonite	1958
Bethel Mennonite	1960
Hoffnungsau Mennonite	1961

*Mixed congregations with outside minister from the beginning.

SOURCE: Compiled from a list of WDC ministers taken from David A. Haury, Prairie People (Newton, Kansas: Faith and Life Press, 1981), pp. 454-66.

"vote and lot" method of selection and extended an invitation to an elder outside the local church. As other congregations became less homogeneous and the demands of the ministry increased, outgroup candidates received serious consideration. Other congregations reverted to a call beyond the local constituency due to a lack of local candidates. A number of smaller churches were hardpressed to maintain a steady supply of ingroup ministers. They grew weary of relying on the elders of nearby congregations to administer communion, baptisms, and congregational meetings.[35]

One reason that the transition from ingroup to outgroup elders took so long was due to the longevity of the last ingroup elder. At Goessel, Peter Buller served from 1920 to 1956 before he was replaced by a minister from outside the congregation. The elder at Johannestal, John Plenert, presided forty-four years before the church called a minister from Pennsylvania. The last ingroup elder at First Mennonite of Christian served thirty-three years; at First Mennonite of Pretty Prairie, thirty years; at Bergthal Mennonite, thirty-eight years, and at Grace Hill Mennonite, fifty-three years. Thus, what started in 1911 at Halstead ended fifty years later when Hoffnungsau called its first outgroup minister in 1961.[36]

There were a number of other changes that accommodated the transition to a called outsider. One had to do with the length of a ministerial term. Under the farmer-patriarch system, elders usually served until death or physical incapacity. Thus, tenure often covered four or five decades. With the advent of the outgroup call, the length was significantly reduced. A tally of all ministers in central Kansas

(Aelteste and Prediger) who began serving before 1925 reveals that the average length of service was 19.8 years. The average tenure for a minister who began serving after 1925 was only 6.5 years. Since the call was no longer a lifetime summons, elders in the second quarter of the twentieth century were more willing to leave a congregation when called elsewhere.[37]

Another impact of the outgroup elder was the infusion of new ideas. In some cases, the new elder accelerated the language transition, encouraged the use of musical instruments, and introduced non-Mennonite Sunday school curriculum. The Pretty Prairie congregation adopted a new constitution upon the arrival of an outgroup elder; Alexanderwohl abandoned footwashing under their first outgroup elder; several churches published their first English constitution shortly after calling an outgroup elder. Many of the local traditions of the church were lost under the ministry of outsiders.[38]

The call of outgroup elders also had the effect of reducing the number of ministers in a local congregation. Under the farmer-patriarch system, an elder usually headed a team of several ministers. Since none were full-time, the local church rotated responsibilities in an attempt to lighten the load. The outgroup call resulted in a full-time salaried minister capable of investing full attention to the church.

Another evidence of the impact of Americanization on Mennonite clergy was the appearance of formally educated ministers in the twentieth century. Few educated elders accompanied Mennonites to Kansas in the 1870s. The organization of Halstead Seminary (1883) and Bethel

College (1893) for the education of ministers, teachers, and missionaries was an extremely progressive step for nineteenth century Mennonites. The usual ministerial preparation entailed no more than having
an elementary education and observing the local elder. The systematically trained seminarian was the product of the twentieth century.

The issue of an educated clergy first produced a serious conflict
around the turn of the century. In 1901 the report of the Bethel
College representative to the WDC revealed the nature of the problem.
Since local churches were exclusively responsible for calling ministers,
the college was in a quandary trying to decide whom to allow into
pastoral ministries classes. Technically, if a student did not have
a call from a local church, Bethel had no right to prepare that student
for the ministry. The college, careful not to encroach upon the local
church, requested guidance from the WDC.[39]

The conference responded with a suggestion that all students
produce a recommendation from a local church before enrolling in ministerial courses. At the same time, a recommendation did not guarantee
a subsequent call from the local church. This agreement between the
conference and the college allowed churches theoretically to maintain
their system of calling leaders without regard to their education.
Practically speaking, however, the demand for a formal ministerial
training accompanied the transition from farmer-patriarch to professional clergy.[40]

The earliest formal Mennonite pastoral preparation programs
were modest by contemporary standards. Bethel College organized a
two year evangelist's course designed to produce homiletically prepared

preachers. By the turn of the century a number of local congregations accepted the practice of ordaining young men as evangelists for the sole purpose of preaching. Many of these completed the evangelist's course. By 1917 Edmund G. Kaufman noted that a formal education for ministers was considered valuable, although not yet essential. In 1930 a survey revealed that eleven (out of fifty-seven) WDC church leaders received some formal ministerial training.[41] Gradually, formally educated ministers replaced self-taught elders in Kansas Mennonite congregations.

Another aspect of the lay-to-professional transition was the question of financial support. Few Kansas elders initially received compensation for their labors, at least not enough to live on. The concept of a paid minister did not gain acceptance until after the First World War. Even as late as 1950 some Kansas congregations offered only irregular gifts rather than a prearranged salary.

The farmer-patriarch system had inherent weaknesses. It was commonly said in the nineteenth century that the elder was either a good preacher and a miserable farmer, or a good farmer who amounted to little as a minister. As early as 1888 an article in the Mennonite called for a regular salary for Mennonite ministers. It referred to traditional reservations of financial compensation as unscriptural.[42] However, Kansas Mennonites were slow to change. After all, the farmer-patriarch system had worked well in southern Russia and eastern Europe, where the Bible and plow (Bibel under Pflug) had been inseparable partners.

Nineteenth century elders often received compensation by means of a "love offering." This might be in the form of a cash gift or produce and livestock. Although these gifts subsidized a farming income, they did not serve as a regular salary. The first evidence of a regularly salaried ministry surfaced during the first decade of the twentieth century. When the Alexanderwohl congregation requested one of its evangelists to accept ordination as a minister in 1905, he agreed on the condition that he be salaried. However, the congregation was not ready to take such an unprecedented step, and therefore the voluntary support basis continued at Alexanderwohl until 1912 when the church established a policy of regular remuneration from the church treasury.[43]

In 1909 the Tabor Mennonite Church (Goessel), a daughter congregation of the Alexanderwohl group, agreed to assess each member one dollar per year for the support of the elder. In turn, they directed the elder to "devote more time to pastoral care in the congregation than is usually done in our churches."[44] Ministers at the Zion Mennonite Church (Elbing) received five dollars per sermon in 1919.[45] By 1929 forty of the fifty-four WDC churches paid a regular salary. The average annual salary of these forty congregations just before the Depression was $838. In 1935 three congregations owned parsonages. With the disappearance of the farmer-patriarch as elder, the practice of paying the minister a salary gained wider acceptance among Kansas Mennonites.[46]

The matter of salaried ministers was a part of the entire clerical transition in Kansas Mennonite churches during the first half

267

of the twentieth century. In most Kansas congregations the educated,
salaried, outgroup minister of 1939 replaced the unpaid, uneducated,
ingroup farmer-patriarch elder of 1874. Even the traditional distinction between elders and ministers had faded by 1939. A 1922 decision
of the WDC removed the previously existing elder-minster rank; the
1923 conference roll listed all ordained ministers by "Rev." Although
the term elder still appeared in later WDC minutes, by 1939 church
leaders were commonly referred to as "reverend" in local
congregations.[47]

The role of women in Kansas Mennonite congregations of the
1870s bore evidence of a patriarchal European heritage. They were
not allowed to vote or speak in congregational meetings. Their input
was primarily in a supportive role. Although they organized sewing
societies as early as 1881 to support the work of the missionaries,
they neither held church offices nor preached.

Mennonite women in the nineteenth century did not display discontent with their status. However, there was a growing need of fulfillment for a certain group of single women. These "unsullied gems"
were often single by circumstances, left by other family members to
tend to ailing parents. Following the death of parents, they were
trapped into a social structure that identified a woman's worth by
the number of children she bore. There seemed to be no appropriate
place for energetic, creative single women in the church. The deaconess
movement in Kansas arose out of these circumstances.

Actually, the deaconess work had historical precedent in the
Anabaptist-Mennonite tradition. Seventeenth century Dutch and German

Mennonite churches had the office of deaconess. Usually the deaconess was an elderly widow who visited the sick, comforted the poor, and took care of orphans and widows.[48] Among the Mennonites arriving in Kansas in the 1870s, the deaconess work had long been dormant. A revival of the deaconess work among Kansas Mennonites paralleled a growing trend in mainline Protestant churches in nineteenth century America.[49]

The deaconess cause had a champion in the person of David Goerz. This pioneer, publisher, and founder of Bethel College recommended deaconess work to the General Conference as early as 1890. In 1898 the WDC investigated the deaconess movement and referred all requests for deaconesses to the Home Missions Committee. In 1900 the first candidate, Frieda Kaufman, entered Bethel College in preparation for deaconess work. A year later Bethel College designed a deaconess course of study and in 1905 the WDC resolved "to take up the deaconess work as a branch of its activity."[50]

The original intent of the deaconess cause was to provide the local church with persons capable of ministering to the physical needs of the congregation. In 1905 the Deaconess Committee placed Sister Martha Richert in the Alexanderwohl congregation. As a graduate of a deaconess institute in Cincinnati, Ohio, Richert was a qualified nurse and received a number of requests from shut-ins in the Alexanderwohl community. Her quiet and sacrificial efforts did much to silence critics of the deaconess work. In 1907 she was ordained in the Alexanderwohl church.[51]

The 1912 report of the Deaconess Committee indicated the general acceptance of the deaconess work by Kansas Mennonites. Hospitals operated by deaconesses existed in Newton and Goessel. However, in less than a decade the deaconess movement developed contrary to the intent of Goerz and the WDC. The two hospitals occupied nearly all the deaconess energy, while little evidence existed of deaconess work in local congregations. The Deaconess Committee frequently expressed frustration with this development, complaining that the two Deaconess hospitals (plus one in Beatrice, Nebraska) left little opportunity for deaconesses "to devote themselves entirely to . . . the work in the church."[52]

Eventually the hospital boards took over the deaconess work since most of the effort was no longer invested in local churches. Even though it took a course different than originally intended, the deaconess movement allowed a number of Kansas Mennonite women to engage in a ministerial activity not available to their counterparts in the nineteenth century. The WDC deaconess cause was part of a nation-wide trend toward women church workers in city missions, overseas missionary enterprises, and even pastoral experiences in some denominations. Although Mennonite women did not gain the right to preach in Kansas congregations by 1939, the deaconess work represented a part of the larger female emergence in twentieth century American Protestant churches.

In 1917 a young Kansas Mennonite completing a master's thesis reflected on the clerical transition of the Western District:

> In the last few decades some transformation has taken place
> in the expression of the religious life of these people.
> In earlier times their preachers and ministers were uneducated
> and unsalaried men; today many of them receive at least a
> small salary, and education is considered very valuable, but
> as yet not essential. Then, the ministers were chosen mostly

by lot, each congregation having two or three men of their
own number to serve as ministers at the same time. Today
the ministers are often called from some other congregation
or from some educational institute, and more and more it is
considered best that only one man serve a congregation at
a time and devote his whole time to that work while he is
in service.[53]

Nowhere was the transition from a lay clergy to a professional
more noticeable than the First Mennonite Church of Christian (Moundridge). P. P. Wedel served this congregation from 1904 until he retired
in 1950. His departure marked the end of an era. He was the last
pastor chosen by lot; the last to be chosen from within; the last
to receive a lifetime call to a church; the last of the farmer-patriarch, authoritarian pastors. During the next fifteen years under
the leadership of educated, salaried, outgroup pastors, the congregation
experienced a rapid, somewhat painful transition. This shift, postponed
by Wedel's lengthy service, was representative of the clerical transition in all Mennonite congregations of central Kansas from 1874 to
1939.[54]

The clerical transition of Kansas Mennonites had several conse-
quences for the local congregation. First, it signaled an end to
an Old World hierarchal theocracy. In the absence of a home-grown
elder, local congregations hired outside clergy who inherited far
less authority and prestige than the farmer-patriarch. This had the
effect of encouraging lay involvement; the congregational meeting
and its offspring, the church board, gained new strength under the
professional clergy.

Secondly, the clerical transition served to accelerate change
in the local church. The end of the farmer-patriarch era also signaled

the end to a number of local traditions. As guardian of an ethnoreligious heritage, the nineteenth century elder maintained Old World traditions in America. With the advent of the first outside church leader, the local congregation experienced a number of changes.

A third consequence of the clerical transition for the local church was a broadening of their Mennonite identity. The nineteenth century Mennonite experience reflected a great deal of provincialism. In Kansas this meant Dutch Prussian, South Russian, Galician, Dutch Volhynian, Swiss Volhynian, Polish Russian, South German, and Swiss Mennonites each kept largely to themselves. Many of the first churches to call an outsider chose individuals with backgrounds different from their own. Seminary graduates and Pennsylvania-born ministers had been called to serve a growing number of Kansas congregations in the 1930s. Other ministers were graduates of fundamentalist Bible institutes. This had the effect of expanding the identity of the local Mennonite church. It also contributed to a loss of local group identity characteristic of nineteenth century "family congregations."

A fourth consequence of the clerical transition was the inclusion of women in the ministry through the deaconess movement. Although Mennonite women did not gain the status of the Prediger, the deaconess cause marked a major breakthrough for a female ministry in the Kansas Conference.

Conclusion

By 1939 little evidence of nineteenth century Mennonite church customs still remained in most Kansas congregations. A few unused footwashing basins reminded older members of a practice once common to many of their group. Common chalices remained in some churches. Only a few elders discouraged baptismal candidates to wait until their late teens. A handful of farmer-patriarch elders still presided as unsalaried, self-educated leaders in WDC congregations. Changing church customs by 1939 far outweighed the similarities with the immigrant church of the 1870s.

Mennonite congregations in central Kansas could hardly be referred to in 1939 as "immigrant churches." Distinctive Old World customs had been replaced by contemorary American practices. The temperance movement forced Mennonites to substitute grape juice for wine. The gradual infiltration by outside Mennonites into "family congregations" contributed to an unwillingness to further use the common cup. Footwashing rapidly disappeared. Baptismal ages continually dropped from the traditional adult baptism in the nineteenth century to the level of adolescent and even child baptism in the twentieth century. The transition from a farmer-patriarch elder, who served as a guardian of traditionally observed church customs, to a salaried, formally educated, outside minister was well underway in the WDC by 1939.

The Canadian sociologist E. K. Francis claimed that European Mennonites were a religious group until forced into a segregated existence in South Russia, at which point they became an ethnic group.[55] It would appear that in light of the transition of church customs in America, by 1939 Kansas Mennonites once again were more akin to a religious group than an ethnic entity. H. Richard Niebuhr referred to this process in Social Sources of Denominationalism:

The process of accommodation as a whole gradually transforms the churches of immigrants into American denominations with marked similarities and with remarkable dissimilarities from the parent churches of Europe.[56]

The loss of certain Old World church customs characterized the transition of Mennonite identity from 1874 to 1939. Their identity was that of an American denomination, not an immigrant church. Although ethnic traits still existed in local congregations by 1939, Kansas Mennonites were less an ethnic group than a religious group.

CHAPTER VII - ENDNOTES

1. Henry Peter Krehbiel, The History of the Mennonite General Conference, vol. 2 (Newton, Kansas: Herald Publishing House, 1939), p. 254.

2. Mennonite Encyclopedia, s.v. "Nonconformity," by Harold S. Bender; "Bruederlich Vereinigung," by Harold S. Bender and John C. Wenger; H. Richard Niebuhr, The Social Sources of Denominationalism (New York: New American Library, Inc., 1929), pp. 37-39; Robert Friedmann, The Theology of Anabaptism (Scottdale, Pennsylvania: Herald Press, 1973); John C. Wenger, tran., "The Schleitheim Confession of Faith," Mennonite Quarterly Review 4 (October 1945): 244-53.

3. Friedmann, p. 41.

4. H. Richard Niebuhr, Christ and Culture (New York: Harper and Brothers, 1951), p. 56; John C. Bennett, Christian Ethics and Social Policy (New York: Charles Scribner's Sons, 1946), pp. 42-46.

5. Roy Vogt, "The Impact of Economics and Social Class on Mennonite Theology," in Mennonite Images, ed. Harry Loewen (Winnipeg: Hyperion Press Limited, 1980), pp. 137-40.

6. Mennonite Encyclopedia, s.v. "Nonconformity," by Harold S. Bender and John C. Wenger.

7. David A. Haury, Prairie People (Newton, Kansas: Faith and Life Press, 1981), pp. 25-57; Martin Schrag, "The Swiss-Volhynian Mennonite Background," Mennonite Life 9 (October 1954): 156, 158-61; Mennonite Encyclopedia, s.v. "Nonconformity," by Harold S. Bender and John C. Wenger.

8. Andrew M. Greeley, The Denominational Society (Glenview, Illinois: Scott, Foresman and Company, 1972), p. 3; Will Herberg, Protestant, Catholic, and Jew (Garden City, New York: Doubleday and Company, Inc., 1955).

9. John C. Wenger, Glimpses of Mennonite History and Doctrine (Scottdale, Pennsylvania; Herald Press, 1947), pp. 149-50.

10. Mennonite Encyclopedia, s.v. "Baptism," by Harold S. Bender.

11. Minutes of the Western District Conference, 11-13 October 1886; 15-16 October 1888, Mennonite Library and Archives, Bethel College, North Newton, Kansas (typescript, English translation): Haury, pp. 172-73.

12. Loris A. Habegger, ed., The Flock and the Kingdom (n.p., 1975), p. 24.

13. J. Winfield Fretz, "Separation or Infiltration" in The Seventy-Fifth Anniversay Services of the Swiss Mennonites, comp. Harley J. Stucky (North Newton, Kansas: Mennonite Press, Inc., 1950), p. 51.

14. John F. Schmidt, interview at the Mennonite Library and Archives, North Newton, Kansas, June 19, 1983. Schmidt pastored the Buhler (GC) Mennonite Church (1939-41) which is located in the center of a Mennonite Brethren community.

15. Fretz, p. 51; Haury, p. 260.

16. Records of the Alexanderwohl, Hoffnungsau, Emmaus, Burrton, and Arlington congregations, Mennonite Library and Archives, Bethel College, North Newton, Kansas.

17. Mennonite Encyclopedia, s.v. "Communion," by Cornelius Krahn.

18. Ibid.

19. James C. Juhnke, A People of Two Kingdoms (Newton, Kansas: Faith and Life Press, 1975), p. 43; Kenneth S. Davis, Kansas: A Bicentennial History (New York: W. W. Norton and Company, Inc., 1976), pp. 143-47; Haury, pp. 68, 259.

20. "Secretary's Report of the Congregational Meetings of the Tabor Mennonite Church 1907-1926," trans. Dan. S. Thiesen (Mennonite Library and Archives, Bethel College, North Newton, Kansas), p. 30; John M. Janzen, "Schisms and Renewal in Three Mennonite Parishes" (Unpublished paper, Mennonite Library and Archives, Bethel College, North Newton, Kansas, 1978), pp. 15-16; Albert M. Gaeddert, Centennial History of the Hoffnungsau Mennonite Church (North Newton, Kansas: Mennonite Press, Inc., 1975), p. 54.

21. Peter S. Goertz and Harley J. Stucky, Our Church Past and Present (North Newton, Kansas: Mennonite Press, 1954), p. 13.

22. Clarence R. Hiebert, "The History of the Ordinance of Feetwashing in the Mennonite Churches" (S.T.B. thesis, New York Biblical Seminary, 1954), pp. 59,95.

23. Mennonite Encyclopedia, s.v. "Footwashing," by Harold S. Bender.

24. Ray N. Funk, Brudertal, 1883-1964 (North Newton, Kansas: Mennonite Press, 1964), p. 8.

25. Minutes, 21-22 October 1931; Samuel Floyd Pannabecker, "The Development of the General Conference of the Mennonite Church of North America in the American Environment" (Ph.D. dissertation, Yale University, 1944), p. 601; "Secretary's Report," p. 3.

26. David C. Wedel, The Story of Alexanderwohl (North Newton, Kansas: Mennonite Press, Inc., 1974), p. 60; C. Henry Smith, The Coming of the Russian Mennonites (Berne, Indiana: Mennonite Book Concern, 1927), p. 146; Richard F. Schmidt and Tena Schmidt, Memories of Baptism and Communion with the Rite of Footwashing at Alexanderwohl (Emporia, Kansas: Emporia State Press, 1980), pp. 22-25.

27. Clarence R. Hiebert, "The History of the Ordinance," pp. 72, 74.

28. John D. Unruh, "A Century of Mennonites in Dakota," South Dakota Historical Collections 36 (October 1972): 103.

29. Mennonite Encyclopedia, s.v. "Elder," by Cornelius Krahn.

30. C. Henry Smith, The Coming of the Russian Mennonites (Berne, Indiana: Mennonite Book Concern, 1927), p. 18; The Story of the Mennonites (Newton, Faith and Life Press, 1981), p. 174; Cornelius Krahn, "The Office of Elder in Anabaptist-Mennonite History," Mennonite Quarterly Review 30 (April 1956): 120-27.

31. Andrew M. Greeley, The Catholic Experience: An Interpretation of the History of American Catholicism (New York: Doubleday and Company, Inc., 1967).

32. Robert Kreider, "The Anabaptist Conception of the Church in the Russian Mennonite Environment," Mennonite Quarterly Review 25 (January 1951): 100; Mennonite Encyclopedia, s.v. "Lot," by Harold S. Bender. Dutch Prussian and Russian Mennonites did not use lot as Swiss and South Germans did to select church leaders.

33. See various South Russian Church histories such as Albert M. Gaeddert, Hoffnungsau Mennonite Church, 1874-1974 (North Newton, Kansas: Mennonite Press, 1974), p. 63; David C. Wedel, The Story of Alexanderwohl (North Newton, Kansas: Mennonite Press, 1974), pp. 58-60.

34. Jonas A. Stucky, Epochs of History of First Mennonite Church of Pretty Prairie, Kansas (n.p., 1954), p. 17.

35. Loris Habegger, The Flock and the Kingdom (n.p., 1975), p. 23.

36. Compiled from a list of WDC ministers in David A. Haury, Prairie People (Newton, Kansas: Faith and Life Press, 1981), pp. 454-66.

37. Ibid.

38. Jonas A. Stucky, p. 73; David C. Wedel, pp. 60-61; see table 4-2.

39. Minutes, 24-26 October 1901.

40. Ibid.

41. Edmund G. Kaufman, "Social Problems and Opportunities of the Western District Conference Communities of Mennonites of North America" (A.M. thesis, Bluffton College and Mennonite Seminary, 1917), p. 138; Minutes, 22-23 October 1930.

42. P. K. Regier, "Values and Problems of the Lay and the Supported Ministry," Proceedings of the Study Conference on the Believer's Church (Newton, Kansas: General Conference Mennonite Church, 1955), pp. 198-99; C. H. A. van der Smissen, "Ministerial Support," Mennonite 4 (November 1888): 17-19.

43. Minutes of the Congregational Meeting, 1912 in David C. Wedel, pp. 57-60.

44. "Secretary's Report of the Congregational Meetings of the Tabor Mennonite Church, 1907-1926" (Mennonite Library and Archives, Bethel College, North Newton, Kansas), p. 9.

45. Ronald J. Andres, Centennial Reflections: Zion 100 (n.p., 1983), p. 16.

46. Minutes, 16-17 October 1929; 23-25 October 1935.

47. Minutes, 18-20 October 1922; 17-18 October 1923; Interview with Hilda Voth, Mennonite Library and Archives, Bethel College, North Newton, Kansas, 26 September 1984; Krahn, "The Office of Elder," p. 127.

48. Mennonite Encyclopedia, s.v. "Deaconess," by Lena Mae Smith.

49. Haury, p. 156-60; "The Deaconess and Her Ministry," Mennonite Life 3 (January 1948): 30-37.

50. Minutes, 1-2 November 1898; 7-9 November 1905; Haury, pp. 156-60.

51. Minutes, 7-9 November 1905; 24-26 October 1906; 16-18 October 1907.

52. Minutes, 23-24 October 1912.

53. Edmund G. Kaufman, "Social Problems," p. 133.

54. Centennial Chronicle: First Mennonite Church of Christian (n.p., 1978), p. 12.

55. E. K. Francis, "The Russian Mennonites: From Religion to Ethnic Group," American Journal of Sociology 54 (September 1948): 101-07.

56. H. Richard Niebuhr, The Social Sources of Denominationalism, p. 213.

CHAPTER VIII

THE FINE ARTS: MENNONITE ARCHITECTURE AND MUSIC

Our church architecture is extremely modest; probably modest
to a fault.[1]

Henry Peter Krehbiel
1926

As evidenced in the previous chapter, the assimilation of Mennonites in central Kansas significantly altered the historic emphases
of Anabaptist conformity from 1874 to 1939. Assimilation was also
manifest in the evolution of American Mennonite church architecture
and music. Both architecture and music were vital to a distinctive
Mennonite ethnoreligious identity. Upon their arrival in Kansas in
1874, Mennonite churches established architectural patterns and a
musical style that stood in contrast to that of the American religious
environment. However, during the next six decades the contrasts faded
and growing similarities emerged.

Church Architecture

One of the most visible aspects of a distinctive ethnoreligious
identity was the architectural characteristics of Mennonite church
buildings. Traditionally, Mennonite church architecture was quite
modest. A precedent existed for this tradition. In the Reformation
era when Anabaptists were forbidden from constructing churches, many
met in homes. In Holland "hidden churches" were intentionally designed

to take on the appearance of living quarters. Steeples, stained-glass windows, and ornate structures were avoided for the purpose of seclusion and anonymity. Architectural simplicity, however, was more than a matter of practicality. There was a theological issue involved. The "Radical Reformation" objected to the ritualistic adornment of the sixteenth century state churches. In the eyes of Anabaptists, Roman Catholic cathedrals had become centers of idolatrous worship.[2]

East European and Russian Mennonites who settled in nineteenth century Kansas brought with them a severely plain rectangular European meetinghouse design. To outsiders, Mennonite simplicity in architecture may have been misinterpreted as an expression of poverty. However, the first meetinghouses in central Kansas were purposefully plain. In this vastly different new world, simple Mennonite church structures served to remind immigrants of their distinctive ethnoreligious heritage. In the twentieth century, however, important changes in church architecture reflected the general impact of Americanization.

Many of the original congregations of the 1870s followed a three-phase architectural development pattern (table 8-1). The first phase involved the inexpensive construction of a church in the first decade. It was usually rectangular in shape with two sets of doors for separate entry by men and women. Devoid of stained-glass windows, steeples, or Gothic design, the first structures also had a plain interior. No art or decoration graced the sanctuary. Some congregations used schoolhouses, immigrant houses, or remodeled stores before erecting a permanent structure.

The second phase of architectural development took place around the turn of the century. By this time local congregations were firmly

TABLE 8-1

THREE-PHASE ARCHITECTURAL DEVELOPMENT OF MENNONITE
CHURCHES IN CENTRAL KANSAS

Church	First structure	Second structure	Third structure
Bergthal Mennonite	1891-1905[a]	1905-1927	1927-
Bethel Mennonite	1880-1897	1897-1928	1928-1953[b]
Buhler Mennonite	1913-1927	1927-1955	1955- [c]
Eden Mennonite	1898-1924	1924-1949	1949- [c]
Emmaus Mennonite	1878-1908	1908-1928	1929-
First Mennonite, Halstead	1877-1885	1885-	1927, 1952, 1964[d]
First Mennonite, Newton	1881-1902	1902-1932[c]	1932-
Hoffnungsau Mennonite	1880-1898	1898-1948[e]	1950-
West Zion Mennonite	1888-1907	1907-1963	1963-
Zion Mennonite	1883-1924	1924-1963	1963-

[a]Tornado destroyed first structure in 1897; a duplicate structure was
rebuilt and used until destroyed by fire in 1905.
[b]Third structure destroyed by fire in 1953; rebuilt from same plans.
[c]Major addition and remodeling.
[d]Various remodeling projects and additions in third phase.
[e]Destroyed by fire.

SOURCE: Compiled from church records and photographs, Mennonite
Library and Archives, Bethel College, North Newton, Kansas.

established in their new homeland and had experienced various levels of prosperity. The second church building seldom retained the simple rectangular design of the first structure. Although still relatively plain by American standards, it was better planned, a bit more lavish, and always bigger. Some congregations chose to add to or remodel the original structure. In either case, distinctive Mennonite modesty was usually retained in the second stage.

The third phase of architectural development began after the First World War and continues up to the present. It usually reflected the influence of both American church architecture and the general prosperity of Mennonites in central Kansas. In some cases churches were constructed without any indication of Mennonite tradition. Steeples, stained-glass windows, and kitchens were frequently included, sometimes over the objections of older members. Some congregations added to or remodeled the second structure during this phase. Often additions radically altered the simple appearance of the original immigrant church structure.

There were numerous variations and some exceptions to this three-phase architectural development process. A few congregations required only two phases while others experienced four or five distinct stages in the transition. Two churches best illustrate the typical three-phase transition from plain Anabaptist, rectangular churches to elaborate structures with typically American design: Emmaus Mennonite Church (Whitewater) and Hoffnungsau Mennonite Church (Inman).

The Emmaus congregation came from West Prussia and organized a church at Whitewater in 1876. In 1878 it constructed a church building after worshipping for two years in a granary, private homes, and public schoolhouses.[3] This structure was quite simple and reflected the modest financial status of the congregation as well as a plain Old World Mennonite church design (fig. 8-1).

In 1908 the congregation constructed a second church. This structure revealed a combination of Mennonite and non-Mennonite features. It was much larger than the first church building but maintained the familiar rectangular shape and added the traditional dual entryway that segregated men and women. At the same time, the 1908 structure included a bell tower and Gothic windows, both relatively uncommon to the immigrants' West Prussian experience.

In 1929 Emmaus constructed a third building. It no longer reflected traditional Mennonite characteristics. Gone were the dual entryway and the rectangular shape. It included a basement along with an even larger bell tower and more decorative steeple. Gothic style windows remained with slight modification. Although modest by contemporary standards, the Emmaus church had nothing that clearly identified it as distinctively Mennonite.

Another example of the three-phase architectural transition is the Hoffnungsau Mennonite Church. The Hoffnungsau congregation was a part of the Alexanderwohl Church in Russia. Upon the arrival of the Alexanderwohlers in central Kansas in 1874, two separate congregations organized. At first the Hoffnungsau group met in an immigrant house, but that was destroyed by a storm in 1880. In the same year Hoffnungsau constructed an adobe brick structure as their first house of worship (fig. 8-2). It was typical of the Russian meetinghouse with its rectangular shape, hip roof, and obvious plain design.

Fig. 8-1

ARCHITECTURAL DEVELOPMENT OF THE EMMAUS MENNONITE CHURCH

First building, 1878-1908

Second building, 1908-1928

Third building, 1929-present

Fig. 8-2

ARCHITECTURAL DEVELOPMENT OF THE HUFFNUNGSAU MENNONITE CHURCH

First building, 1880-1898

Second building, 1898-1948

Third building, 1948-present

By 1898 the congregation had outgrown the first building and built a second structure intended to appear more like the Alexanderwohl Church in Russia. However, it lacked the hip roof, window shutters, and the rectangular shape of the mother church. Gothic windows and a whitewashed exterior further deviated from the Old World structure. Still, the second structure had the traditional dual entry and printed high above the front center window were the words, "Die Mennoniten Kirche der Hoffnungsauer Gemeinde - 1898."

When the second building burned to the ground in 1948, Hoffnung-sau built a third edifice. It deviated dramatically from distinctively plain Mennonite architecture. The dual entry was replaced by a double door. The new church was T-shaped rather than rectangular. Stained-glass windows adorned the sanctuary. Hoffnungsau took on the appearance of a modern American church structure. To a passerby, only the name revealed an immigrant identity.[4]

In part, the transition in Mennonite church architecture was due to modernization. Electric lights were capable of lighting larger structures. Gas and electric heating systems more adequately controlled the temperature in multi-shaped buildings than the old wood burning stove. Twentieth century Mennonite architecture was also a response to the growing impact of Sunday schools. The old one room, rectangular-shaped church building was not conducive to the needs of individual Sunday school classes. In 1924 the Western District Conference Commit-tee for School and Education recommended that congregations erecting new church buildings take into consideration the need for Sunday school space.[5] Several churches in the second phase and nearly all in the

third phase included a church basement for Sunday school classrooms.
Others added educational wings to existing structures. In either
case, Mennonite church buildings in the twentieth century noticeably
departed from the simple immigrant church of the nineteenth century.

In 1928 the Western District Conference included a statistical
report on church buildings. Eight WDC churches had steeples, six
included a kitchen, twenty-one had basements, two had telephones,
and eight constructed slanting floors.[6] There was concern expressed
in the statistical report regarding Mennonite imitation of American
practices. Few elders recalled the Old World church buildings. However, Mennonites still maintained certain reservations regarding lavish
church adornments. When the First Mennonite Church of Newton constructed a new church in 1931-32, some members took issue with its
ornate semi-Gothic style and stained-glass windows. However, no costs
were spared during the Depression to construct such an edifice.[7]

A photograph that clearly reveals the stark differences between
the nineteenth century Old World structure and the twentieth century
American design is that of the newly built West Zion Mennonite Church
in 1907 (fig. 8-3), complete with decorative, Gothic windows and a
contrast with the old church pictured at the rear. Not only was the
first building smaller, it was completely devoid of any decorative
characteristics.

It was not until most churches of the WDC moved into the final
phase of the transition that alarm cries were sounded with regard
to the Americanization of Mennonite church architecture. Mennonite
historian Cornelius Krahn complained in 1957 that the willingness

FIGURE 8-3

WEST ZION MENNONITE CHURCH

c. 1907 with old structure behind new building

of Mennonites to accept any architectural patterns in America produced some "very odd mixtures and contradictions." He used the example of steeples or bell towers found on almost all Mennonite churches of the prairie states to illustrate his point:

> When and how did these towers become the adornment of Mennonite churches and what connection is there between them and a church in which the gospel of redemption and the nonresistance way of life is proclaimed?[8]

In 1950 J. Winfield Fretz, professor at Bethel College, reflected upon the feeble efforts of architects to symbolize such principles as simplicity, nonconformity, and nonresistance in church structures. He concluded that non-Mennonite architects were hired to construct churches without cognizance of Mennonite distinctions.[9] One Mennonite complained that his brethren had lost their apostalic simplicity in church architecture by the middle of the twentieth century. Contemporary Mennonite churches emphasized "comfort, escape, and fine feelings," rather than distinctive traditions.[10]

The influence of the American environment was not limited to the exterior style of Mennonite churches; in time the interior revealed non-Mennonite influences. Mennonites traditionally avoided altars since they presumably violated the "universal priesthood of all believers" concept. Anabaptists abhorred any symbolic separation between the clergy and the laity. They traced the altar to the medieval chancel used to separate believers from the "holy of holies," as in the Old Testament. Likewise, early Mennonites avoided the inclusion of communion tables in their sanctuaries. According to church tradition, first century Christians used coffins as tables to serve communion in the catacombs. The Roman Catholic Church placed strong symbolic value on the communion table and built them in a coffin-shaped design as centers of worship and shrines. In an attempt to avoid veneration of "graven images," Anabaptists greatly restricted the use of symbols in the church. However, by the 1930s, both altars and communion tables appeared in Mennonite churches in central Kansas.[11]

Altars and communion tables were not the only additions to the sanctuary in the twentieth century. Even more noticeable was the presence of American flags. Over the centuries Mennonites retained an adamant stand for complete separation between church and state. American flags were not mounted in churches of Kansas Mennonites before World War I. Patriotic pressure brought American flags into the church. The Bethel College Church reluctantly mounted a flag in the sanctuary to assure the community of its patriotic loyalty. In an attempt to reduce the encroachment of the American flag, a Christian flag was also added. Both were removed after the war. Other churches received American flags from local American Legions. The Zion Mennonite Church (Elbing) displayed a flag during the war in the form of a decal displayed in the front window. Most removed them after the First World War only to take them out of storage when patriotic pressure mounted in World War II. The placement of American flags in sanctuaries signaled the advance of civil religion and Americanization.[12]

Another distinctive practice related to church architecture was that of separate seating for men and women. The practice was so strictly enforced that in time separate doors for men and women were designed at the entry of the church. Nearly all Mennonite churches of the Kansas Conference had a dual entryway and maintained separate seating well into the twentieth century. Men sat on the right side and women on the left. Children were either scattered throughout the congregation or located in the first few pews. Occasionally a visiting couple unfamiliar with separate seating visited a Mennonite church. Ushers usually made urgent requests to seat separately; on at least one occasion the embarrassed couple immediately left the service.[13]

Separate seating was difficult to give up. Mennonites generally preferred to maintain doing things as they had for centuries. Mixed seating actually resulted from other innovations. With the advent of electric lighting and the adoption of Sunday evening services, some couples took the less formal atmosphere as an opportunity to sit together. At first this applied only to married couples.[14] In other churches separate seating came to an end with the transition to a new building without the dual entryway.

Mixed seating was accepted in 1932 at the First Mennonite Church of Newton with the dedication of a new edifice. Hoffnungsau encouraged families to sit together around the same time the congregation moved into a modern structure in 1950.

Although the transition to mixed seating was gradual, as with other changes it caused some incidents of conflict. One such event occurred at the Eden Mennonite Church (Moundridge) early in its history. The congregation assembled to address the matter of mixed seating. A suggestion had been made that families sit together. This was intolerable to some. A college student triggered an outburst by stating that he had recently attended a YMCA meeting where people sat together

in family units and it seemed appropriate. When he sat down an older
gentleman thundered:

> What do we care about that XYZ? We are not an XYZ! We are
> in a Christian Church and in a Christian Church the men sit
> on one side and the women on the other side![15]

Many of the earliest incidents of mixed seating occurred among
engaged couples who sat together on the men's side at the rear. Young
people were usually outspoken in their support for mixed seating.
As with Sunday schools and Christian Endeavor Societies, the church
gradually accepted mixed seating in part to retain its young people.
Although the rate of transition from separate to mixed seating varied
with each congregation, the process began shortly before the First
World War in some churches and continued into the 1950s for others.[16]

Church Music

The church music of Mennonites illustrates the confrontation
between the principle of nonconformity and the process of Americanization. Congregational singing was a regular part of Anabaptist-Mennonite
worship from the beginning. However, it was distinctly different
from that of the Roman Catholic and Lutheran churches in both form
and content. The Ausbund, an early collection of Swiss Anabaptist
hymns, contained mostly martyr songs. Many of them were composed
and first sung in prisons. Early Anabaptist music distinctively included the use of vernacular, homophonic singing in a nonliturgical
style devoid of musical instruments. The Lutheran Reformation, which
first restored singing in the vernacular, retained both musical instruments and a liturgical type of worship service.[17]

When East European and Russian Mennonites arrived in Kansas
in the 1870s, they continued to honor the musical traditions of their

past. Church music was, as a rule, in unison (homophonic) and restricted to congregational singing without instrumental accompaniment. The early hymnbooks were in German, had no notes, but indicated a melody which was transmitted by rote from generation to generation. The singing was very slow and followed the leading of a Vorsaenger, or songleader. Choirs did not exist in the original Kansas congregations.[18]

The adoption of musical instruments, the demise of the Vorsaenger, the development of choirs, and the use of American "gospel" hymns and hymnals were evidence of the acculturation of Mennonite music in America.

Early Anabaptists associated musical instruments with the Catholic mass and thus did not include them in their worship services. Although Dutch Mennonite churches introduced pipe organs in their churches during the eighteenth century, East European and Russian Mennonite churches generally did not have musical instruments before World War I. The pietistic revivals of the 1860s resulted in the incorporation of musical instruments in Mennonite Brethren churches in the second half of the nineteenth century. However, the Kirchliche Mennonites who settled in central Kansas in the 1870s, for the most part, were unfamiliar with musical instruments in church services.

The introduction of musical instruments followed a familiar pattern in most congregations. Usually an organ was installed first (table 8-2). Its tonal qualities were less obtrusive than that of the piano. Often musical instruments came into the church via Sunday school. Since Sunday school was an American addition to nineteenth

TABLE 8-2

FIRST MUSICAL INSTRUMENTS INSTALLED IN WESTERN DISTRICT
CONFERENCE MENNONITE CHURCHES

Church	Year Organ	(Piano)
First Mennonite of Halstead.	1882	(1919)
First Mennonite of Newton.	1897	
Bergthal Mennonite	1898	
Zion Mennonite	1899	
Bethel College Mennonite	1900*	
Johannestal Mennonite.	1907	
Emmaus Mennonite	1908	(1926)
Hopefield Mennonite.	1909	
First Mennonite of Pretty Prairie.	1905	(1914)
Alexanderwohl Mennonite.	1910	(1922)
Tabor Mennonite.	1912	(1924)
Eden Mennonite	1912	(1924)
Brudertal Mennonite.	1913	(1923)
First Mennonite of Christian		(1919)

* Approximate date.

SOURCE: Compiled from church records, Mennonite Library and
Archives, Bethel College, North Newton, Kansas.

294

century immigrant churches, fewer objected to such nontraditional improvisions as organs or pianos. The use of musical instruments in tradition laden worship services was another matter. Some congregations eased the entry of musical instruments by accepting them as personal gifts rather than spending funds from the church treasury. Most churches realized the delicate nature of including something that had been prohibited for centuries.

In 1881 the Kansas Conference discussed the issue of musical instruments in worship services. In typical General Conference fashion, a resolution was passed leaving the decision to the individual congregation.[19] The conference recognized that each church had different views on the issue and the matter was best dealt with at the local level.

Bethel College was a strong influence with regard to musical instruments in Mennonite churches. From its beginning, the school offered piano and organ lessons. In 1902 three of the eleven faculty members taught music. The music department was commonly referred to as the best equipped department at the school.[20] In 1896 the School and College Journal, a monthly publication of the Bethel's board of directors, featured a three part series on church music. It based the distinction of church music from worldly music on the "dignity, seriousness, and spiritual nature" of the former. Although somewhat critical of rhythmical Sunday school and gospel songs, no mention was made of musical instruments in the church.[21]

The presence of musical instruments in worship services did not occur without controversy. In 1908 a proposal for an organ at Alexanderwohl was stalled by the Vorsaenger Committee for two years before the church purchased an instrument. At the Eden Mennonite Church, a debate resulted from a 1912 Bruderschaft decision to select an organ committee to solicit funds. Edmund G. Kaufman recalled the controversy:

> . . . Eden argued whether or not to have an instrument in church. Oh there was a hot argument! "After all, organs and pianos are worldly things. Why bring them into the church?" But the instrument won.[22]

The First Mennonite Church of Halstead was the first Kansas congregation to introduce a musical instrument in 1882 (table 8-2). Several members of the Halstead congregation had previously resided in Iowa and Illinois and were more progressive than other Kansas Conference churches. By World War I the vast majority of WDC churches had either a piano or an organ. In 1928 the conference statistician reported that thirty-seven of forty WDC churches had either a piano, organ, or both. By 1939 few, if any, Mennonite congregations remained without a musical instrument.[23]

The demise of the Vorsaenger was directly related to the introduction of musical instruments. In the absence of organs and pianos in the nineteenth century, the Vorsaenger led singing during worship. He usually sat on a front bench across from the ministers and kept time and tune by singing loudly. Occasionally the Vorsaenger "lined" the hymns by reading each line before the congregation sang it. In large churches several persons served as Vorsaenger and alternated in this role for each hymn. A member was selected to this esteemed position for life.

The organ or piano rendered the position of Vorsaenger unnecessary. After the advent of musical instruments, the only aspect of the position remaining was the selection of hymns. Gradually the minister accepted this responsibility. In some churches, the Vorsaenger attempted to function in conjunction with musical instruments. This seldom worked. The last Vorsaenger at the Alexanderwohl Church resigned in 1927, seventeen years after the congregation purchased an organ.[24] By 1939 the Vorsaenger was a mere memory in most WDC churches.

Historically, European Mennonites looked down on choirs because of their worldly and professional appearance. The traditional emphasis upon congregational singing and simplicity of worship restricted the introduction of choirs for centuries in Mennonite churches. Early Anabaptists emphasized worship services that avoided all forms of liturgy common to Roman Catholic churches. They identified clerical choirs of the Catholic Church as a violation of the "priesthood of all believers" concept.[25]

The introduction of choirs into Kansas Conference churches actually began in Russia. Although none of the Kirchliche Mennonites who came to America developed choirs in Russia, they were exposed to their adoption in Mennonite Brethren congregations by 1870. The actual development of choirs by Kirchliche Mennonite churches in Russia took place around the beginning of the twentieth century.[26]

None of the Kansas Conference congregations were organized in central Kansas with a choir. However, their introduction in America occurred within the first decade. The first choir organized in a Kansas Conference congregation (1876) was in the Hopefield Mennonite Church (Moundridge).[27] The First Mennonite Church of Halstead organized a choir a year later (1877). By the First World War, church choirs in WDC congregations were common (table 8-3).

TABLE 8-3

FIRST CHOIRS ORGANIZED IN WDC MENNONITE CHURCHES

Church	Year
Hopefield Mennonite.	1876
First Mennonite of Halstead.	1877
Brudertal Mennonite.	1877
First Mennonite of Newton.	1888
Bethel College Mennonite	1900*
First Mennonite of Pretty Prairie.	1900*
Johannestal Mennonite.	1900*
Buhler Mennonite	1913
Emmaus Mennonite	1914
Alexanderwohl Mennonite.	1915
Zion Mennonite	1922
First Mennonite of Christian	1922

* Approximate date.

SOURCE: Compiled from church records in the Mennonite Library and Archives, Bethel College, North Newton, Kansas.

Although the first choirs usually sang a cappella, the addition of musical instruments aided their growth. Bethel College also served to encourage the development of choirs in local congregations. The earliest choral organization on campus occurred in the 1890s. The college choir became well known in the early twentieth century for its performance of the "Messiah."[28]

At the 1914 Western District Conference, the delegates were entertained by two choir numbers.[29] This marked the general acceptance of church choirs in Kansas Mennonite congregations. For the most part, choral singing met little opposition in most churches. This may be due to its previous existence in Russia. However, there was often considerable controversy surrounding the type of music sung by church choirs. The introduction of American gospel hymns was a stylistic departure from the traditional Anabaptist hymns of the sixteenth and seventeenth centuries.

Choirs were not the only segment of the Mennonite Church to adopt American gospel hymns. Sunday schools found their lighter and catchy English phrases and tunes particularly useful for children's classes. As early as 1896 a School and College Journal editorial complained that gospel hymns and Sunday school choruses were lowering the quality of Mennonite church music.

> If we give them a careful estimate, we find them lacking in
> strength, in solidity and dignity, elements which are very
> essential to good church music, and which are found in the
> old German church and in the standard English hymns.[30]

The editorial urged Mennonite congregations to avoid the "rhythmic," and "light and flimsy style" of gospel hymns common to revivalistic America in the late nineteenth century.

Mennonites from the Old World frequently brought their own hymnals to America and continued using them during the nineteenth century. Swiss Volhynian congregations used the Ausbund while Prussian and Russian congregations used various editions of Gesangbuch in Welchem eine Sammlung geistreicher Lieder befindlich zur all gemeinen Erbauung und zum Lobe Gottes (Songbook Containing a Collection of Hymns Intended for a General Edification and to the Praise of God). In 1892 the General Conference Mennonite church published the Gesangbuch mit Noten (Songbook with Notes). It was widely accepted by WDC congregations and served as the final German-language hymnal in most churches. Hoffnungsau (Inman) and Alexanderwohl (Goessel) adapted Gesangbuch mit Noten around the turn of the century and used it until 1940 when they both adopted English-language hymnals.[31]

During the early twentieth century, a common trend in WDC Mennonite churches was the use of two hymnals: a German-language Mennonite hymnal and an English-language American gospel hymnal. American gospel hymns developed in the middle of the nineteenth century and became popular largely as the result of the great Moody revivals of 1870-1890. Several collections of gospel hymns including the Moody and Sankey songbook, Gospel Hymns and Spiritual Songs (1875), made their way into Mennonite congregations across North America. The most popular in central Kansas Mennonite churches was Tabernacle Hymns (1921). A survey in the 1940s revealed that 75 percent of WDC churches owned Tabernacle Hymns. The survey also revealed that 86 percent had the English-language Mennonite Hymnary while only 18 percent still used Gesangbuch mit Noten. This seems to indicate that most WDC had two hymnals - a Mennonite hymnal for worship service and an American gospel hymnal for Sunday school.[32]

Tabernacle Hymns contained revivalistic songs by Wesley, Bliss, Sankey, Knapp, Palmer, Crosby, and others. Such hymns as "Onward Christian Soldiers" must have seemed awkward alongside the hymns of sixteenth century Anabaptist martyrs. Walter H. Hohmann, professor of music at Bethel College, complained that gospel songs "lowered the standards" of Mennonite church music. He berated "cheap commercial hymnbooks" which left congregations "definitely weaker and spiritually poorer."[33]

Hohmann's 1946 criticisms were a matter of too little, too late. By 1939 American gospel hymns had infiltrated Mennonite church music in central Kansas. When the General Conference Mennonite Church decided to publish an English-language hymnal, they chose Hohmann to serve as one of its editors. In 1940 the conference released the first edition of the Mennonite Hymnary. Included was an entire section entitled "Gospel Songs," featuring the works of Wesley, Bliss, Sankey, Knapp, Palmer, Crosby, and others.[34]

The development of Mennonite music in central Kansas from 1874-1939 clearly reveals the impact of Americanization. The introduction of musical instruments, choirs, and gospel hymns replaced simple Old World homophonic singing led by a Vorsaenger. Consequently, the influence of American church music eroded a distinctive form of nineteenth century Mennonite church music.

Conclusion

With an emphasis upon simplicity, sincerity, and humility, any development of the fine arts seemed to Mennonites to be at the best artificial and pretentious, and at the worst dangerous and wasteful. In the Old World Mennonite church architecture and music were merely functionable. The simplicity of fine arts was due in part to a desire to abstain from any worldly appearance. A rural character and cultural isolation also accounted for simple artistic taste among those who arrived in central Kansas in 1874.

Although Mennonite architecture was modest by 1939 American standards and church music still revealed traces of an Anabaptist tradition, Kansas congregations in the twentieth century gradually took on a number of American characteristics. Mennonites increasingly worshipped in churches that reflected their surroundings. Tall steeples outlined against the flat Kansas prairie betrayed the impact of Americanization. In 1939 Mennonites sang American gospel hymns accompanied by musical instruments and choral arrangements. The Russian Mennonite immigrant of 1874 would have felt out of place in many of the Kansas congregations six decades later. Mixed seating and the obtrusive sound of musical instruments in the worship service certainly would have stood in stark contrast to the standard nineteenth century Mennonite concept of worship.

The development of American Mennonite church architecture and music from 1874 to 1939 was a gradual process. Architectural and musical transitions took place in several stages, not always without controversy. However, the first sixty-five years in America produced far more changes in the immigrant church than had a full century of Mennonite sojourn in Russia. To an observer passing by a Mennonite church in central Kansas on a Sunday morning in 1939, there was little external evidence of immigrant origins. He was likely to hear American revivalistic hymns coming from a structure typical of rural American churches. Any hint of immigrant roots would have required observation beyond that of Mennonite music and architecture.

CHAPTER VIII - ENDNOTES

1. Henry Peter Krehbiel, The History of the Mennonite General Conference, vol. 2 (Newton, Kansas: Herald Publishing Co., 1939), p. 252.

2. Gerald V. Mussleman, "Architecture and Our Faith," Mennonite Life 20 (October 1965): 158-67; Cornelius Krahn, "Mennonite Church Architecture," Mennonite Life 12 (January 1957): 19-27; Mennonite Encyclopedia, s.v. "Architecture," by Cornelius Krahn.

3. David A. Haury, Prairie People (Newton, Kansas: Faith and Life Press, 1981), p. 32.

4. Albert M. Gaeddert, Centennial History of Hoffnungsau Mennonite Church (North Newton, Kansas: Mennonite Press, Inc., 1975), pp. 57-60, 93-95.

5. Minutes of the Western District Conference, 29-31 October 1924, Mennonite Library and Archives, Bethel College, North Newton, Kansas (typescript, English translation).

6. Minutes, 17-18 October 1928.

7. John D. Thiessen, "The More Things Change, the More They Stay the Same: a History of the First Mennonite Church, Newton, Kansas 1878-1982" (Unpublished paper, Mennonite Library and Archives, Bethel College, North Newton, Kansas, 1982), p. 81; Menno Schrag, First Mennonite Church (n.p., 1978).

8. Krahn, "Mennonite Church Architecture," p. 34.

9. J. Winfield Fretz, "Separation or Infiltration" in The Seventy-fifth Anniversary Services of the Swiss Mennonites, comp. Harley J. Stucky (North Newton, Kansas: Mennonite Press, Inc., 1950), p. 51.

10. Don E. Smucker, "Building the Lord's House," Mennonite Life 12 (January 1957): 18.

11. Mussleman, p. 162; Elmer Ediger, "What is Central in Worship," Mennonite Life 12 (January 1957): 29-30; Krahn, "Mennonite Church Architecture," p. 34.

12. Ronald Andres, Centennial Reflections: Zion 100 (n.p., 1983), p. 16; Henry A. Fast, "The Witness of Our Congregation Over Seventy-five Years" (Unpublished paper, Mennonite Library and Archives, Bethel College, North Newton, Kansas, 1972), p. 7.

13. Cornelius Cicero Janzen, "Americanization of Russian Mennonites in Central Kansas" (M.A. thesis, University of Kansas, 1914), pp. 88-89.

14. Ibid., p. 89.

15. William Juhnke, ed., The Seventy-fifth Anniversary: the Eden Church in Mission - Past, Present, and Future (n.p., 1970), p. 36.

16. Edmund G. Kaufman, "Social Problems and Opportunities of the Western District Conference Communities of Mennonites of North America" (M.A. thesis, Bluffton College and Mennonite Seminary, 1917), p. 134; Willis Linscheid, "The History of the Emmanuel Mennonite Church" (Unpublished paper, Mennonite Library and Archives, Bethel College, North Newton, Kansas, 1950), p. 12. Kaufman states in 1917 that separate seating was already in transition in some churches. Linscheid discovered in 1950 that the Emmanuel Church still maintained separate seating.

17. Mennonite Encyclopedia, s.v. "Church Music," by Harold S. Bender.

18. Mennonite Encyclopedia, s.v. "Church Music," by Cornelius Krahn.

19. Minutes, 10-11 October 1881.

20. Minutes, 8-9 October 1902.

21. David Goerz, "Church Music," School and College Journal 5 (May 1896): 33-35.

22. William Juhnke, ed., p. 36.

23. Edmund G. Kaufman, "Social Problems," p. 134; Minutes, 17-18 October 1928; Otto D. Unruh, "Schisms of the Russian Mennonites of Harvey, McPherson, and Reno Counties, Kansas" (M.A. thesis, University of Kansas, 1939), p. 98.

24. David C. Wedel, The Story of Alexanderwohl (North Newton, Kansas: Mennonite Press, Inc., 1974), p. 64.

25. Calvin D. Buller, "The Development of Singing Amongst the Dutch-German Mennonites of Central Kansas" (M.A. thesis, Wichita State University, 1965), p. 19; Mennonite Encyclopedia, s.v. "Choirs," by Harold S. Bender and Cornelius Krahn.

26. Wesley Berg, "The Development of Choral Singing Among the Mennonites of Russia to 1895," Mennonite Quarterly Review 55 (April 1981): 132.

27. Menno Kaufman, The Challenging Faith (Newton, Kansas: United Printing, Inc., 1975), p. 35.

28. Peter J. Wedel, The Story of Bethel College (North Newton, Kansas: Bethel College, 1954), pp. 124, 148.

29. Minutes, 28-30 October 1914.

30. David Goerz, "Church Music," p. 34.

31. Mennonite Encyclopedia, s.v. "Hymnology of the Swiss, French, and South German Mennonites," by Harold S. Bender; "Hymnology of the Mennonites of West and East Prussia, Danzig, and Russia," by Cornelius Krahn; "Hymnology of American Mennonites," by Harold S. Bender; Buller, pp. 14-16; Albert Gaeddert, p. 67.

32. Margie Wiebe, "Hymnals Used by the General Conference," Mennonite Life 3 (April 1948): 36, 38.

33. Walter H. Hohmann, "Transition in Worship," Mennonite Life 1 (January 1946): 8; Tabernacle Hymns, no. 2 (Chicago: Tabernacle Publishing Company, 1921).

34. Walter H. Hohmann and Lester Hostetler, eds., The Mennonite Hymnary (Newton, Kansas: Mennonite Publications Office, 1940), pp. 437-504.

CHAPTER IX

CONCLUSION

In 1949 Kansas Mennonites observed the seventy-fifth anniversary
of their arrival in America. At that time, nearly every Mennonite
community organized a celebration honoring the few surviving first
generation immigrants. For Kansas Mennonites the occasion was one
of reflection. Despite America's crusades against all things German
during World War I, the vast majority of Mennonites were content with
their lot in Kansas. America had offered nineteenth century immigrants
religious toleration and economic opportunity beyond their greatest
expectations.

By the middle of the twentieth century, numerous Mennonite
churches dotted the Kansas countryside and Mennonite farmers flourished
in America's agricultural heartland. However, success in America
came with a price -- a loss of Mennonite distinctiveness. Bethel
professor and one time pastor of a German Congregational church, Ralph
C. Kaufman, acknowledged this loss of ethnoreligious separation in
an anniversary address to a group of Swiss Volhynians: "I am inclined
to say that the difference between Mennonites as a whole and the outside
world is often grossly exaggerated."[1] In pursuit of religious freedom
and economic gain, Kansas Mennonites by the middle of the twentieth
century no longer retained the same ethnoreligious distinctiveness
that allowed them to establish an autonomous peoplehood in Russia

and east Europe for nearly a century. Whereas Russification with its conscription and educational requirements failed, Americanization, via prosperity and toleration, infiltrated the Mennonite ethos and successfully produced loyal American citizens.

The immigrant church played a significant role in the Americanization of Mennonites. In the absence of the Old World village social structure, the local congregation in Kansas served as a center for identity formation. As the pressures of Americanization mounted, immigrants turned to the church for support. In this way the congregation facilitated the Americanization process, easing the pain of adjustment through the maintenance of certain Old World customs while forsaking other traditions that did not fit in the American Protestant environment. At the same time, the very institution that served as a repository of sacred symbols also experienced a transition.

The Mennonite churches of central Kansas in 1939 were significantly altered in both appearance and content after six decades in America. With the gradual abandonment of German as an ecclesiastical language, the church lost an important essence (Wesen) of Mennonite peoplehood as well as a barrier to worldly conformity. When parochial schools were supplanted by public schools, the church was left with Sunday school and two weeks of Vacation Bible School each summer to instill traditional Mennonite values. American revivalism made inroads into Kansas congregations by means of protracted meetings, an emphasis on evangelism, the temperance movement, and Sunday schools. The church bore the impact of American modernism as evidenced by a brief affiliation with the Federal Council of Churches. Even such church customs as footwashing, communion, and baptism were altered by Americanization. Mennonite church architecture and music lost much of its distinctive character from 1874 to 1939.

The story of Mennonite acculturation in central Kansas contains a paradox. Immigrants in search of religious toleration in 1874 discovered an American freedom different from what they had envisioned. They sought community autonomy; instead, they were offered individual self-sufficiency. This individualistic freedom eroded Mennonite community autonomy. However, World War I awakened Americanizing Mennonites to a revitalization of an Anabaptist heritage. Bethel College, the General Conference, and Mennonite benevolence, all agents of Americanization, provided a vision for progressive Mennonite life. This was the type of progressive Mennonitism C. H. Wedel, president of Bethel College, had called for in 1904. It represented "the merging of new and old ideas" and challenged Mennonites to "enrich their knowledge and widen their horizons."[2] To nineteenth century immigrants this meant the forfeiture of social separation and group autonomy and an emphasis on such Anabaptist ideals as nonresistance and collective benevolence. Thus exists the paradox: as Mennonite churches in central Kansas took on characteristics of American Protestantism, there emerged a revitalization of progressive Mennonitism.

E. G. Kaufman, former missionary to China and one time president of Bethel College, recognized that the greatest threat to progressive Mennonitism was "rampant individualism." Kaufman predicted in his 1917 thesis that the failure of Mennonites to cooperate collectively would result in the complete loss of a historical ethnoreligious identity.[3] The First World War brought Kansas Mennonites to the shocking realization that group survival required a cooperative, organized effort to foster group beliefs systematically. They could no longer rely upon the German language, parochial schools, and the farmer-patriarch elder to preserve the Mennonite ethos. The transforming impact of Americanization had already taken its toll on the essence of Mennonite identity by 1920. Western District Conference leaders were challenged to develop new agents of group preservation. The WDC responded by incorporating Bethel College as a conference-controlled institution in 1921 and developing a variety of relief programs in the 1920s and 1930s. Both of these measures were indicative of a desire by conference leaders to respond creatively to difficult situations facing Mennonites in the twentieth century.

In some respects the experiences of Mennonites in central Kansas conforms to the model of assimilation formed by the sociologist, Milton Gordon. Gordon contends that first generation immigrants initiate behavioral assimilation (language shift and acceptance of American behavioral patterns), while the second generation moves on to the structural assimilation stage (large-scale entrance into institutions of the host society on a primary level). Once structural assimilation occurs all other types of assimilation, including marital assimilation, will naturally follow. Thus, by the third generation all evidences of ethnic identity are replaced by mere memories. Gordon makes two exceptions for his generalizations: 1) minority groups who are spatially isolated and segregated in a rural area; and 2) racially distinct minorities easily marked for discrimination. In both instances, behavioral assimilation is slowed while structural assimilation is postponed for at least a generation.[4]

Mennonites in central Kansas were spatially isolated and segregated in a rural area. True to Gordon's model, their Americanization was delayed but not halted. Behavioral assimilation began gradually with the first generation, but it was the second generation that made the language transition. Structural assimilation began with the second generation but moved slowly until World War I forced an emerging third generation leadership to pursue a progressive Mennonitism in the 1920s and 1930s. The third generation adopted select aspects of American Protestantism and incorporated them in the Mennonite ethos.

The decision to drop certain traditional characteristics (German language, footwashing, parochial schools) and adopt those characteristics of American Protestantism (English language, gospel hymns, musical instruments, protracted meetings, public schools) was at times painful. In her novel about Russian Mennonites in Paraguay, Ingrid Rimland depicts the pain encountered in the structural assimilation of second and third generation immigrants. Young Karin vents the frustrations of a granddaughter torn between her love for a Paraguayan man and the long held Anabaptist values of nonconformity and social segregation:

> In time Oma, we will have to leave the past. We cannot forever and ever cling to ways of doing things and believing things just because they had meaning in Russia. There is more to life than that. I am only now beginning to realize how much more there is to life than what I have known. Carlitos believes that occasional work is justified only in order to make leisure possible. But he says we glorify the virtues of work while life passes us by.[5]

America's entry into World War I reminded Kansas Mennonites of their "Christ-against-culture" heritage. However, a mass exodus from the United States was not a feasible solution after four decades of acculturation. Instead WDC leaders chose to pursue a course between superpatriotism and emigration. Kansas Mennonites cautiously observed their Anabaptist heritage while simultaneously displaying all of the evidences of good citizenship. The result was an _American_ denomination with an _Anabaptist_ doctrine.

The prophetic observation of journalist Nobel Prentis in 1882 was fulfilled by many Kansas Mennonites in the twentieth century. As predicted, they prospered and became the richest farmers in the state. Several left the farm, as Prentis said they would, and took up city life. Some married "American gentiles" and rapidly assimilated. Others took up politics and, as Prentis described them, went "about like a roaring lion, seeking nomination for Congress." However, Prentis was not completely accurate in his prediction. Although some left and others completely assimilated, the vast majority opted to pursue a life Prentis could not envision -- "of a peaceful, quiet, wealthy, people . . . dwelling in great content . . . in the grassy, wind-swept wilderness."[6]

Thus, by 1939 many of the descendants of the original immigrants continued to reside in central Kansas. Their experience offered little hope of escaping acculturation. After more than six decades in America, these folk were both Mennonites and Americans, what Mennonite historian James C. Juhnke describes as "a people of two kingdoms."[7]

CHAPTER IX - ENDNOTES

1. Ralph C. Kaufman, "A Critical Evaluation of Ourselves," in Addresses and Items of Interest Connected with the Seventy-fifth Anniversay Services of the Swiss Mennonites, ed. Harley J. Stucky (North Newton, Kansas: Mennonite Publishing, 1950), p. 53.

2. C. H. Wedel, Abriss der Geschichte der Mennoniten, IV (North Newton, Kansas: Bethel College, 1904), p. 199.

3. Edmund G. Kaufman, "Social Problems and Opportunities of the Western District Conference Communities of Mennonites of North America" (A.M. thesis, Bluffton College and Mennonite Seminary, 1917), p. 110.

4. Milton M. Gordon, Assimilation in American Life (New York: Oxford University Press, 1964), pp. 70-71.

5. Ingrid Rimland, The Wanderers (St. Louis: Concordia, 1977), p. 313.

6. Nobel L. Prentis, Kansas Miscellanies (Topeka: Kansas Publishing House, 1899), pp. 147-54.

7. James C. Juhnke, A People of Two Kingdoms (Newton, Kansas: Faith and Life Press, 1975).

BIBLIOGRAPHY

Books

Ahlsrom, Sydney. A Religious History of the American People. New
    Haven: Yale University Press, 1972.

Anderson, Barbara. Internal Migration During Modernization in Late
    Nineteenth-Century Russia. Princeton: Princeton University
    Press, 1980.

Andres, Ronald J. Centennial Reflections: Zion 100. n.p., 1983.

Barrett, Lois. The Vision and the Reality. Newton, Kansas: Faith
    and Life Press, 1983.

Bartel, Helen, and Quiring, Walter. In the Fullness of Time: 150
    Years of Mennonite Sojourn in Russia. Waterloo, Ontario: Reeve
    Bean Limited, 1974.

Bartel, H. J.; Bartel, L. F.; and Ewert, D. P. Historical Sketch of
    the First Mennonite Church, Hillsboro, Kansas. Hillsboro,
    Kansas: Mennonite Brethren Publishing House, 1944.

Bartlett, Roger P. Human Capital: the Settlement of Foreigners in
    Russia 1762-1804. Cambridge: Cambridge University Press, 1979.

Bender, D. H.; Erb, T. M.; and King, L. O. Conference Record Contain-
    ing the Proceedings of the Kansas-Nebraska Mennonite Conference,
    1876-1914. n.p., 1914.

Bender, Harold S., and Smith, C. Henry. Mennonites and their Heritage.
    Scottdale, Pennsylvania: Herald Press, 1964.

Bender, Harold S. Two Centuries of American Mennonite Literature.
    Goshen, Indiana: Mennonite Historical Society, Goshen College,
    1929.

Bennett, John C. Christian Ethics and Social Policy. New York: Charles
    Scribner's Sons, 1946.

Blum, Jerome. Lord and Peasant in Russia from the 9th to the 19th
    Century. Princeton, Princeton University Press, 1961.

Buenker, John D., and Burkel, Nicholas C. Immigration and Ethnicity:
    A Guide to Information Sources. Detroit: Gale Research Company,
    1977.

Carman, J. Neale. Foreign-Language Units in Kansas. Lawrence, Kansas:
    University of Kansas Press, 1962.

Centennial Chronicle: First Mennonite Church of Christian. n.p., 1978.

Connelley, William E. History of Kansas Newspapers. Topeka: Kansas
    State Printing Plant, 1916.

Davis, Kenneth S. Kansas: A Bicentennial History. New York: W. W.
    Norton & Company, 1976.

Dieter, Melvin Easterday. The Holiness Revival in the Nineteenth
    Century. Metuchen, New Jersey: Scarecrow Press, Inc., 1980.

Dyck, Cornelius J. An Introduction to Mennonite History. Scottdale,
    Pennsylvania: Herald Press, 1981.

Estep, William R. The Anabaptist Story. Grand Rapids, Michigan:
    William B. Eerdmans Publishing Company, 1975.

Ewert, Jacob; Ewert, John A.; Plenert, Albert; Unruh, Mrs. Harrison.
    Sixtieth Anniversary of the Johannestal Mennonite Church, 1882-
    1942. Hillsboro, Kansas; n.p., 1942.

Fiftieth Anniversary of Buhler Mennonite Church, 1920-1970. North
    Newton, Kansas: Mennonite Press, Inc., n.d.

Friedmann, Robert. The Theology of Anabaptism. Scottdale, Pennsyl-
    vania: Herald Press, 1973.

Friesen, Peter M. The Mennonite Brotherhood in Russia (1789-1910).
    Fresno, California: Board of Christian Literature, General Con-
    ference of the Mennonite Brethren Churches, 1978.

Funk, Ray N. Brudertal, 1873-1964. North Newton, Kansas: Mennonite
    Press, 1964.

Funk, Ruby, ed. Peace, Progress, Promise: A 75th Anniversary of Tabor
    Mennonite Church. North Newton, Kansas: Mennonite Press, 1983.

Gaeddert, Albert M. Centennial History of Hoffnungsau Mennonite Church.
    North Newton, Kansas: Mennonite Press, Inc., 1975.

Gaeddert, G. R., and Reimer, Gustav E. Exiled by the Czar. Newton,
    Kansas: Mennonite Publication Office, 1956.

Galpin, Charles Josiah. Rural Life. New York: Century Company, 1918.

Gerig, Jared F., and Lugibihl, Walter H. The Missionary Church Association. Berne, Indiana: Economy Printing Concern, 1950.

Giesinger, Adam. From Catherine to Khrushchev. Battleford, Saskatchewan: Marian Press, 1974.

Goering, Gladys V. Women in Search of Mission. Newton, Kansas: Faith and Life Press, 1980.

Goertz, P. S., and Stucky, Harley J. Our Church Past and Present. North Newton, Kansas: Mennonite Press, 1954.

Gordon, Milton M. Assimilation in American Life. New York: Oxford University Press, 1964.

_____. Human Nature, Class, and Ethnicity. New York: Oxford University Press, 1978.

Greeley, Andrew M. The Catholic Experience: An Interpretation of the History of American Catholicism. New York: Doubleday and Company, Inc., 1967.

_____. The Denominational Society. Glenview, Illinois: Scott, Foresman and Company, 1972.

Greeley, Andrew M., and Rossi, Peter H. The Education of American Catholics. Chicago: Aldine Publishing Company, 1966.

Habegger, Loris A., ed. The Flock and the Kingdom. n.p., 1975.

Handlin, Oscar. The Uprooted. Boston: Little, Brown and Company, 1973.

Harcave, Sidney. Russia, a History. Philadelphia: J. B. Lippencott Company, 1964.

Hartzler, John E. Education Among the Mennonites of America. Danvers, Illinois: Central Mennonite Publishing Board, 1925.

Haury, David A. Prairie People: A History of the Western District Conference. Newton, Kansas: Faith and Life Press, 1981.

Haxhausen, August von. Studies on the Interior of Russia. Chicago: The University of Chicago Press, 1972.

Heitman, Sidney, ed. Germans from Russia in Colorado. Ft. Collins, Colorado: The Western Social Science Association, 1978.

Herberg, Will. Protestant, Catholic, Jew; an Essay in American Religious Sociology. New York: Doubleday and Company, 1955.

Hiebert, Clarence. The Holdeman People. South Pasadena, California: William Carey Library, 1973.

316

_____, ed. Brothers in Deed to Brothers in Need. Newton, Kansas: Faith and Life Press, 1974.

Higham, John. Strangers in the Land. New York: Atheneum, 1977.

Hohmann, Walter H., and Hostetler, Lester, eds. The Mennonite Hymnary. Newton, Kansas: Mennonite Publications Office, 1940.

Horsch, John. Mennonites in Europe. Scottdale, Pennsylvania: Mennonite Publishing House, 1942.

Huffman, Jasper A. History of the Mennonite Brethren in Christ. New Carlisle, Ohio: The Bethel Publishing Company, 1920.

Jensen, Richard. The Winning of the Midwest. Chicago: The University Press, 1971.

Jones, Charles E. Perfectionist Persuasion: The Holiness Movement and American Methodism. Metuchen, New Jersey: Scarecrow Press, Inc., 1974.

Juhnke, James C. A People of Mission. Newton, Kansas: Faith and Life Press, 1979.

_____. A People of Two Kingdoms. Newton, Kansas: Faith and Life Press, 1975.

Juhnke, William, ed. The 75th Anniversary: The Eden Church in Mission - Past, Present, Future. n.p., 1970.

Kaufman, Edmund G. General Conference Mennonite Pioneers. North Newton, Kansas: Bethel College Press, 1973.

Kaufman, Menno. The Challenging Faith. Newton, Kansas: United Printing, Inc., 1975.

Keller, Ludwig. Die Reformation und die Aelteren Reformparteien. Leipzig: S. Hirzel, 1885.

Klaasen, Walter. Anabaptism: Neither Catholic nor Protestant. Waterloo, Ontario: Conrad Press, 1973.

Krahn, Cornelius, and Schmidt, John F., eds. A Century of Witness: General Conference Mennonite Church. Newton, Kansas: Mennonite Publishing Office, 1959.

Krahn, Cornelius, ed. From the Steppes to the Prairies. Newton, Kansas: Mennonite Publication Office, 1949.

Krehbiel, Christian. Prairie Pioneer. Newton, Kansas: Faith and Life Press, 1961.

317

Krehbiel, Henry Peter. History of the Mennonite General Conference. Vol. 1. St. Louis: A. Wieblisch & Sons Printing Company, 1898.

_____. The History of the General Conference of the Mennonite Church of North America. Vol. 2. Newton, Kansas: Herald Publishing Company, 1938.

Lageer, Eileen. Merging Streams: The Story of the Missionary Church. Elkhart, Indiana: Bethel Publishing Company, 1979.

Lenski, Gerhard E. The Religious Factor. Garden City, New York: Doubleday and Company, 1961.

Littell, Franklin H. The Anabaptist View of the Church. Boston: Star King Press, 1958.

Loewen, Harry, ed., Mennonite Images. Winnipeg: Hyperion Press, 1980.

Long, James. The German-Russians: A Bibliography. Santa Barbara: Cleo Press, 1978.

Luebke, Frederick C. Bonds of Loyalty; German-Americans and World War I. DeKalb, Illinois: Northern Illinois University Press, 1974.

_____. Immigrants and Politics: The Germans of Nebraska 1880-1900. Lincoln: University of Nebraska Press, 1969.

_____, ed. Ethnicity on the Great Plains. Lincoln: University of Nebraska Press, 1980.

Madariaga, Isabel de. Russia in the Age of Catherine the Great. London: Yale University Press, 1981.

Marsden, George M. Fundamentalism and American Culture: The Shaping of Twentieth Century Evangelicalism: 1870-1925. New York: Oxford University Press, 1980.

Meakin, Annette M. B. Russia: Travels and Studies. Philadelphia: J. B. Lippincott Company, 1906.

Mennonite Encyclopedia. Scottdale, Pennsylvania: Mennonite Publishing House, 4 vols. 1955-1959.

Niebuhr, H. Richard. Christ and Culture. New York: Harper and Brothers, 1951.

_____. The Social Sources of Denominationalism. New York: New American Library, Inc., 1929.

Norwood, Frederick. Strangers and Exiles. 2 vols. Nashville: Abingdon Press, 1969.

Pannabecker, Samuel F. Open Doors: The History of the General Confer-
    ence Mennonite Church. Newton, Kansas: Faith and Life Press,
    1975.

_____. Faith in Ferment. Newton, Kansas: Faith and Life Press,
    1968.

Parish, Arlyn John. Kansas Mennonites During World War I. Hays,
    Kansas: Fort Hays Kansas State College, 1968.

Peters, Gerhard. Heritage: First One Hundred Years, 1874-1974. North
    Newton, Kansas: Mennonite Press, 1974.

Pipes, Richard. Russia Under the Old Regime. New York: Charles Scrib-
    ner's Sons, 1974.

Prentis, Noble L. A History of Kansas. Topeka: Caroline Prentis, 1909.

_____. Kansas Miscellanies. Topeka: Kansas Publishing House, 1889.

Raeff, Marc. Imperial Russia 1682-1825: The Coming Age of Modern
    Russia. New York: Knopf Inc., 1971.

Riasanosky, Nicholas V. A History of Russia. New York: Oxford Uni-
    versity Press, 1963.

Rimland, Ingrid. The Wanderers. St. Louis: Concordia, 1977.

Risser, Emma K. History of the Pennsylvania Mennonite Church in Kansas.
    Scottdale, Pennsylvania: Mennonite Publishing House, 1958.

Sallet, Richard. Russian-German Settlements in the United States.
    Minneapolis: Lund Press, 1974.

Sanford, Elias B. Federal Council of the Churches of Christ in America.
    Hartford: S. S. Scranton Company, 1916.

Schach, Paul, ed. Languages in Conflict. Lincoln: University of
    Nebraska Press, 1980.

Schmidt, John F. From Michalin to Gnadenberg: 1811-1950. North Newton,
    Kansas: Mennonite Press, 1950.

Schmidt, Richard F., and Schmidt, Tena. Memories of Baptism and Com-
    munion with the Rite of Footwashing at Alexanderwohl. Emporia,
    Kansas: Emporia State Press, 1980.

Schock, Adolph. In Quest of Free Land. Assen, Netherlands: Royal
    Vangorcum Ltd., 1964.

Schrag, Martin. The European History of the Swiss Mennonites from
    Volhynia. North Newton, Kansas: Mennonite Press, 1974.

319

Schrag, Menno. First Mennonite Church. n.p., 1978.

Self, Huber, and Socolofsky, Homer E. Historical Atlas of Kansas.
    Norman: University of Oklahoma Press, 1972.

Seller, Maxine. To Seek America: A History of Ethnicity in the United
    States. Englewood, New Jersey: Jerome S. Ozer, 1977.

Siebert, Grant. History of the Bergthal Mennonite Church Pawnee Rock,
    Kansas. Great Bend, Kansas: n.p., 1976.

Sixtieth Anniversary of the West Zion Mennonite Church. n.p., n.d.

Smith, C. Henry. The Coming of the Russian Mennonites. Berne,
    Indiana: Mennonite Book Concern, 1927.

_____. The Story of the Mennonites. Newton, Kansas: Faith and
    Life Press, 1981.

Smith, Timothy L. Called Unto Holiness. Kansas City: Nazarene Pub-
    lishing House, 1962.

_____. Revivalism and Social Reform in Mid-Nineteenth Century
    America. New York: Abingdon Press, 1957.

Srole, Leo, and Warner, W. Lloyd. The Social Systems of American Ethnic
    Groups. New Haven: Yale University Press, 1945.

Stucky, Harley J. Addresses and Items of Interest Connected with the
    Seventy-fifth Anniversary Services of the Swiss Mennonites.
    Newton, Kansas: Mennonite Publishing, 1950.

Stucky, Jonas A. Epochs of History of First Mennonite Church of Pretty
    Prairie, Kansas. n.p., 1954.

Stumpp, Karl. The German-Russians: Two Centuries of Pioneering. Bonn:
    Edition Atlantic-Forum, 1967.

_____. The Emigration from Germany to Russia in the Years 1763 to
    1862. Lincoln: American Historical Society of Germans from
    Russia, 1973.

Synan, Vinson. The Holiness-Pentecostal Movement in the United States.
    Grand Rapids, Michigan: William B. Eerdman's Publishing Company,
    1971.

Tabernacle Hymns, no. 2. Chicago: Tabernacle Publishing Company, 1921.

Taylor, Philip. The Distant Magnet: European Emigration to the United
    States. London: Eyre and Spottiswoode, 1971.

Toews, John A. A History of the Mennonite Brethren Church. Hillsboro,
    Kansas: Mennonite Brethren Publishing House, 1975.

Toews, John B. Czars, Soviets, and Mennonites. Newton: Faith and Life Press, 1982.

_____. Lost Fatherland. Scottdale, Pennsylvania: Herald Press, 1967.

Unrau, Ruth. Who Needs an Oil Well? New York: Abingdon Press, 1968.

Walker, Mack. Germany and the Emigration 1816-1885. Cambridge: Harvard University Press, 1964.

Wedel, Cornelius H. Abriss der Geschichte der Mennoniten. 4 vols. North Newton, Kansas: Bethel College, 1904.

_____. Bilder aus der Kirchengeschichte fur Mennonitische Gemeindeschulen. 7th ed. Newton, Kansas: Herald Book and Printing Company, 1951.

Wedel, David C. The Story of Alexanderwohl. North Newton, Kansas: Mennonite Press, 1974.

Wedel, Peter J. The Story of Bethel College. North Newton, Kansas: Mennonite Press, 1954.

Wedel, Peter P. Church Chronicle of the First Mennonite Church of Christian, Kansas. By the Author, 1957.

Weiss, Bernard J., ed. American Education and the European Immigrant: 1840-1940. Urbana: University of Illinois Press, 1982.

Werger, John C. History of the Mennonites of the Franconia Conference. Scottdale, Pennsylvania: Mennonite Publishing House, 1938.

_____. The Mennonite Church in America. Scottdale, Pennsylvania: Herald Press, 1966.

_____. Glimpses of Mennonite History and Doctrine. Scottdale, Pennsylvania: Herald Press, 1947.

Wiebe, David V. Grace Meadows. Hillsboro, Kansas: Mennonite Brethren Publishing House, 1967.

Williams, George H. The Radical Reformation. Philadelphia: Westminster Press, 1967.

Wilson, Don W. Governor Charles Robinson of Kansas. Lawrence, Kansas: The University of Kansas Press, 1975.

Wittke, Carl. The German-language Press in America. Lexington: University of Kentucky Press, 1957.

Wulhnow, Robert, ed. The Religious Dimension: New Directions in Quantative Research. New York: Academic Press, 1979.

Articles

Adrian, Walter. "A Thrilling Story from an Old Diary." Mennonite Life 3 (January 1948): 23-44.

Bender, Harold S. "Outside Influences on Mennonite Thought." Mennonite Life 10 (January 1955): 45-48.

Berg, Wesley. "The Development of Choral Singing Among the Mennonites of Russia to 1895." Mennonite Quarterly Review 55 (April 1981): 131-42.

Bernap, C. L. "Among the Mennonites of Kansas in 1878." Mennonite Life 4 (October 1949): 20-25, 39.

Bodnar, John. "Materialism and Morality: Slavic-American Immigrants and Education, 1890-1940." The Journal of Ethnic Studies 3 (Winter 1976): 1-19.

Brand, D. J. "The Federal Council - What is it? What does it do?" Mennonite 32 (March 1917): 2.

Braun, Peter. "The Educational System of the Mennonite Colonies in South Russia." Mennonite Quarterly Review 3 (July 1929): 169-82.

Buchheit, Robert H. "Language Maintenance and Shift Among Mennonites in South-Central Kansas." Yearbook of German-American Studies 17 (1982): 111-21.

Carruth, W. "Foreign Settlements in Kansas." Kansas University Quarterly 1 (October 1892): 71-84.

_____. "Foreign Settlements in Kansas." Kansas University Quarterly 3 (October 1894): 159-63.

"The Coming Inter-church Conference." Mennonite 20 (October 1905): 4.

Conzen, Kathleen Neils. "Historical Approaches to the Study of Rural Ethnic Communities." In Ethnicity on the Great Plains, pp. 1-18. Edited by Frederick C. Luebke. Lincoln: University of Nebraska Press, 1980.

Coultis, Hugh P. "The Introduction and Development of Hard Red Winter Wheat in Kansas." Kansas State Board of Agriculture, Biennial Report 15 (1905-1906): 945-48.

"The Deaconess and Her Ministry." Mennonite Life 3 (January 1948): 30-37.

"The Dry Issue Has Won." Mennonite Weekly Review, 7 November 1928, p. 4.

Duerksen, Jacob A. "Transition from Dutch to German in West Prussia."
Mennonite Life 22 (July 1967): 107-09.

Ediger, Elmer. "What is Central in Worship." Mennonite Life 12
(January 1959): 28-30.

"Editorial." Mennonite 23 (December 1908): 4.

Enns, Adolf. "The Public School Crisis Among Mennonites in Saskatchewan
1916-25." In Mennonite Images, pp. 73-82. Edited by Harry
Loewen. Winnipeg: Hyperion Press, 1980.

Encyclopedia Americana, 1978 ed. S.v. "Masonic Fraternity," by Henry
Wilson Coil.

"The Federation of Churches." Mennonite 28 (February 1913): 4.

Francis, E. K. "The Russian Mennonites: From Religious to Ethnic
Group." American Journal of Sociology 54 (September 1948):
101-07.

Fretz, J. Winfield. "Separation or Infiltration." In The Seventy-
fifth Anniversary Services of the Swiss Mennonites, pp. 50-55.
Compiled by Harley J. Stucky. North Newton, Kansas: Mennonite
Press, Inc., 1950.

Friesen, Isaac I. "Values and Problems of the Lay and Supported Minis-
try." In Proceedings of the Study Conference on the Believer's
Church, pp. 205-10. Newton, Kansas: General Conference Mennonite
Church, 1955.

Funk, D. L. "What is Temperance?" Mennonite 15 (July 1900): 75.

Giesinger, Adam. "The Migrations of Germans from Russia to America."
Journal of the American Historical Society of Germans from
Russia 9 (October 1972): 33-40.

Gingerich, Melvin. "The Reaction of the Russian Mennonite Immigrants
of the 1870s to the American Frontier." Mennonite Quarterly
Review 34 (April 1960); 137-46.

Goering, Jacob D., and Williams, Robert. "Generational Drift on Four
Variables Among the Swiss-Volhynian Mennonites in Kansas."
Mennonite Quarterly Review 50 (October 1976): 190-97.

Goerz, David. "Church Music." School and College Journal (May 1896):
33-35.

Harder, M. S. "A Pioneer Educator--Johannes Cornies." Mennonite Life
3 (October 1948): 5-7, 44.

Hertzler, Silas. "Early Mennonite Sunday Schools." Mennonite Quarterly
Review 2 (April 1928): 123-24.

Higham, John. "Current Trends in the Study of Ethnicity in the United States." Journal of American Ethnic History 2 (Fall 1982): 5-15.

Hohmann, Walter H. "Transition in Worship." Mennonite Life 1 (January 1946): 8.

Juhnke, James C. "Except the Lord Build the House: Halstead Seminary Centennial." Mennonite Life 38 (December 1983): 4-7.

_____. "Freedom for Reluctant Citizens." Mennonite Life 29 (January 1974): 30-32.

_____. "Gemeindechristentum and Bible Doctrine: Two Mennonite Visions of the Early Twentieth Century." Mennonite Quarterly Review 57 (July 1983): 208-10.

_____. "General Conference Mennonite Missions to the American Indians in the Late Nineteenth Century." Mennonite Quarterly Review 54 (April 1980): 117-34.

_____. "Kansas Mennonites During the Spanish-American War." Mennonite Life 26 (April 1971): 70-72.

_____. "Mennonite Benevolence and Civic Identity: The Post-War Compromise." Mennonite Life 25 (January 1970): 34-37.

Koop, Albert P. "Some Economic Aspects of Mennonite Migration: With Special Emphasis on the 1870s Migration from Russia to North America." Mennonite Quarterly Review 55 (April 1981): 143-56.

Krahn, Cornelius. "The Ethnic Origin of the Mennonite from Russia." Mennonite Life 3 (July 1948): 45-48.

_____. "Mennonite Church Architecture." Mennonite Life 12 (January 1957): 19-27.

_____. "The Office of Elder in Anabaptist-Mennonite History." Mennonite Quarterly Review 30 (April 1956): 120-27.

_____. "Some Letters of Bernhard Warkentin Pertaining to the Migration of 1873-1875." Mennonite Quarterly Review 24 (June 1950): 248-63.

_____. "Some Social Attitudes of the Mennonites of Russia." Mennonite Quarterly Review 9 (October 1935): 165-77.

Krehbiel, Christian E. "Historical-Sketch: First Mennonite Church, Halstead, Kansas." Mennonite Weekly Review, 5 May 1925, pp. 3-4.

Kreider, Robert. "The Anabaptist Conception of the Church in the Russian Mennonite Environment." Mennonite Quarterly Review 25 (January 1951): 17-33.

_____. "Environmental Influences Affecting the Decision of Mennonite
     Boys of Draft Age." Mennonite Quarterly Review 16 (October
     1942): 247-259, 275.

Kuhn, Walter. "Cultural Achievements of the Chortitza Mennonites."
     Mennonite Life 3 (January 1948): 35-38.

Leibbrandt, George. "The Emigration of the German Mennonites from
     Russia to the United States and Canada in 1873-1880." Mennonite
     Quarterly Review 6 (October 1932): 205-226.

_____. "The Emigration of the German Mennonites from Russia to the
     United States and Canada in 1873-1880." Mennonite Quarterly
     Review 7 (January 1933): 5-41.

Lederach, Paul M. "The History of the Young People's Bible Meeting in
     the Mennonite Church." Mennonite Quarterly Review 26 (July
     1952): 216-31.

Luebke, Frederick C. "Ethnic Group Settlement on the Great Plains."
     Western Historical Quarterly 8 (October 1977): 405-30.

_____. "German Immigrants and the Churches in Nebraska, 1889-1915."
     Mid-America 1 (April 1968): 116-30.

_____. "German Immigrants and Parochial Schools." Issues 2 (Spring
     1967): 11-18.

_____. "Legal Restrictions on Foreign Languages in the Great Plains
     States, 1917-1923. In Languages in Conflict, pp. 8-16. Edited
     by Paul Schach. Lincoln: University of Nebraska Press, 1980.

"Maessiges Trinken." Christlicher Bundesbote, 1 January 1896, p. 3.

Marty, Martin. "Ethnicity: The Skeleton of Religion in America."
     Church History 41 (March 1972): 5-21.

Mennonite Yearbook and Almanac for 1897. Quakertown, Pennsylvania:
     U. S. Stauffer, 1897.

"Mrs. Carrie Nation." Mennonite 16 (April 1901): 51.

Musselman, V. Gerald. "Architecture and Our Faith." Mennonite Life 20
     (October 1965): 158-67.

Neufeld, Vernon. "The Musical Instrument in Worship." Mennonite Life
     3 (April 1948): 33-34.

"Our Conference." Mennonite 32 (September 1917): 4.

Parsons, Talcott. "Christianity and Modern Industrial Society." In
     Religion, Culture and Society, pp. 273-78. Edited by Louis
     Schneider. New York: John Wiley and Sons, Inc., 1964.

Penner, Horst. "West Prussian Mennonites Through Four Centuries."
    Mennonite Quarterly Review 23 (October 1949): 232-45.

Quiring, Walter. "Johannes Cornies--a Great Pioneer." Mennonite Life
    3 (July 1948): 30-34, 38.

Redekop, Calvin. "Patterns of Cultural Assimilation Among Mennonites."
    In Proceedings of the Eleventh Conference on Mennonite Educa-
    tional and Cultural Problems, pp. 99-112. North Newton, Kansas:
    n.p., 1957.

Regier, P. K. "Values and Problems of the Lay and the Supported Min-
    istry." In Proceedings of the Study Conference on the Believer's
    Church, pp. 197-204. Newton, Kansas: General Conference Mennonite
    Church, 1955.

Rempel, David G. "The Mennonite Migration to New Russia, 1787-1870."
    Mennonite Quarterly Review 9 (April 1935): 71-91.

_____. "The Mennonite Migration to New Russia, 1787-1870." Mennonite
    Quarterly Review 9 (July 1935): 109-28.

_____. "The Mennonite Commonwealth in Russia, a Sketch of its Found-
    ing and Endurance." Mennonite Quarterly Review 47 (October
    1973): 259-308.

_____. "The Mennonite Commonwealth in Russia, a Sketch of its Found-
    ing and Endurance." Mennonite Quarterly Review 48 (January
    1974): 5-54.

Saul, Norman E. "The Migration of the German-Russians to Kansas."
    The Kansas Historical Quarterly 40 (Spring 1974): 38-62.

Schaefer, P. J. "Heinrich H. Ewert--Educator of Kansas and Manitoba."
    Mennonite Life 4 (October 1948): 18-23.

Schmidt, C. B. "Reminiscences of Foreign Immigration Work for Kansas."
    Kansas Historical Collection 9 (1905-1906): 485-497.

Schrag, Martin. "The Swiss-Volhynian Mennonite Background." Mennonite
    Life 9 (October 1954): 156, 158-61.

Shelly, Maynard. "Practices and Trends in Mennonite Congregations."
    In Proceedings of the Study Conference on the Believer's Church,
    pp. 23-39. Newton, Kansas: General Conference Mennonite Church,
    1955.

Smissen, C. H. A. van der. "Ministerial Support." Mennonite Life 4
    (November 1888): 17-19.

Smith, C. Henry. "Mennonite and Culture." Mennonite Quarterly Review
    12 (April 1938): 71-84.

Smith, Timothy L. "Religion and Ethnicity in America." American Historical Review 83 (December 1978): 1155-85.

_____. "Religious Denominations as Ethnic Communities: A Regional Case Study." Church History 35 (June 1966): 207-26.

Smucker, Don E. "Building the Lord's House." Mennonite Life 12 (January 1957): 18.

"The Special Meeting of the Federal Council." Mennonite 32 (May 1917): 3-5.

Stout, Harry. "Ethnicity: The Vital Center of Religion in America." Ethnicity 2 (June 1975): 202-24.

Sudermann, Jacob. "The Origin of Mennonite State Service in Russia, 1870-1880." Mennonite Quarterly Review 17 (January 1943): 23-46.

Thomas, George M. "Rational Exchange and Individualism: Revival Religion in the United States, 1870-1890." In The Religious Dimension, pp. 351-372. Edited by Robert Wulhnow. New York: Academic Press, 1979.

Tschetter, Paul. "The Diary of Paul Tschetter, 1873." Translated by J. M. Hofer. Mennonite Quarterly Review 5 (April 1931): 112-28.

_____. "The Diary of Paul Tschetter, 1873." Translated by J. M. Hofer. Mennonite Quarterly Review 5 (July 1931): 198-220.

Umble, John. "Early Mennonite Sunday School Lesson Helps." Mennonite Quarterly Review 2 (April 1938): 98-113.

_____. "Seventy Years of Progress in Sunday School Work Among the Mennonites of the Middle West." Mennonite Quarterly Review 8 (October 1934): 166-79.

Unruh, Benjamin H. "Dutch Background of the Mennonite Migration of the Sixteenth Century to Prussia." Mennonite Quarterly Review 10 (July 1936): 173-81.

Unruh, John D., Jr. "The Burlington and Missouri Railroad Brings the Mennonites to Nebraska, 1873-1878." Nebraska History 45 (March 1964): 3-30.

_____. "The Burlington and Missouri Railroad Brings the Mennonites to Nebraska, 1873-1878." Nebraska History 45 (June 1964): 177-206.

Vogt, Roy. "The Impact of Economics and Social Class on Mennonite Theology." In Mennonite Images, pp. 137-40. Edited by Harry Loewen. Winnipeg; Hyperion Press, 1980.

Wedel, Cornelius H. "Bethel College." In Mennonite Yearbook and Almanac, p. 28. Quakertown, Pennsylvania: U. S. Stauffer, 1895.

Wedel, David C. "Contributions of Pioneer David Goerz." Mennonite Life 7 October 1952): 170-75.

Wedel, P. J. "Beginnings of Secondary Education in Kansas." Mennonite Life 3 (October 1948): 14-17.

Wedel, Theodore O. "Reminiscences and Reflections." Mennonite Life 3 (October 1948): 39-40.

Wenger, John C., trans. "The Schleitheim Confession of Faith." Mennonite Quarterly Review 4 (October 1945): 244-53.

Wiebe, Margie. "Hymnals Used by the General Conference." Mennonite Life 3 (April 1948): 36, 38.

Ph.D. Dissertations, M.A. Theses, and Unpublished Papers

Albrecht, Abraham. "Mennonite Settlements in Kansas." Master's thesis, Kansas University, 1924.

Buchheit, Robert H. "Mennonite 'Plautdietsch': A Phonological and Morphological Description of a Settlement Dialect in York and Hamilton Counties, Nebraska." Ph.D. dissertation, University of Nebraska, 1978.

Buller, Calvin D. "The Development of Singing Amongst the Dutch-German Mennonites of Central Kansas." Master's thesis, Wichita State University, 1965.

Carman, J. Neale. "Language Transition Amongst the Kansas Mennonites." Unpublished paper, Mennonite Library and Archives, Bethel College, North Newton, Kansas, n.d.

Fast, Henry A. "The Witness of Our Congregation Over 75 Years." Unpublished paper, Mennonite Library and Archives, Bethel College, North Newton, Kansas, 1972.

Franzen, Jacob. "Survey of the West Zion Mennonite Church Moundridge, Kansas." Unpublished paper, Mennonite Library and Archives, Bethel College, North Newton, Kansas, 1950.

Friesen, Loren, and Janzen, Mary E. "A Kansas Community and the Election of 1932." Unpublished paper, Mennonite Library and Archives, Bethel College, North Newton, Kansas, 1967.

Gaeddert, Carol D. "A Study in the Change of Baptismal Age in the Alexanderwohl and Hoffnungsau Churches." Unpublished paper, Mennonite Library and Archives, Bethel College, North Newton, Kansas, 1953.

Goerzen, Jakob W. "Low German in Canada: A Study of 'Plauldietsch'." Ph.D. dissertation, University of Toronto, 1952.

Graebner, Alan Niehaus. "The Acculturation of an Immigrant Lutheran Church." Ph.D. dissertation, Columbia University, 1965.

Harder, Richard. "A Comparison of the Gospel Missionary Union and the General Conference Commission of Overseas Missions." Unpublished paper, Mennonite Library and Archives, Bethel College, North Newton, Kansas, 1969.

Haury, David A. "German-Russian Immigrants and Kansas Politics: A Comparison of the Catholic and Mennonite Immigration to Kansas and Their Politics." Unpublished paper, Mennonite Library and Archives, Bethel College, North Newton, Kansas, 1972.

Hiebert, Clarence R. "The History of the Ordinance of Footwashing in the Mennonite Churches." S.T.B. thesis, New York Biblical Seminary, 1954.

Janzen, Cornelius Cicero. "Americanization of Russian Mennonites in Central Kansas." Master's thesis, Kansas University, 1914.

_____. "A Social Study of the Mennonite Settlements in the Counties of Marion, McPherson, Harvey, Reno, and Butler, Kansas." Ph.D. dissertation, University of Chicago, 1926.

Janzen, John M. "Schisms and Renewal in Three Mennonite Parishes." Unpublished paper, Mennonite Library and Archives, Bethel College, North Newton, Kansas, 1975.

_____. "Schism and Renewal in Three Central Kansas Mennonite Congregations." In Quest for Community: Mennonite Separation and Integration. Edited by Leo Driedger and Calvin Redekop, forthcoming.

Janzen, Louis A. "Forbid Him Not." Unpublished paper, Mennonite Library and Archives, Bethel College, North Newton, Kansas, 1978.

Kaufman, Edmund G. "Social Problems and Opportunities of the Western District Conference Communities of Mennonites of North America." Master's thesis, Bluffton College and Mennonite Seminary, 1917.

Linscheid, Willis. "The History of the Emmanuel Mennonite Church." Unpublished paper, Mennonite Library and Archives, Bethel College, North Newton, Kansas, 1950.

Lohrentz, Tim. "But What Are the Charges?" Unpublished paper, Mennonite Library and Archives, Bethel College, North Newton, Kansas, 1982.

McQuillan, David Aidan. "Adaptation of Three Immigrant Groups to Farming in Central Kansas 1875-1925." Ph.D. dissertation, University of Wisconsin-Madison, 1975.

Niles, Jan. "H. D. Penner and the Hillsboro Preparatory School." Unpublished paper, Mennonite Library and Archives, Bethel College, North Newton, Kansas, 1978.

Pannabecker, Samuel F. "The Development of the General Conference of the Mennonite Church of North America in the American Environment." Ph.D. dissertation, Yale University, 1944.

Peters, H. P. "History and Development of Education Among the Mennonites in Kansas." Master's thesis, Bluffton College, 1925.

Rempel, David G. "The Mennonite Colonies in New Russia--A Study of Their Settlement and Economic Development from 1789 to 1914." Ph.D. dissertation, Stanford University, 1933.

Saul, Norman E. "The Settlement and Assimilation of German from Russia; the Kansas Experience, 1874-1880." Unpublished paper, Mennonite Library and Archives, Bethel College, North Newton, Kansas, 1977.

Sawatsky, Rodney J. "The Influence of Fundamentalism on Mennonite Nonresistance 1908-1944." Master's thesis, University of Minnesota, 1973.

Smith, Elma Ruth. "A Brief History of the Bergthal Mennonite Church, Pawnee Rock, Kansas." Unpublished paper, Mennonite Library and Archives, Bethel College, North Newton, Kansas, 1943.

Smith, Marlyn. "A Brief History of the Mennonites of Barton County, Kansas." Unpublished paper, Mennonite Library and Archives, Bethel College, North Newton, Kansas, 1940.

Stucky, Harley J. "Cultural Interaction Among the Mennonites Since 1870." Master's thesis, Northwestern University, 1947.

Thiesen, John D. "The More Things Change the More They Stay the Same: A History of the First Mennonite Church, Newton, Kansas 1878-1982." Unpublished paper, Mennonite Library and Archives, Bethel College, North Newton, Kansas, 1982.

Wedel, David C. "The Contributions of C. H. Wedel to the Mennonite Church Through Education." Th.D. dissertation, Iliff School of Theology, 1952.

Unruh, Otto D. "Schisms of the Russian Mennonites of Harvey, McPherson, and Reno Counties, Kansas." Master's thesis, Kansas University, 1939.

Urry, James. "The Transformation and Polarization of the Mennonites
in Russia, 1789-1914." Paper presented to the Conference on
Russian Mennonite History, Winnipeg, November 1977.

Voth, John J. "Religious Education in the Mennonite Churches Comprising
the Western District Conference." Master's thesis, Witmarsum
Theological Seminary, 1922.

Newspapers and Religious Periodicals

Bethel College Monthly 1903-1935.

Christlicher Bundesbote 1882-1956 (Merged with Der Bote in 1947).

Herold (Newton) 1897-1914.

Kansan-Republican (Newton) 1876- .

Monatsblaetter aus Bethel College 1903-1912.

McPherson Republican 1879- .

Mennonite 1885- .

Mennonite Weekly Review 1922.

Review 1898-1904.

School and College Journal 1896-1903.

Zur Heimath (Halstead) 1875-1881.

Primary Materials and Collections

Note: The following holdings of the Mennonite Library and Archives at
Bethel College represent a small portion of the vast resources
of that library. Nearly all of the churches of the Western
District Conference have turned over records to the MLA.

Ewert, Wilhelm J. Collection.

Friesen, H. B. Collection.

Friesen, J. J. Collection.

Halstead Mennonite Seminary Reports and Accounts, Collection.

Krehbiel, C. E. Collection.

Krehbiel, H. P.   Collection.

"Minutes of the Kansas Conference, 1877-1892" and the "Western District Conference, 1892-1939."

Richert, P. H.   Collection.

"Secretary's Report of the Congregational Meetings of the Tabor Mennonite Church, 1907-1926."

"Selected Items from a Survey of the Committee on Education, Western District Conference, 1925-1936."

Suderman, John M. Collection.

Interviews

Schmidt, John F. Mennonite Library and Archives, Bethel College, North Newton, Kansas. Interview, 19 June 1983.

Schmidt, Richard H. Mennonite Library and Archives, Bethel College, North Newton, Kansas. Interview, 20 July 1984.

Schrag, Menno. Mennonite Library and Archives, Bethel College, North Newton, Kansas. Interview, 30 July 1984.

Voth, Hilda. Mennonite Library and Archives, Bethel College, North Newton, Kansas. Interview, 26 September 1984.

Printed in Great Britain
by Amazon

38814394R00192